The quest for freedom from hunger and repression has triggered in recent years a worldwide movement toward political democracy and economic rationality. Never have so many people experimented with democratic institutions. At the same time, traditional strategies of economic development have collapsed in Eastern Europe and Latin America and entire economic systems are being transformed on both continents.

What should we expect in the countries that venture on the paths to democracy and markets? Will these transitions result in democracies or in new dictatorships? What economic system, new or old, will emerge?

This important book analyzes recent events in Eastern Europe and Latin America, focusing on transitions to democracy and market-oriented economic reforms. The author underscores the interdependence of political and economic transformations and draws on extensive local data for his analysis. A distinctive feature of the book is that it employs models derived from political philosophy, economics, and game theory.

*Democracy and the Market* will be of particular interest to scholars and graduate students in political science, economics, and sociology.

# DEMOCRACY
# AND THE MARKET

STUDIES IN RATIONALITY AND SOCIAL CHANGE

Editors: Jon Elster and Michael S. McPherson

*Editorial Board:*
Fredrik Barth
Amartya Sen
Arthur Stinchcombe
Amos Tversky
Bernard Williams

*Titles in the series:*

Adam Przeworski
*University of Chicago*

# DEMOCRACY
# AND THE MARKET

## POLITICAL AND ECONOMIC REFORMS IN
## EASTERN EUROPE AND LATIN AMERICA

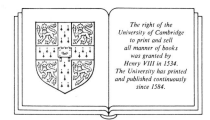

The right of the
University of Cambridge
to print and sell
all manner of books
was granted by
Henry VIII in 1534.
The University has printed
and published continuously
since 1584.

**Cambridge University Press**

Cambridge

New York    Port Chester    Melbourne    Sydney

Published by the Press Syndicate of the University of Cambridge
The Pitt Building, Trumpington Street, Cambridge CB2 1RP
40 West 20th Street, New York, NY 10011-4211, USA
10 Stamford Road, Oakleigh, Victoria 3166, Australia

First published 1991
Reprinted 1992

Printed in the United States of America

*Library of Congress Cataloging-in-Publication Data*

Przeworski, Adam
Democracy and the market : political and economic reforms in
Eastern Europe and Latin America / Adam Przeworski.
p.  cm. – (Studies in rationality and social change)
Includes bibliographical references.
1. Europe, Eastern – Economic policy.  2. Europe, Eastern – Politics
and government – 1989 –  3. Latin America – Economic policy.  4. Latin
America – Politics and government – 1980 –  5. Mixed economy – Europe,
Eastern.  6. Mixed economy – Latin America.  7. Democracy.
I. Title.  II. Series.
HC244.P8  1991
338.947–dc20                                          91-7524
                                                          CIP

*British Library Cataloguing in Publication Data*

Przeworski, Adam
Democracy and the market : political and economic reforms
in Eastern Europe and Latin America. – (Studies in
rationality and social change).
1. South America. Central America. Eastern Europe.
Economics, related to politics
I. Title  II. Series
330

ISBN 0-521-41225-0 hardback
ISBN 0-521-42335-X paperback

*To Molly, her friends, and their friends*

# Contents

# Introduction

To eat and to talk – to be free from hunger and from repression: These elementary values animate a worldwide quest for political democracy and economic rationality. In the past fifteen years, Greece, Portugal, Spain, Argentina, Bolivia, Brazil, Chile, Paraguay, Peru, Uruguay, South Korea, Pakistan, the Philippines, Turkey, Poland, Hungary, Czechoslovakia, Bulgaria, Slovenia, Albania, and Algeria have held democratic elections, the first ever, or at least the first in decades. Even in the Soviet Union, the first timid opening met with a massive expression of popular will and forced democracy onto the political agenda. Never have so many countries enjoyed or at least experimented with democratic institutions.

At the same time, models of economic development that were successful over several decades collapsed in some countries. The economic crises facing Argentina, Brazil, and Mexico as well as Hungary, Poland, and Yugoslavia are without precedent in the history of these nations. As a result, we witness a frantic search for new models and new strategies that could generate sustained growth. In many countries, after many failed reforms, entire economic systems are now being transformed.

In the realm of both politics and economics we observe attempts to make a radical break with the past; in fact, in both realms the word "transitions" best describes the processes launched in a number of countries. These are transitions from authoritarianism of several varieties to democracy and from state-administered, monopolistic, and protected economic systems, again of several varieties, to a reliance on markets. Both transitions are radical, and they are interdependent.

What should we expect to happen to the countries that have ventured on the path to democracy and markets? The purpose of studying transitions is to answer questions about the conditions and the paths that lead to political democracy and material prosperity. Will transitions end in a democracy or in a dictatorship, new or old? Will the new democracy be a stable one?

Which institutions will constitute it? Will the new political system be effective in generating substantive outcomes? Will it be conducive to individual freedom and social justice? What economic systems will emerge: Which forms of property will prevail, which mechanisms will allocate resources, which development strategies will be pursued? Will these systems generate development with material security for all?

There are no simple answers to such questions. There is too much we social scientists still do not know. And yet to speculate about the future, to understand the choices we face at present, we have to make assumptions. Specifically, we need to offer answers to the four question about democracy and development we seem to have been asking forever:

1. What kinds of democratic institutions are most likely to last?
2. What kinds of economic systems – forms of property, allocation mechanisms, and development strategies – are most likely to generate growth with a humane distribution of welfare?
3. What are the political conditions for the successful functioning of economic systems, for growth with material security for all?
4. What are the economic conditions for democracy to be consolidated, allowing groups to organize and pursue their interests and values without fear and under rules?

My book begins with a prologue: the story of the fall of communism. This event, not anticipated by anyone, in a few weeks opened a new world to millions of people in Eastern Europe. But which world will it be? Will the postcommunist countries find their way to democracy and to prosperity, to the "West"? Or will they find themselves struggling against misery and oppression, like billions of people inhabiting the "South"? This is the question posed in the Prologue.

Chapter 1 offers a theory of durable democratic institutions. I argue that democracies last when they evoke self-interested spontaneous compliance from all the major political forces. I then show that to evoke such compliance, democracy must simultaneously offer to all such forces a fair chance to compete within the institutional framework and to generate substantive outcomes: It must be fair and effective. Yet under some historical conditions, these requirements cannot be simultaneously fulfilled by any system of democratic institutions. Foremost among such conditions are periods of profound economic transformation.

Even if durable democratic institutions are possible under given circumstances, there is no guarantee that the political forces in conflict about their future chances under democracy will adopt such institutions. After a prologue concerning the liberalization of authoritarian regimes, Chapter 2 focuses on the choice of institutions during the transition to democracy. I argue that such institutions always emerge from negotiation. What differentiates particular cases of transition is whether these negotiations involve the forces associated with the previous authoritarian regimes or only the allies in the struggle against authoritarianism. "Extrication" – transitions negotiated with the previous authoritarian regimes – is likely to leave institutional traces, foremost among them the autonomy of the armed forces. Yet even if they are free from the fear of repression, the proto-democratic forces seeking to constitute the new regime are prone to adopt an institutional framework that some of them will see only as a temporary expedient. Therefore, basic institutional issues are unlikely to be resolved at the time of transition. Finally, I claim, when institutional issues continue to be present in minor political conflicts, ideological factors come to the fore. And the dominant ideologies of many nascent democracies are not conducive to tolerating the divisions and conflicts inherent in democratic competition.

The discussion shifts to economic issues in Chapter 3. The central question is what kinds of economic systems – forms of property and allocation mechanisms – are most likely to generate growth with a humane distribution of welfare. I argue that capitalism suffers from a particular kind of irrationality: When self-interested economic agents allocate scarce resources in a decentralized way, the productive potential cannot be fully utilized unless they receive full return on their endowments. But socialism – allocation of resources by centralized command – is not feasible because it rests on untenable assumptions concerning the behavior of planners, of workers, and of consumers. Faced with this dilemma, I argue that forms of property are less important than mechanisms of allocation. The most rational and humane economic system is one that relies on regulated markets to allocate resources and on the state to assure a minimum of material welfare for everyone. This system may still involve quite a lot of inefficiency and inequality, but I find none better.

Even if we know which economic system is best, the road to it is not an easy one. Chapter 4 is devoted to the political dynamics of economic reforms. I show that transitional effects of reforms are likely to include inflation, unemployment, allocative inefficiencies, and volatile changes in relative incomes. The question is whether such transitional costs will be tolerated politically. Adopting some simple assumptions, I demonstrate that the reform strategy that is most likely to advance the farthest and that will be preferred by politicians is not the one that minimizes social costs. Yet even if this strategy enjoys widespread popular support at the outset, political counterreactions set in once the costs are experienced. In response, governments begin to vacillate between a technocratic style inherent in market-oriented programs and the participatory style needed to maintain political support. These vacillations erode confidence in reforms and may threaten democratic stability.

As these previews intimate, the mood of what follows is sober, maybe even somber. Perhaps pessimism, as Poles say, is merely informed optimism. But my intention is not to offer forecasts, pessimistic or not, only to illuminate the obstacles typically confronted in building democracy and transforming economies. Many of these obstacles, I believe, are the same everywhere, for they are determined by a common destination, not by the different points of departure. Yet the outcomes will differ, for outcomes depend on historically inherited conditions, on good will, on intelligence, and on luck.

# A prologue: The fall of communism

Transitions to democracy occurred in Southern Europe – in Greece, Portugal, and Spain – in the mid 1970s. They were launched in the Southern Cone of Latin America, except for Chile – in Argentina, Brazil, and Uruguay – in the early 1980s. And they were inaugurated in Eastern Europe during the "Autumn of the People" of 1989. Can we draw on the earlier experiences to understand the later ones? Are there lessons to be learned from history?

In spite of the waves of democratization in Southern Europe and Latin America, the fall of communism took everyone by surprise. No one had expected that the communist system, styled by some as totalitarian precisely because it was supposed to be immutable, would collapse suddenly and peacefully. What made the transition to democracy in Eastern Europe possible? What made it happen so quickly and so smoothly?

Since the fall of communism in Eastern Europe is the prologue to the analyses that follow, let me reconstruct the story as I see it. Yet first we need a warning against facile analyses. The "Autumn of the People" was a dismal failure of political science. Any retrospective explanation of the fall of communism must not only account for the historical developments but also identify the theoretical assumptions that prevented us from anticipating these developments. For if we are wise now, why were we not equally sage before?

Most terminal cancer patients die of pneumonia. And social science is not very good at sorting out underlying causes and precipitating conditions; witness the fifty years of controversy over the fall of Weimar. For the response to the question "Why did communism collapse?" is not the same as to "Why did it collapse in the autumn of 1989?" It is easier to explain why communism had to fall than why it did.

"Totalitarianism" could not answer either question: It could not diagnose the cancer and hence the vulnerability to pneumonia. The totalitarian model was more ideological than the societies it depicted as such. This model denied the possibility of conflict within communist societies because it saw them as based on dogma and repression. Yet from the late 1950s, ideology was no longer the cement, to use Gramsci's expression, that held these societies together. I remember how startled I was by the leading slogan of May Day 1964 in Poland: "Socialism is a guarantee of our borders." Socialism – the project for a new future – was no longer the end; it had become an instrument of traditional values. And by the 1970s, repression had subsided: As the communist leadership became bourgeoisified, it could no longer muster the self-discipline required to crush all dissent. Party bureaucrats were no longer able to spend their nights at meetings, to wear working-class uniforms, to march and shout slogans, to abstain from ostentatious consumption. What had developed was "goulash communism," "Kadarism," "Brezhnevism": an implicit social pact in which elites offered the prospect of material welfare in exchange for silence. And the tacit premise of this pact was that socialism was no longer a model of a new future but an underdeveloped something else. Khrushchev set it as the goal of the Soviet Union to catch up with Great Britain; by the 1970s, Western Europe had become the standard of comparison, and the comparisons became increasingly humiliating.

As Polish and Hungarian surveys showed, the outcome was a society that was highly materialistic, atomized, and cynical. It was a society in which people uttered formulas they did not believe and that they did not expect anyone else to believe. Speech became a ritual. I am haunted by a Soviet joke. A man is distributing leaflets in Red Square. He is stopped by a policeman, who confiscates them, only to discover that they are blank. "What are you spreading? They are blank. Nothing is written!" the surprised guardian of order exclaims. "Why write?" is the answer. "Everybody knows . . ."

Words became dangerous, so dangerous that the five armies to invade Czechoslovakia in 1968 cited as one reason Ludvik Vaculik's "Two Thousand Words." And most subversive were the very ideals that founded this social order: rationality, equality, even the working class. As early as the 1960s, Polish surveys showed that engineering students were most radical in criticizing the socialist economy; they were the ones imbued with the value of rationality. Polish dissidents adopted in the mid 1970s a simple strategy to subvert the political system: They decided to use the rights proclaimed by the Communist constitution. And the decisive threat to this system originated from those on behalf of whom it had always claimed legitimacy: the working class. Communist ideology became a threat to the social order in which it was embodied. People need some modicum of cognitive consistency; when their thoughts and their words perpetually diverge, life becomes intolerable.

This is why the cry for "truth" became at least as important in imploding this system as the clamor for bread, why history became an obsession when the regime began to crumble, why a leading opponent of the Communist regime in the Soviet Union has been the director of the National Archive, why high school history examinations were suspended for two years in the Soviet Union, why writers and intellectuals became the leaders of the postcommunist regimes.

But those of us who saw no reason to distinguish between authoritarianism and totalitarianism, those of us who found in the transition to democracy in Spain, Greece, Argentina, Brazil, or the Philippines a ready-made model for Hungary, Poland, or the Soviet Union, were looking for the symptoms of pneumonia but did not diagnose the cancer. We knew how to analyze the dynamic of conflicts once they flared up, but not the conditions ensuring that they would. Although Timothy Garton Ash (1990: 252) cautiously wrote, in September of 1988, about the possibility of the "Ottomanization" – "emancipation by decay" – of the Soviet empire, no one sensed how feeble the communist system had become, no one expected that just a little push would cause it to collapse.

The "Autumn of the People" constitutes one event, or perhaps one and a half. Henry Kissinger's domino theory triumphed; all he missed was the direction in which the dominoes would fall. What happened in Romania was caused by what had occurred in Czechoslovakia; what ensued in Czechoslovakia resulted from the breakdown in East Germany; what stimulated masses of people to fill the streets in East Germany followed the political changes in Hungary; what showed Hungarians a way out was the success of the negotiations in Poland. I know that hundreds of macrohistorical comparative sociologists will write thousands of books and articles correlating background conditions with outcomes in each country, but I think they will be wasting their time, for the entire event was one single snowball. I mean it in a technical sense: As developments took place in one country, people elsewhere were updating their probabilities of success, and as the next country went over the brink, the calculation was becoming increasingly reassuring. And I have no doubt that the last hold-outs will follow.

The open rebellion began in Poland in 1976 and flared up for the first time in 1980. The first instance of collapse of a communist system does not date to 1989 but to December 13, 1981. The coup d'état of General Jaruzelski was proof that Communist parties could no longer rule with passive acquiescence, that from now on power must be based on force. As the economic strategy of the 1970s collapsed, as intellectuals found their voices and workers took over their factories, party bureaucrats were unable to preserve their rule. To continue to enjoy privileges, they had to abdicate political power in favor of organized forces of repression. Communist rule became militarized because only in this form could it survive the revolt of the society.

From then on it was only the fear of physical force, external and internal, that held the system together. Even this force turned out to be insufficient when Polish workers struck again in the summer of 1988, and it is to the credit of General Jaruzelski that he understood it. The decision to compro-mise with the opposition was imposed on the Polish party by the military. The Hungarian party split from the top, without the same pressure from below and without being coerced by the armed forces. The success of the Polish negotiations in the spring of 1989 showed Hungarians a road to peaceful transfer of power. By that time party bureaucrats in both countries began to realize that if they could hold onto political power, perhaps they could, to use Elemer Hankiss's felicitous phrase, "convert it" into eco-nomic power before it was too late.

The spark that ignited the subsequent chain of events was the Hungarian decision to let East German refugees proceed to West Germany. Having learned that the road was open from Budapest, East Germans tried Prague. At this moment, the East German leadership made a fatal mistake. They agreed that the refugees could transit to the West but decided to "humili-ate" them. They had them pass by train through East Germany to be exposed to the scorn of organized demonstrations. But instead of condemn-ing the refugees, the masses turned the demonstrations against the regime, as they would later do in Bulgaria and Romania. The rest is history. Once hundreds of thousands of people had flooded the streets of Leipzig, Dres-den, and Berlin, once the wall had fallen, the pressure on Czechoslovakia was irresistible, and all the Bulgarian communists could do was to limit the damage.

The Gorbachev revolution in the Soviet Union obviously played a crucial role in unleashing the events in Eastern Europe. It was the single precipitating event, the pneumonia. But this platitude easily leads to confusion.

The threat of Soviet intervention, imprinted in the memories of 1956 in Hungary and 1968 in Czechoslovakia, was the constraint on internal developments in Eastern Europe. But it was only that: the constraint, a dam placed against pressing waters. When this dam cracked, it was the pent-up waters that overran its remains. The change in the Soviet Union did not propel transformations in Hungary and Poland; what it did was to remove the crucial factor that had been blocking them. The constraint was external, but the impetus was internal. This is why the "Soviet factor" does not render invalid the application of Latin American models to Eastern Europe.

Moreover, the Gorbachev revolution was not a fluke of history. The Soviet Union was not exempt – in retrospect it is obvious – from the same pressures that made the system crack in Eastern Europe. Unable to persuade, incapable of silencing dissident voices, inept at feeding its own people, impotent against an amalgam of tribes in the mountains of Afghanistan, indolent in international technological competition – was this not the Soviet Union of 1984? And had we made this list, would we not have concluded, whatever theoretical differences divide us, that no such system could last?

Could the Soviet Union have invaded Poland in 1981? Could it have maintained its empire? At what cost to its internal peace and prosperity? In my view, the changes in the Soviet Union, including the shift of the Soviet strategic posture with regard to Eastern Europe, were to a large extent endogenous; that is, they were brought about in part by the developments in Eastern Europe, by the increasing political and economic costs of maintaining the empire.

Everyone, not only marxists, used to believe that political change of this magnitude could only be violent. Yet except in Romania and in the nationalistic flare-ups in the Soviet Union and Yugoslavia, not a single person was killed in this revolution. Why?

The reasons the system collapsed so rapidly and so quietly are to be found both in the realm of ideology and in the realm of physical force. For me, again the most striking aspect of this collapse is that party bureaucrats had nothing to say to defend their power. They were simply mute; they did not speak about socialism, progress, the future, prosperity, rationality, equality, the working class. They only calculated how many thousands of people they could beat up if they persevered, how many ministerial posts they would have to yield if they compromised, how many jobs they could retain if they surrendered. The most they could muster were declarations of patriotic commitment, but their credentials were dubious. And even now, when the relabeled or transformed Communist parties declare their devotion to democratic socialism, they still do not mean what they say: The founding Program of the Polish Social Democratic Party begins with the statement that Poland is the highest value the party adheres to, affirms its commitment to political democracy, and goes on to express the preference for "whatever forms of property . . . are economically most efficient." These declarations may serve the party in finding a place in the new system, but these are not the values with which it could have defended the old one. By 1989, party bureaucrats did not believe in their speech. And to shoot, one must believe in something. When those who hold the trigger have absolutely nothing to say, they have no force to pull it.

Moreover, they did not have the guns. In no country did the army, as distinct from the police forces, come to the rescue. In Poland, the armed forces led the reforms; only when three generals walked out of the February 1989 meeting of the Central Committee did party bureaucrats understand that their days were over. In all the other countries, including Romania, the army refused to repress. I have a cynical view of the reason for this posture, although I admit that perhaps patriotic motivations did play a role. Educated by the Latin American experience, I find the canonical phrase uttered by the generals all over Eastern Europe foreboding. When the military proclaim, "The army does not serve a political party, but the nation," I see them jumping at the chance to free themselves from civilian control, to establish themselves as the arbiter of the national fate. Yet whether or not I am correct, in fact party bureaucrats did not control the guns. I cannot stop myself from recounting a Polish joke that encapsulates the entire story. An older man ventures to buy meat. A long line has already formed. The delivery is not coming; people are getting impatient. The man begins to swear: at the leader, at the party, at the system. Another man approaches him and remarks, pointing to his head: "You know, comrade, if you said things like this in the old days, we would just go 'Paf' and it would all be over." The old man returns home empty-handed. His wife asks, "They have no more meat?" "It is worse than that," the man replies; "they have no more bullets."

What was it that collapsed in Eastern Europe? "Communism" is a neutral answer to this question, since it is a label that has no more advocates. But was it not socialism? Many of those who believe that there can be no socialism without democracy contend that the system that failed in Eastern Europe was perhaps Stalinism, statism, bureaucracy, or communism, but not socialism. Yet I fear that the historical lesson is more radical, that what died in Eastern Europe is the very idea of rationally administering things to satisfy human needs – the feasibility of implementing public ownership of productive resources through centralized command; the very project of basing a society on disinterested cooperation – the possibility of dissociating social contributions from individual rewards. If the only ideas about a new social order originate today from the Right, it is because the socialist project – the project that was forged in Western Europe between 1848 and 1891 and that had animated social movements all over the world since then – failed, in the East and in the West. True, the values of political democracy and of social justice continue to guide social democrats such as myself, but social democracy is a program to mitigate the effects of private ownership and market allocation, not an alternative project of society.

Now several countries in Eastern Europe, again led by Poland, have ventured or are about to venture into the greatest experiment in history since the forced Stalinist industrialization of 1929. Although the prevailing mood follows Adenauer's dictum of *keine Experimenten,* the economic transformations envisaged in these countries ironically mirror the communist project. They implement an intellectual blueprint, a blueprint developed within the walls of American academia and shaped by international financial institutions. They are radical; they are intended to turn upside down all the existing social relations. And they offer a single panacea, a magic wand that, once waved, will cure all ills. Replace "nationalization of the means of production" with "private property" and "plan" with "market," and you can leave the structure of the ideology intact. Perhaps revolutions are shaped by the very systems against which they are directed?

What, then, is the future of Eastern Europe? As I see it, Eastern European societies can follow three roads: their own, that of Southern Europe, or that of Latin America and other countries of the capitalist South. This is what future discussions of Eastern Europe will be all about: Which of these three roads is most likely?

The Left sees in these countries a historic chance to realize what used to be called the third and today should be counted as the second way: a chance to develop a social system alternative to both capitalism and communism. This system would be democratic market socialism: democracy in the political realm and an economy that combines a large cooperative sector with allocation by markets. Although blueprints for this system animate political discussions in Czechoslovakia, Hungary, and Poland, I believe that if such a system does develop it will be mainly by default. Plans for selling the entire public sector to private owners are simply unrealistic, given the low level of domestic savings and fears of foreign domination. Hence, a large number of firms may either remain in state hands or be transferred to employees for lack of private buyers. Whether this property structure will have profound consequences for firm performance, for the role of workers in the enterprise, for their political organization outside the firm, and for political institutions is still a matter of controversy. I remain skeptical.

Whatever mix of ownership patterns emerges, the road the new elites and the people in Eastern Europe want to take is the one that leads to Europe. "Democracy, market, Europe" is the banner. The optimistic scenario is to retrace the path of Spain. Since 1976, in only fifteen years Spain has succeeded in irreversibly consolidating democratic institutions, allowing peaceful alternation in power; in modernizing its economy and making it internationally competitive; in imposing civilian control over the military; in solving complicated national questions; in extending citizenship rights; and in inducing cultural changes that made it part of the European community of nations. And this is what everyone in Eastern Europe expects to happen. Eastern Europeans deeply believe that if it had not been for "the system," they would have been like Spain. And now this system is gone. They will thus reenter Europe. They will become a part of the West.

But Spain is a miracle: one of a handful of countries that since World War I have escaped the economics, the politics, and the culture of poor capitalism. Portugal did not match this achievement; Greece is experiencing profound economic difficulties and a shaky political situation. And note the case of Turkey, which tried and failed to generate the economic, political, and cultural transformations that would have brought it into Europe.

Should we, then, expect these hopes to be fulfilled? Is Eastern Europe on its way to the West, or will the Hungarians, the Poles, and the Romanians join billions of people who inhabit the capitalist South? See the last chapter, "Conclusions."

# 1. Democracy

## Democracy

In his opening speech to the Constituent Assembly, Adolfo Suárez, the prime minister of the Spanish transition to democracy, announced that henceforth "the future is not written, because only the people can write it" (Verou 1976). Heralding this plunge into the unknown, he caught two quintessential features of democracy: Outcomes of the democratic process are uncertain, indeterminate ex ante; and it is "the people," political forces competing to promote their interests and values, who determine what these outcomes will be.

Democracy is a system in which parties lose elections.[1] There are parties: divisions of interests, values, and opinions. There is competition, organized by rules. And there are periodic winners and losers. Obviously not all democracies are the same; one can list innumerable variations and distinguish several types of democratic institutions. Yet beneath all the institutional diversity, one elementary feature – contestation open to participation (Dahl 1971) – is sufficient to identify a political system as democratic.[2]

Democracy is, as Linz (1984) put it, government pro tempore. Conflicts

---

[1] Note that the presence of a party that wins elections does not define a system as democratic: The Albanian People's party has regularly produced overwhelming victories. It is only when there are parties that lose and when losing is neither a social disgrace (Kishlansky 1986) nor a crime that democracy flourishes.

[2] Most definitions of democracy, including Dahl's own, treat participation on a par with contestation. Indeed, there are participationist and contestationist views of democracy. The emphasis on participation is essential if one wants to understand the development of democracy in Western Europe, where battles over suffrage evoked more conflicts than the issue of governmental responsibility. Moreover, such an emphasis is attractive from the normative point of view. Yet from the analytical point of view, the possibility of contestation by conflicting interests is sufficient to explain the dynamic of democracy. Once political rights are sufficiently extensive to admit of conflicting interests, everything else follows, even if effective participation is far from universal. And since, except in South Africa, broad restrictions of political rights are inconceivable under present conditions, a focus on contestation is sufficient to study current transitions to democracy.

are regularly terminated under established rules. They are "terminated" (Coser 1959), temporarily suspended, rather than resolved definitively. Elections fill offices, legislatures establish rules, bureaucracies issue decisions, associations arrive at agreements, courts adjudicate conflicts, and these outcomes are binding until and unless they are altered according to rules. At the same time, all such outcomes are temporary, since losers do not forfeit the right to compete in elections, negotiate again, influence legislation, pressure the bureaucracy, or seek recourse to courts. Even constitutional provisions are not immutable; rules, too, can be changed according to rules.

In a democracy, multiple political forces compete inside an institutional framework. Participants in the democratic competition dispose unequal economic, organizational, and ideological resources. Some groups have more money than others to use in politics. Some may have more extensive organizational skills and assets. Some may have greater ideological means, by which I mean arguments that persuade. If democratic institutions are universalistic – blind to the identity of the participants – those with greater resources are more likely to win conflicts processed in a democratic way.[3] Outcomes, I am arguing, are determined jointly by resources and institutions, which means that the probability that any group, identified by its location in the civil society, will realize its interests to a specific degree and in a particular manner is in general different from any other group's.

The protagonists in the democratic interplay are collectively organized; that is, they have the capacity to formulate collective interests and to act strategically to further them (Pizzorno 1978). Furthermore, they are organized in a particular way entailed in the institutional framework within which they act. To represent, political parties must be stratified into leaders and followers; by definition, representative institutions seat individuals, not masses. A relation of representation is thus imposed on the society by the very nature of democratic institutions (Luxemburg 1970: 202). Individuals do not act directly in defense of their interests; they delegate this defense. Masses are represented by leaders; this is the mode of collective organization in democratic institutions.[4] Moreover, as Schmitter (1974),

---

[3] This is not to say that institutions are not biased. Institutions have distributional consequences. Much more on this topic will follow.

[4] Note that social movements are an ambiguous actor under democracy, and always short-lived. Unions have a place to go: industrial relations institutions and the state; parties have parliaments; and lobbies have bureaus; but movements have no institutions to direct themselves to.

Stepan (1978), Offe (1985), and others have insisted, most interests are organized in a coercive and monopolistic fashion. Interest associations acquire the capacity to act on behalf of their members because they can coerce these members, specifically because they can sanction any individuals or subgroups who attempt to advance their particular goals at the cost of the collective interest. To have market power, unions must be able to punish workers who are eager to replace their striking colleagues; to have a strategic capacity, employers' associations must be able to control the competition among firms in the particular industry or sector. Democratic societies are populated not by freely acting individuals but by collective organizations that are capable of coercing those whose interests they represent.

Democracy is a system of processing conflicts in which outcomes depend on what participants do but no single force controls what occurs. Outcomes of particular conflicts are not known ex ante by any of the competing political forces, because the consequences of their actions depend on actions of others, and these cannot be anticipated uniquely. Hence, from the point of view of each participant, outcomes are uncertain: Democracy appears to be a system in which everyone does what he or she expects is for the best and then dice are thrown to see what the outcomes are. Democracy generates the appearance of uncertainty because it is a system of decentralized strategic action in which knowledge is inescapably local.

The fact that uncertainty is inherent in democracy does not mean everything is possible or nothing is predictable. Contrary to the favorite words of conservatives of all kinds, democracy is neither chaos nor anarchy. Note that "uncertainty" can mean that actors do not know what can happen, that they know what is possible but not what is likely, or that they know what is possible and likely but not what will happen.[5] Democracy is uncertain only in the last sense. Actors know what is possible, since the possible outcomes are entailed by the institutional framework;[6] they know what is likely to happen, because the probability of particular outcomes is deter-

---

[5] These distinctions are based on Littlechild 1986.

[6] I mean "know" in the logical sense: They have the information from which they can deduce each consequence. They can deduce it because the possible outcomes are entailed by rules, and rules can change only according to rules. The "institutional framework," understood as the entire system of rules, is not fixed; it is repeatedly modified as a result of conflicts. But these conflicts always occur within a system of rules that delimit the feasible set. Obviously, none of the above implies that political actors always know what is possible in the psychological sense: They err and they are surprised, particularly because the logical relations involved are often "fuzzy."

mined jointly by the institutional framework and the resources that the different political forces bring to the competition. What they do not know is which particular outcome will occur. They know what winning or losing can mean to them, and they know how likely they are to win or lose, but they do not know if they will lose or win. Hence, democracy is a system of ruled open-endedness, or organized uncertainty.

The uncertainty inherent in democracy does permit instrumental action. Since actors can attach probabilities to the consequences of their actions, they form expectations and calculate what is best for them to do. They can participate, that is, act to advance their interests, projects, or values within the democratic institutions. Conversely, since under the shared constraints outcomes are determined only by actions of competing political forces, democracy constitutes for all an opportunity to pursue their respective interests. If outcomes were either predetermined or completely indeterminate, there would be no reason for groups to organize as participants. It is the uncertainty that draws them into the democratic interplay.

Results of democratic processes are read by applying the particular rules that make up the institutional framework to the joint consequences of decentralized actions. Yet in spite of its majoritarian foundations, modern representative democracy generates outcomes that are predominantly a product of negotiations among leaders of political forces rather than of a universal deliberative process. The role of voting is intermittently to ratify these outcomes or to confirm in office those who brought them about.[7] In all modern democracies, the deliberative process and day-to-day supervision over the government are well protected from the influence of the masses. Indeed, a direct recourse to voters about specific policy issues is often referred to as plebiscitarianism, a term with negative connotations. Hence, voting – majority rule – is only the ultimate arbiter in a democracy.

Outcomes consist of indications to each political force to follow specific courses of action, different for winners and losers. If these indications are followed, losers get less of what they want than winners. To follow these indications is to comply.

Because outcomes cannot be predicted exactly under democracy, com-

---

[7] As Bobbio (1989: 116) put it, "collective decisions are a fruit of negotiation and agreements between groups which represent social forces (unions) and political forces (parties) rather than an assembly where voting operates. These votes take place, in fact, so as to adhere to the constitutional principle of the modern representative state, which says that individuals and not groups are politically relevant . . .; but they end up possessing the purely formal value of ratifying decisions reached in other places by the process of negotiation."

mitment to rules need not be sufficient for compliance once the results are known. If outcomes were certain, that is, if participants could predict them uniquely, they would have known that in committing themselves to particular rules they were accepting specific outcomes; commitment to rules would have been sufficient for compliance with results. Yet under democracy commitment to rules constitutes at most a "willingness to accept outcomes of an as yet undetermined content" (Lamounier 1979: 13). This is why procedural evaluations of democracy diverge from consequentialist judgments. As Coleman (1989: 197) put it, "consenting to a process is not the same thing as consenting to the outcomes of the process." Since outcomes are uncertain for the participants, their ex ante and ex post evaluations must diverge. And, as Lipset and Habermas agree, ex post evaluations modify the ex ante commitments.[8] Hence, compliance is problematic.

In sum, in a democracy all forces must struggle repeatedly for the realization of their interests. None are protected by virtue of their political positions.[9] No one can wait to modify outcomes ex post; everyone must subject interests to competition and uncertainty. The crucial moment in any passage from authoritarian to democratic rule is the crossing of the threshold beyond which no one can intervene to reverse the outcomes of the formal political process. Democratization is an act of subjecting all interests to competition, of institutionalizing uncertainty. The decisive step toward democracy is the devolution of power from a group of people to a set of rules.

---

[8] Lipset (1960) makes the distinction between "legitimacy" – ex ante commitment – and "effectiveness" – ex post evaluation of outcomes. Habermas (1975) distinguishes "legality" – ex ante acceptance of rules – and "legitimacy" – for him, the ex post evaluation. Both maintain that ex post evaluations modify ex ante commitments, but neither notices that the very problem of compliance arises only because the outcomes generated by rules are uncertain ex ante.

[9] Some interests, notably of those who own productive resources, may be protected by their structural position in the economy: If everyone's material welfare depends on the decisions of capitalists to employ and to invest, all governments may be constrained from adopting policies that lower employment and investment. This is the theory of the structural dependence of the state on capital. The controversial question is whether this dependence is so binding on all democratically elected governments that the democratic process can have no effect on the policies followed by governments. My view is that all governments are to some degree dependent on capital but that this dependence is not so binding as to make democracy a sham. There is room for the democratic process to affect the outcomes. See Przeworski and Wallerstein 1988 for a formal analysis of this theory.

## How are outcomes enforced under democracy?

*The question: democracy, rationality, and compliance*

With these preliminaries, we are ready to pose the central question concerning the durability of democracy: How does it happen that political forces that lose in contestation comply with the outcomes and continue to participate rather than subvert democratic institutions? Suppose a government seeks to establish control over the military. Why would the military obey? Imagine that a legislature passes a law granting workers extensive rights within enterprises. Why would the bourgeoisie not defend property by antidemocratic means? Envisage a government policy that causes massive unemployment and widespread impoverishment. Why would the poor not take to the streets to overturn it? Why would they all continue to channel their actions via the democratic institutions that hurt their interests? Why would they comply?

To understand why these questions matter, we need first to clear away some underbrush. If democracy were rational in the sense of eighteenth-century democratic theory, the problem of compliance would not emerge at all, or at least it would assume a different form. If societal interests were harmonious – the central assumption of the democratic theory of the eighteenth century – conflicts would be but disagreements about identifying the common good. They could be overcome by rational discussion: The role of the political process would be only epistemic, a search for the true general will. Politics, Wood (1969: 57–8) noted concerning American political thought between 1776 and 1787, "was conceived to be not the reconciling but transcending of the different interests of the society in the search for the single common good." If representatives could free themselves from the passion of particular interests, if institutions were properly designed, and if the process of deliberation were sufficiently unhurried, unanimity would prevail – the process would have converged to the true general will. Even today some theorists see recourse to voting as only a time-saving device: Voting merely economizes on the transaction costs inherent in deliberation.[10] In this view, as Coleman (1989: 205) characterized it, "the minority

---

[10] Summarizing with approval the views of Buchanan and Tullock (1962), Brennan and Lomasky (1989; 3) present the argument as follows: "If the rule of unanimity were also employed at the postconstitutional level, such that each individual possessed an effective veto

does not consist of losers, and the majority winners. Instead, minority members have false beliefs about the general will; members of the majority have true beliefs."

Is democracy in any sense rational?[11] Democracy would be collectively rational in the eighteenth-century sense if (1) there exists some unique welfare maximum over a political community: common good, general interest, public interest, and the like (Existence); (2) the democratic process converges to this maximum (Convergence). Moreover, democracy would be superior to all its alternatives if (3) the democratic process is the unique mechanism that converges to this maximum – no benevolent dictator could know what is in the general interest (Uniqueness).

The question whether democracy is rational in this sense evokes five distinct responses, depending on whether (1) (a) such a welfare maximum is thought to exist prior to and independent of individual preferences, (b) it is thought to exist only as a function of individual preferences, whatever these might happen to be, or (c) it is thought not to exist at all, because of class or some other irreconcilable division of society; and whether (2) the democratic process is thought to converge to this maximum. Rousseau believed that general interest is given a priori and that the democratic process converges to it. Conservatives in France and England at the time of the French Revolution, as well as contemporary ideologists of various authoritarianisms, maintain that such a welfare maximum does exist but that the democratic process does not lead to it. Economic theorists of democracy, notably Buchanan and Tullock (1962), have maintained that the public interest is tantamount to the verdict of the democratic process, which does identify it. Arrow (1951) demonstrated, under some assumptions, that even if such a maximum does exist, no process of aggregating individual preferences will reveal it. Finally, Marx and his socialist followers argued that no such general interest can be found in societies divided into classes. Note that Schmitt (1988: 13, 6) simultaneously sided

over every collective determination, exorbitant bargaining costs would ensue. . . . Balloting thus emerges as an efficiency-enhancing device itself resting on a foundation that eschews majoritarianism."

[11] To follow distinctions made by economists, we might first distinguish technical from collective rationality. Democracy would be said to be technically rational if it effectively served some otherwise desirable objectives, such as promoting economic development, or (a view to which I adhere) minimized arbitrary violence. But in the present discussion our interest is in the notion of collective, rather than technical, rationality.

with Marx when he rejected Rousseau's assumption that "a true state . . . only exists where the people are so homogeneous that there is essentially unanimity" and attacked convergence when he observed that "the development of modern mass democracy has made argumentative public discussion an empty formality."

Recent discussions focus on the issue of convergence. In the light of social choice theory, as argued particularly by Riker (1982), the democratic process would not converge to a unique welfare maximum even if one existed. The reasons are those offered by Arrow (1951): There is no procedure for aggregating preferences that would guarantee a unique outcome. Hence, one cannot read voting results as identifying any unique social preference. Moreover, McKelvey (1976) demonstrated that voting results may be collectively suboptimal. Yet this view of the democratic process relies on a tacit assumption that individual preferences are fixed and exogenous to the democratic process. Economists take preferences as fixed and adjustment to equilibrium as instantaneous; this is why many of them consider the democratic process as "rent seeking," that is, a waste of resources (see, for example, Tollison 1982).

Yet the assumption that preferences are exogenous to the democratic process is patently unreasonable. As Schumpeter (1950: 263) observed, "the will of the people is the product, not the motive power of the political process." Democracy may still discover or define the social welfare maximum if preferences change as a result of communication. Deliberation is the endogenous change of preferences resulting from communication.[12] The question, then, is whether deliberation leads to convergence.

Habermas and Joshua Cohen (1989) think it does. Their assumptions are, however, too strong to be realistic. They have to claim that (1) the messages are true or false, (2) people will accept the truth when confronted with it, and (3) messages are issued in a disinterested way. The last assumption is most dubious: If people behave strategically in pursuit in their interests, they also emit messages in this way. But even if these assump-

---

[12] To make this discussion less abstract, imagine that three young ladies venture to buy ice cream, with enough money to buy only one flavor. Their initial preferences are respectively $C > V > S > N$, $V > S > C > N$, $S > C > V > N$, where C stands for chocolate, V for vanilla, S for strawberry, and N for none, and $>$ should be read as "prefers over." Now, suppose that the chocolate fan is told that this flavor leaves indelible spots on her dress. Having received this information, she alters her preference, relegating chocolate to second place, from $C > V > S > N$ to $V > C > S > N$. This is deliberation.

tions are granted, it does not follow that there is only one truth. The first two assumptions may not suffice to lead the process to a unique welfare maximum.[13]

In turn, Manin (1987), who offered a more realistic description of the way deliberation works, concluded that deliberation stops short of convergence to a unique maximum. In his view, deliberation educates preferences and makes them more general: It leads to the broadest agreement possible at a particular time. But it stops there, leaving conflicts unresolved. Indeed, it is not apparent whether or not the intensity of conflicts is reduced by Manin's process of deliberation. Perhaps conflicts between two groups that are educated to believe that their interests are opposed are more difficult to resolve than conflicts among fragmented "wanton" desires, to use a term of Hirschman's (1985). After all, this was precisely socialists' understanding of the deliberative process. In their view, this process leads to a recognition of class identity and results in class conflict that cannot be resolved by deliberation (see Przeworski and Sprague 1986).

Indeed, the coup de grâce against theory of democracy as rational deliberation was administered in 1923 by Schmitt (1988), who argued that not all political conflicts can be reconciled by discussion.[14] At some point, reasons and facts are exhausted, yet conflicts remain. At this point, Schmitt observed, issues are decided by voting, which is an imposition of one will upon a resisting will. From this observation, he concluded that conflicts can be resolved only by recourse to physical force: Politics is an antagonistic relation between "us" and "them" in which the ultimate arbiter is violence.

The puzzle is thus the following. If one accepts, as I do, that not all conflicts can be resolved by deliberation and that therefore democracy generates winners and losers, can one ever expect the losers to comply with the verdict of democratically processed conflicts? Why would those who

---

[13] Go back to ice cream. Suppose that in response to the message about chocolate, the strawberry devotee informs others that vanilla makes one fat. In turn, the vanilla lover notes that strawberry contains red dye number 5, which causes cancer. Suppose further that all the rational arguments are exhausted by these messages. Then the preferences that result from rational deliberation may still cycle. Democracy will have educated the participants but will not have led to a unique solution.

[14] "Parliament," Schmitt (1988: 4–5) argued, "is in any case only 'true' as long as public discussion is taken seriously and implemented. 'Discussion' here has a particular meaning and does not simply mean negotiation. . . . Discussion means an exchange of opinion that is governed by the purpose of persuading one's opponent through the argument of the truth or justice of something, or allowing oneself to be persuaded of something as true and just."

suffer as the result of the democratic interplay not seek to subvert the system that generates such results?

Interests are often in conflict. Hence, there are winners and losers, and compliance is always problematic. Yet Schmitt drew a conclusion that is too strong because he failed to understand the role of institutions.[15] Democratic institutions render an intertemporal character to political conflicts. They offer a long time horizon to political actors; they allow them to think about the future rather than being concerned exclusively with present outcomes. The argument I develop below is the following: Some institutions under certain conditions offer to the relevant political forces a prospect of eventually advancing their interests that is sufficient to incite them to comply with immediately unfavorable outcomes. Political forces comply with present defeats because they believe that the institutional framework that organizes the democratic competition will permit them to advance their interests in the future.

## Competing views of compliance

Before this argument is developed, it may be helpful to consider alternative views of compliance.[16]

Think of democracy in the following way. To advance their interests, all have to get past a particular intersection by any means of locomotion they can put their hands on. Some people always arrive from the east; others always from the south. Once they do arrive, a random device chooses the lights: green is a signal to advance, red to wait.[17] The probability of getting the signal to pass or the signal to stop depends on the direction from which one comes and the way the lights are set. If the lights are green in the east–

---

[15] Indeed, his contemporary polemicist had already pointed out that Schmitt "has by no means proven that Europe is confronted by the dilemma: parliamentarism or dictatorship. Democracy has many other organizational possibilities than parliamentarism" (Thoma 1988: 81).

[16] The question I pose is an empirical one: What are the conditions concerning the institutions and the circumstances under which they operate that make political forces comply with the outcomes of the democratic process and hence cause democracy to endure? There is an enormous philosophical literature concerning moral justifications of democracy, in particular of the coercion applied to force compliance. Since philosophers tend to confuse their normative opinions with reality, one often reads that democracy "is" this or that, rather than that it would be this or that if people were guided by the morality of the particular author. While some distinctions introduced in this literature clarify the issues, I find it largely irrelevant to the empirical question at hand.

[17] This allegory is derived from Moulin (1986: ch. 8).

west direction 80 percent of the time, those coming from the east have a good chance to advance. If they are coming from the south, they are likely to be told to wait. But if the lights are green 80 percent of the time in the south–north direction, the situation is reversed. Hence, the likely outcome depends on where one is coming from and on how the lights are set: the resources that participants bring to the democratic competition and the institutional framework within which they compete.

What will happen at any particular moment is uncertain in the sense specified above: Actors know that the possible outcomes are the four combinations of advance and wait, and they know the probability that the light will be green or red (depending on where they are coming from) and hence the probabilities of the two equilibrium outcomes, but they do not know whether they will pass unobstructed or wait while others pass.

Suppose that participants obey the light. They pass alternatively, avoiding collisions.[18] Why do they do it? Why does a big car not force its way through the intersection despite the signal?

Three alternative answers to this question are plausible. One is that compliance is spontaneous – decentralized and voluntary. The second is that there is a policeman at the intersection ready to send back to the end of the queue anyone who tries to barge through out of turn. The last answer is that people observe their turn because they are motivated by a moral commitment to this social order even when it is not in their interest and even when there is no one to punish them.

Elementary game theoretic terminology helps to flesh out these possibilities. Let us distinguish three classes of outcomes of strategic situations.

*(1) Spontaneous self-enforcing outcomes, or equilibria.* Each actor does what is best for her given what others (would) do. A car arrives at the intersection from the south. The driver looks around and comes to the conclusion that it is her turn to wait. She arrives at this conclusion because she thinks that drivers coming from the east expect to pass. Her mental

---

[18] These are the two outcomes that will occur if everyone complies with the signals. The purpose of the institution of traffic lights is to eliminate the collectively suboptimal outcomes: swear at the other {Advance, Advance} and swear at yourself {Wait, Wait}. In this sense, democracy is a Pareto improvement over the state of nature in which everyone tries to force the way. Yet this is a very weak argument for the rationality of democracy, since this state of nature is merely an imaginary counterfact designed to justify the existing order. This is why property rights arguments for efficiency are normatively unpersuasive.

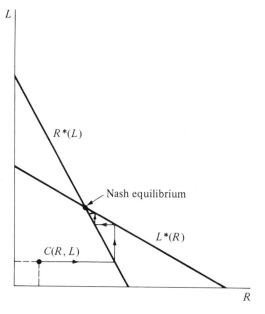

Figure 1.1

signal is "red"; the best response to red is to wait (the alternative is collision), and she waits. Drivers coming from the east interpret the signal as green because they expect those arriving from the south to wait; their best response is to advance (the alternative is to miss a turn and perhaps get hit from behind), and they do. The outcome is {Wait, Advance}. This outcome is equilibrium; no one wants to act differently given expectations of others' actions, and the expectations are mutually fulfilled.

Suppose that leaders of political parties, Left and Right, decide how dirty their campaigns should be. If Right plays clean, it is best for Left to play dirty, and vice versa. If they select their strategies independently and simultaneously, they will adopt some strategy combination {Dirty, Dirty} that will be self-enforcing in the sense that neither party will want to do anything else given what the opponent has done. Their expectations will have been fulfilled: Left will have chosen some degree of dirty on the assumption that Right chose a definite degree, and Right will have chosen this same degree on the assumption that Left chose what it in fact did. This equilibrium is portrayed in Figure 1.1.

Yet another example: Suppose the civilian government anticipates (correctly) that if it tinkers with the military, it will invite a coup, but if it leaves them alone, the military will stay in the barracks. The government reads its preferences as the discovery that it is better off with {Not Tinker, Stay in the Barracks (Not Tinker)} than with {Tinker, Probable Coup (Tinker)}. It decides not to tinker. This is also an equilibrium: The government does not want to do anything else, anticipating the reaction of the military, and the military do not want to do anything else given what the government did.[19] Expectations are again fulfilled: The government expects the military to stay in the barracks, and they do.

What matters about such outcomes is that they constitute equilibria: No one wants to act differently given what others (would) do in response. Such outcomes are thus self-enforcing; they are enforced by independent spontaneous reactions.

*(2) Bargains, or contracts.* An outcome is such that at least one actor would be better off doing something else, and it holds because it is exogenously enforced. There is some third party who punishes "defections" from this outcome.

Suppose the two political parties agree not to engage in a dirty campaign, even though it is most useful for each of them to do so if the other does not. If parties want to win elections, this outcome will not hold without external enforcement. Suppose the parties agreed not to exceed the degree of dirt represented by point $C$ $(R, L)$ in Figure 1.1. Now, the leaders of the Right party look at what the Left has promised to do and ask themselves what it is best for them to do in response. They will smear the Left party all the way to that point on their best response line, $R^*(L)$. But then the Left party will discover that if the Right has begun to talk about the sexual mores of their leader, it is best for them to point out the sources of wealth of their opponents. And so the agreement will unravel until it arrives at the equilibrium outcome. For the initial agreement to stick, a Fair Elections Commission must be able to punish dissuasively everyone who transgresses. Bargains, or contracts, are agreements in which at least one

---

[19] Note that this is a somewhat different equilibrium from the one we used to solve the game between political parties. Political parties chose their strategies simultaneously, whereas in the civilian–military game the government moved first, anticipating the best response of the military. The first equilibrium concept is not very plausible, and the question of what constitutes a reasonable notion of equilibrium is still wide open. But all these niceties need not occupy us at the moment: Nash equilibrium is the simplest and the classic concept of game theory.

party has an incentive to renege but which hold because a third party effectively sanctions defections.

But who is the third party who inflicts punishments under democracy?

In the end, there are two answers to this question. Either enforcement is decentralized – there are enough actors who self-interestedly sanction noncompliance to support the cooperative outcome – or it is centralized – there is a specialized agency that has the power and the motivation to sanction defections, even if this agency is not itself punished for failing to sanction defections or for sanctioning behaviors that constitute compliance.[20] There are only two answers "in the end" because the issue is not whether the state, in the Weberian sense, is necessary to sanction noncompliance. In all democracies, state institutions specialize in doing precisely that. The question concerns the autonomy of the state with regard to the politically organized civil society. If the sanctioning behavior of the state is not itself subject to sanctions from the society, the state is autonomous; the cost of order to society is the Leviathan. But the Leviathan – an externally enforced cooperative agreement – is not democracy.[21] The cost of peace is a state independent of the citizens. In turn, if the state is itself an (albeit imperfect) agent of coalitions formed to assure compliance – a pact of domination – then democracy is an equilibrium, not a social contract. The state enforces compliance because it would itself be punished for not doing so or for using its coercive power to prevent participation. And it would be punished given the interests of the relevant political forces.

Hence, the notion that democracy is a social contract is logically incoherent. Contracts are observed only because they are exogenously enforced; democracy, by definition, is a system in which no one stands above the will of the contracting parties. As Hardin (1987: 2) put it, "A constitution is not a contract, indeed it creates the institution of contracting. Hence, again, its function is to resolve a problem that is prior to contracting."

*(3) Norms.* Equilibria and bargains are the only states of the world that are feasible according to game theory. This theory asserts that all outcomes

---

[20] Enforcement is decentralized if, when a car passes out of turn, someone is willing to pass out of turn from the other direction, this time risking a collision because the present sacrifice will increase his or her expected probability of passing in the future. The result is an equilibrium, a "subgame perfect equilibrium" in game theoretic language.

[21] As Kavka (1986: 181) observed, for Hobbes "the sovereign is not, qua sovereign, a party to the social contract and is therefore not constrained by it." Kavka ended up arguing (p. 229), in the same vein as I do, that this solution is not necessary to evoke compliance if the government is "divided and limited."

hold only because they are mutually enforced in self-interest or are enforced externally by some third party. Specifically, this theory proscribes outcomes that would be supported by something other than a strategic pursuit of interests.

Yet the literature on democracy is full of the language of values and moral commitments.[22] In particular, those writing about transitions frequently report precisely such normatively inspired commitments to democracy. These tend to be called pacts.[23] Institutional pacts are agreements to establish democracy even if a particular system of institutions is not best for some political forces. Political pacts are collusive agreements to stay away from dominant strategies that threaten democracy. Social – in fact, economic – pacts are commitments by unions and firms to restrain present consumption. Military pacts are deals, often secret, between civilian politicians and the military that say, "We will not touch you if you do not touch us." Such outcomes are said to be supported by values: They are collectively optimal, individually irrational, and not externally enforced. Game theory claims they do not exist.

I adopt the game theoretic perspective in what follows. I am not claiming that normative commitments to democracy are infrequent or irrelevant, only that they are not necessary to understand the way democracy works.[24] I am convinced that arguments about whether democracies are supported by acting out of values or by strategic pursuit of interests are not resolvable by direct reference to evidence. The two orientations have to and do compete with each other in making sense of the world around us. The only claim I am trying to substantiate is that a theory of democracy based on the assumption of self-interested strategic compliance is plausible and sufficient.

This claim is made possible by recent developments in game theory that,

---

[22] A typical explanation of the feebleness of democracy in this perspective is well represented by the title of a recent Brazilian book: *A cidadania que no temos* (The citizenry we do not have).

[23] I am not claiming that all "pacts" to be found in the literature on transitions are pacts in this sense. Some are bargains, and some are perhaps even equilibria. Despite its botanical proclivities, this is not a literature distinguished by conceptual clarity.

[24] This assertion does not imply that culture does not matter. Culture is what tells people what to want; culture informs them what they must not do; culture indicates to them what they must hide from others. I take it as an axiom that people function in a communicative and a moral context. Buying votes, for example, is considered immoral in all democracies, though it may be a collectively efficient behavior: If politicians trade promises of future benefits for votes, why cannot they just pay up front?

though still in the midst of a rapid flux, all add up to the message that cooperation can be spontaneously enforced in systems with decentralized self-interested punishments.[25] The variety of circumstances in which this assertion is true include repeated situations in which actors do not discount the future and the probability of the game ending in any particular round is low, repeated situations in which the game is expected to last indefinitely and the actors discount the future at not too high a rate, and repeated situations in which there is even a very low probability that one of the actors is irrational. Many punishment strategies support compliance: tit for two tats, two tits for a tat, three tits for two tats, and so on.[26]

Thus, neither normative commitments nor "social contracts" are necessary to generate compliance with democratic outcomes. Again, in all democracies the state is obviously a specialized agency for enforcing compliance. Moreover, since the state monopolizes instruments of organized coercion, there is a perpetual possibility that it will become independent, that it will act in its own interest without effective supervision by political forces. This is why the threat of the autonomization of the state is perpetual and why institutional frameworks for controlling state autonomy are of fundamental importance in any democracy.[27] The central difficulty of political power in any form is that it gives rise to increasing returns to scale (Lane 1979): On the one hand, incumbency can be used directly to prevent others from contesting office; on the other hand, economic power translates into political power, political power can be used to enhance economic power, and so on. But compliance can be self-enforcing if the institutional framework is designed in such a way that the state is not a third party but an agent of coalitions of political forces. The answer to the question "Who guards the guardian?" is: those forces in the civil society that find it in their

[25] It appears that we were too precipitous in embracing Mancur Olson's (1965) vision of the world as a macrocosm of prisoner's dilemmas generating ubiquitous collective action problems. We now know that in a wide range of repeated situations, cooperative equilibria can be spontaneously supported by self-interested actions. See Fudenberg and Maskin 1986 for several theorems to this effect. Note, in particular, their theorem 2, which shows that under rather mild conditions (payoffs must be sufficiently varied), this result holds for $n$-person games. Their explanation (p. 544) is the following: "If a player deviates [from cooperation], he is minimaxed by the other players long enough to wipe out any gain from his deviation. To induce the other players to go through with minimaxing him, they are ultimately given a 'reward.'" Note furthermore that the punishment strategies that induce cooperation need not depend on a history of past deviations; hence, players need not recognize one another to inflict effective punishment for noncooperation (Abreu 1988).

[26] A tit is a sanction in this language; a tat is an act of noncompliance.

[27] See Przeworski 1990: ch. 2 for a review of literature on this topic.

self-interest. Democracy can be an equilibrium: a system of "self-govern-
ment" in which the distinction between the rulers and the ruled disappears
because, as Montesquieu put it, "le peuple . . . est à certains égards le
monarque; à certains autres, il est le sujet."[28]

### Democracy as an equilibrium

Democracy is consolidated when under given political and economic conditions a particular system of institutions becomes the only game in town,
when no one can imagine acting outside the democratic institutions, when
all the losers want to do is to try again within the same institutions under
which they have just lost. Democracy is consolidated when it becomes self-
enforcing, that is, when all the relevant political forces find it best to
continue to submit their interests and values to the uncertain interplay of
the institutions. Complying with the current outcome, even if it is a defeat,
and directing all actions within the institutional framework is better for the
relevant political forces than trying to subvert democracy. To put it somewhat more technically, democracy is consolidated when compliance –
acting within the institutional framework – constitutes the equilibrium of
the decentralized strategies of all the relevant political forces.[29]

This hypothesis is based on three assumptions. First, institutions matter.
They matter in two ways: as rules of competition and as codes of punishment for noncompliance. That rules affect outcomes needs no discussion.
Just consider the following examples. The Spanish Unión Centro Democrático, the party headed by Adolfo Suárez, and Roh Tae-Woo both received 35 percent of the vote in the first democratic elections in their
respective countries. But Suárez won the election in a parliamentary system: To form a government, he had to build a coalition, and he could
remain in office only as long as this coalition enjoyed sufficient support.
Roh was elected president for a five-year term and could rule during this
period, using decree powers, regardless of the short-term dynamic of political support.[30]

---

[28] I am quoting from a 1905 edition of *L'esprit des lois,* edited and commented on by
Camille Julia, who footnotes this statement with a reference to Aristotle: "All should command each one and everyone all, alternatively."

[29] By "political forces," I mean those groups that are already organized collectively and
those that can be organized under the particular institutional framework, as well as individuals
in their role as voters. I do not suppose that political forces are organized prior to and
independently of the particular institutional framework; institutions do shape political organization.

[30] This example is due to Juan Linz.

The point about institutions as codes of punishment is more complex. Note that I argued earlier that actors may find it individually rational to comply with some (cooperative) outcomes without invoking institutions: When certain conditions are fulfilled, punishing deviations from cooperation by others is the best strategy for each self-interested rational actor. Yet the game theoretic account is based on the implicit assumption that some actors have the capacity to punish. To administer sanctions, actors must be able to undertake actions the effect of which is to lower the payoffs to others. Institutions enable such punishments and make them predictable; they have a priori rules according to which punishments are meted out, the physical means of administering punishments, and incentives for specialized agents to administer them. Just think of taxes. To induce compliance, there must be rules of punishment, a bureaucracy for the detection of noncompliance, and a set of incentives for the bureaucracy to detect it and to apply the rules. If the tax office lacks means of detection and if bureaucrats can be easily bribed, punishment will not be effective. Institutions replace actual coercion with a predictable threat.[31]

Second, there are different ways of organizing democracies. In some democracies, directly elected presidents head governments independent of support in legislative bodies. In other democratic systems, governments must be supported by parliaments and last only as long as they can muster support. Another important distinction concerns the manner in which interests are organized and some aspects of economic policy are determined: The preponderant role of political parties may be countered by the officially recognized role of union federations and employers' associations in representing functional interests and in concerting with each other and with governments about macroeconomic policies. Yet another important difference is between those systems that give almost unlimited powers to current majorities and systems that tightly constrain majority rule, often by providing special guarantees for religious, linguistic, or regional groups. These are just illustrations. The list of important differences could be continued to include electoral formulas, the presence or absence of judicial review, the mode of civilian control over the military, the existence of a professional civil service, and so on.

Finally, contrary to the current fashion, institutions make a difference

---

[31] Game theorists take it for granted that punishment strategies are available to players. Yet the issue is a complex one, as shown by Kavka (1986: ch. 4, sect. 3). In the state of nature, punishments can be administered, but only by physical coercion. Institutions organize this coercion, make it predictable, and rely on the threat.

not only in efficiency but, as Knight (1990) has forcefully reminded us, through their profound distributional effects. It is well known, for example, that first-past-the-post electoral formulas often generate "unearned majorities": majorities of parliamentary seats out of minority electoral support. Collective bargaining frameworks affect the results of wage negotiations; property laws affect the assignment of responsibility for accidental losses; rules governing university admissions determine the class composition of the student body.

Because they have distributional consequences – because they provide different opportunities to particular groups – some institutional frameworks are consolidated under particular economic and political conditions, where others would not have been. The question, then, is what kinds of democratic institutions will evoke the compliance of the relevant political forces?

But what does it mean not to comply? This is not a place for hair splitting; let me just distinguish what matters from what does not. In no system do all individuals comply with all that is expected or required of them. Since the marginal costs of enforcement are typically increasing, all states tolerate some individual noncompliance, sometimes on a massive scale. Noncompliance, in a somewhat counterintuitive sense, can also mean individual withdrawal from participation: indifference to outcomes resulting from democratic institutions. Nonparticipation at times assumes mass proportions: At least 35 percent of the U.S. citizenry remains permanently outside the democratic institutions.

These forms of individual noncompliance can threaten democracy when they are on a mass scale, by creating a potential for sporadic street outbursts or ephemeral antidemocratic movements. But isolated individuals do not shake social orders. This is why "legitimacy" understood in individual terms, even with all the Eastonian distinctions, has little bearing on the issue of regime stability. Only organized political forces have the capacity to undermine the democratic system.

Thus, the only forms of noncompliance that matter for the self-enforcement of democracy are strategies that (1) seek to alter ex post the outcomes of the democratic process and (2) drastically reduce the confidence of other actors in democratic institutions.[32] Thus, not to comply is the same as to subvert the democratic system in order to override its outcomes.

---

[32] If any actor is able to reverse the outcome ex post, other actors must update downward their expectations about winning the game according to the rules.

Let me suggest schematically how spontaneous decentralized self-interested compliance may work.

Examine the situation from the point of view of a particular actor, such as the military or a coalition of the bourgeoisie and the military. At any moment, the outcomes of the democratic process are such that these actors either win or lose, where the value of having won is greater than of having lost ($W > L$). The probability they attach to their chance of winning in any future round is $p$.[33] The courses of action available to these actors are either to comply or to subvert. If they subvert, they get $S$, where $S$ includes the risk that they will fail and will be punished;[34] and if the compliance of these actors is problematic, it must be true that $W > S > L$.[35] Suppose, then, that they have just lost; let this be $t = 0$. If they comply, they will get $L(0)$; if they subvert, they will get $S(0)$. If they were guided only by immediate interests, they would subvert. But institutions offer actors an intertemporal perspective. Although they have just lost, the actors know that if they comply in this round then they can expect to get $C(1) = pW + (1 - p)L$ in the next one, and although $L < S$, it may be true that $L(0) + C(1) > S(0) + S(1)$, which would lead them to comply at $t = 0$.

Let us generalize this argument. It is reasonable to assume that actors discount the future, where the discount factor is $0 < r < 1$, so that the value they attach to compliance in the next round is $rC$, the round after that $r^2C$, and so on. The cumulative value of compliance is $C^*$. If they subvert, they can reverse the loss in this round and can expect to get $S$ now and in the future. The cumulative value of subversion is $S^*$. If $C^* > S^*$, the losers will comply at $t = 0$.

Note that the likelihood of successful subversion and the cost associated with its failure depend on the willingness of other political forces to defend the democratic institutions. One may thus be tempted to think in terms of a "tipping equilibrium": a situation in which each actor's support of democracy depends on the number of other actors who support it. Yet the actors in the democratic game are not identical; democracy is not just a matter of numbers. Obviously, the institutional framework of civilian control over the military constitutes the neuralgic point of democratic consolidation.

---

[33] This is the probability they attach at present; they may update this probability as they learn whether they are losing or winning.

[34] $S$ depends on the probability that an attempt to subvert the outcomes will be successful and on the utilities of success and failure of subversion. If $q$ is this probability, and $D$ is the value of successful subversion and $F$ of its failure, then $S = qD + (1 - q)F$.

[35] Some actors may be such that for them $S > W > L$: They will always try to subvert. Others may be characterized by $W > L > S$: They never will.

One can complicate this story in several ways to make it more realistic, allowing for more differentiated strategies, incomplete knowledge and learning, and a more reasonable notion of victories and defeats.[36] But one fundamental conclusion has already emerged from this simplified model and continues to hold when the model is made descriptively more realistic: Compliance depends on the probability of winning within the democratic institutions. A particular actor $i$ will comply if the probability it attaches to being victorious in democratic competition, $p(i)$, is greater than some minimum; call it $p^*(i)$. This minimum probability depends on the value the particular collective actor attaches to outcomes of the democratic process and to outcomes of subverting democracy and on the risk it perceives for the future. The more confident the actor is that the relationship of political forces will not take an adverse turn within the democratic institutions, the more likely is this actor to comply; the less risky the subversion, the less likely are the potential antidemocratic forces to comply.[37]

None of the above is intended as a description of historical events. "Models" – I frequently feel forced to cite Theil (1976: 3) – "are to be used, not believed." What the model suggests is that in analyzing any concrete situation one should consider the values and the chances the particular political forces attach to advancing their interests under democracy and outside it. Democracy will evoke generalized compliance, it will be self-enforcing, when all the relevant political forces have some specific

---

[36] Note that the concepts of winning and losing are greatly simplified here. Each group defines its interests over a broad spectrum of outcomes and attaches values to particular degrees and specific manners in which each of these interests is realized. Thus, winning and losing are continually defined for multidimensional preference contours. But there is no reason to get mired in mathematics if the logical implications remain the same as in a simple model.

[37] For those who are curious about the reasoning and not just the conclusions, here is the model. If the actor has just lost, at time $t$, set as $t = 0$ for notational convenience, the payoffs from complying are $C^* = L + \Sigma r^t C(t) = L + [r/(1 - r)]C$. The payoffs from subverting are $S^*$ and depend on the probability this actor attaches to the success of subversion and the rate at which it discounts the nondemocratic future. Hence, the actor complies if $C^* > S^*$, or if

$$p > (1/r) \frac{(1 - r)S^* - L}{W - L} = p^*.$$

Note that $dp^*/dr < 0$: The more confidence a particular actor has in its future under democracy, the lower the minimum probability required to evoke its compliance. In turn, let $q$ be the probability of the success of subversion, $dS^*/dq > 0$. Then $dp^*/dq > 0$: The less risky it is for a particular group to subvert, the higher is the probability of winning required to make it obey democratic outcomes.

Finally, observe that if $p^*$ is sufficient to evoke compliance when the actor has just lost, it will be also sufficient if it has just won. Hence, $p > p^*$ is the minimal condition.

minimum probability of doing well under the particular system of institutions.[38]

This probability is different for different groups. We learned earlier that it depends on the specific institutional arrangements and on resources the participants bring into the democratic competition. We now learn that it also depends on the power a particular actor has to cause the downfall of democracy. The military have weak prospects to pursue their interests under democracy, but they can subvert democracy by force: Their $W$ is low, their $S$ high. Hence, their $p*$ may be quite high. The bourgeoisie can do quite well under democracy and well outside it but need the military for successful subversion. Unions and other organizations of wage earners can do quite well in democratic competition, but they are often brutally repressed if democracy falls; they may be the one group for which $L > S$ and which always prefers to comply.[39] Moreover, the guarantees required by a particular group may vary with historical conditions. In post-1976 Spain, the military were almost indifferent as between $S$ and $L$; they were so starved by Franco that even a nonpolitical life under democracy seemed satisfactory to them. In turn, the post-1983 Argentine military saw $L$ as much inferior to $S$; they knew that losing could mean long jail sentences for many of them. These are just seat-of-the-pants speculations; what I want to show is that even the simplified model has some power to distinguish particular actors and different historical conditions.

Hence, the minimal chance required to stay within the democratic system depends on the value of losing in the democratic interplay of interests. Those political forces that have an outside option – the option of subverting democracy or provoking others to subvert it – may stay with the democratic game if they believe that even losing repeatedly under democracy is better for them than a future under an alternative system. After all, democracy does offer one fundamental value that for many groups may be sufficient to prefer it to all alternatives: security from arbitrary violence. As Santiago Carillo, then secretary of the Spanish Communist party, put it in 1974, "One should have the courage to explain to the working class that it is better to pay surplus value to this bourgeois sector than to create a situation that may turn against them" (Carrillo 1974: 187).

Even from the purely economic point of view, faith in the efficacy of

---

[38] The political forces that are relevant are those for which $S > L$. Those for which $L > S$ have no outside option and need no guarantee.

[39] The Peronist unions in Argentina are the most likely exception.

democracy may be a source of commitment among those who see little chance of winning distributional conflicts within democratic institutions. If democracy is believed to be conducive to economic development in the long run, various groups may opt for this system even if they see little chance of winning conflicts about distribution. The higher the anticipated value of losing under democracy, the lower need be the chances of winning.[40]

This last hypothesis has implications for the perennial issue of the social conditions of democracy. Put conversely, the model implies that if some important political forces have no chance to win distributional conflicts and if democracy does not improve the material conditions of losers, those who expect to suffer continued deprivation under democratic institutions will turn against them. To evoke compliance and participation, democracy must generate substantive outcomes: It must offer all the relevant political forces real opportunities to improve their material welfare. Indeed, a quick calculation shows that in South America between 1946 and 1988 any regime, democratic or authoritarian, that experienced positive rates of growth in a given year had a 91.6 percent chance of surviving through the next twelve months, a regime that experienced one year of a negative rate of growth had an 81.8 percent chance, and a regime that experienced two consecutive years of declining incomes had only a 67 percent chance.

Yet it is important to see what this hypothesis does not imply. First, it does not mean that democracy must have a social content if the institutions are to evoke compliance. If democracy is a system in which outcomes always appear uncertain, "social content" cannot mean prior commitments to equality, justice, welfare, or whatever.[41] Such commitments are not feasible; under democracy, outcomes are determined by the strategies of competing political forces and are thus inevitably uncertain ex ante. Constitutions that are an oath to promote the general welfare, enhance national unity, advance the culture of the people, or provide decent conditions of life for everyone[42] may be necessary for catharsis, but they cannot be

---

[40] This is true if the political forces that have a low chance of winning distributional conflicts believe that democracy will result in increasing the total pie. Return to the expression for $p^*$. The derivative $dp^*/dL = -(1/r)[W - (1 - r)S^*]/(W - L)^2$. This derivative is negative.

[41] This has been a topic of my repeated debate with Francisco Weffort. For the most recent salvo, see his "Incertezas da transição na América latina," (1989).

[42] Not to mention such clauses as those requiring every firm that employs more than ten workers to hire at least 10 percent of new employees over forty-five years of age!

complied with. They can be observed only to the extent that they express laws, not oaths.[43] Democracy may end up having a social content if the institutional framework favors social justice in spite of the unequal resources with which different forces enter the democratic competition. But this is a matter of institutions, not of substantive commitments.

Second, the assertion that democracy cannot last unless it generates a satisfactory economic performance is not an inexorable objective law. A phrase one repeatedly hears in newly democratic countries is "Democracy must deliver, or else . . ." The ellipsis is never spelled out, since it is taken as self-evident. When Argentine generals proclaim one after another that "the economic situation is putting democracy at risk" (*New York Times,* 3 January 1990), they appear to be asserting an objective law of which they are just unwitting agents: They expect the economic crisis to turn some civilians against democracy, which will increase the probability of successful subversion, to which they will respond, given their preferences, by overthrowing democracy. Yet whether or not democracy survives adverse economic conditions is a joint effect of conditions and institutions. As the European experience of the Great Depression demonstrates, some institutional frameworks are more resistant than others to economic crisis.

In conclusion, from the static point of view democratic institutions must be "fair": They must give all the relevant political forces a chance to win from time to time in the competition of interests and values. From the dynamic point of view, they must be effective: They must make even losing under democracy more attractive than a future under nondemocratic alternatives. These two aspects are to some extent interchangeable. They constitute different ways of asserting that political forces comply with democratic outcomes when they expect that their future will be better if they continue to follow the rules of the democratic game: Either they must have a fair chance to win or they must believe that losing will not be that bad. Thus, to evoke compliance, to be consolidated, democratic institutions must to some extent be fair and to a complementary degree effective.

Yet under certain conditions these requirements may be contradictory, particularly with regard to economic issues. Fairness requires that all major interests must be protected at the margin; effectiveness may necessitate that they be seriously harmed. To be effective economically, governments may

---

[43] This juxtaposition is derived from the current Polish constitutional debate. See *Trybuna Ludu,* 17 September 1989.

have to violate some property rights – for example, by adopting land reform or by generating massive unemployment in a quest for allocative efficiency. Institutions conducive to major economic transformation cannot protect all interests; institutions that protect all interests are not an appropriate framework for major economic transformation.

Indeed, the traditional dilemma of the Left has been that even a procedurally perfect democracy may remain an oligarchy: the rule of the rich over the poor. As historical experience demonstrates, democracy is compatible with misery and inequality in the social realm and with oppression in factories, schools, prisons, and families. And the traditional dilemma of the Right has been that democracy may turn out to be the rule of the many who are poor over the few rich. Democratic procedures can threaten property; political power in the form of universal suffrage and the right to associate may be wielded to restrict property rights. Hence, the conditions under which democracy becomes the equilibrium of decentralized strategies of autonomous political forces are restrictive. This is why democracy has been historically a fragile form for organizing political conflicts.

## Institutional design

What does this abstract discussion imply about specific institutions? What kinds of institutional arrangements are likely to last and to matter? Should the constitution contain only rules about political competition and about protecting minorities, or should it include substantive commitments? Is the parliamentary system more likely than the presidential one to regulate conflicts?[44] Are some elements of a corporatist organization of interests necessary to mobilize consent to economic policy at a time of crisis?

---

[44] Linz (1984) has developed a number of arguments in favor of parliamentary, as opposed to presidential, systems. I am particularly persuaded by his observation that presidential systems generate a zero-sum game, whereas parliamentary systems increase total payoffs. The reasons are the following. In presidential systems, the winner takes all: He or she can form a government without including any losers in the coalition. In fact, the defeated candidate has no political status, as in parliamentary systems, where he or she becomes the leader of the opposition. Hence, in terms of the model developed above, under *ceteris paribus* conditions (under which $W + L = T$ is the same in both systems), the value of victory, $W$, is greater and the value of defeat, $L$, is smaller under presidential than under parliamentary systems. Now, assume that political actors discount the future at the rate of $r$ per annum. Under the presidential system, the term is fixed for some period ($t =$ PRES), and the expected value of the next round is $r^{PRES} [pW + (1 - p) L]$. Under the parliamentary system, the winner governs only as long as he or she can maintain sufficient support in the parliament, say for the period $t =$ PARL, so that the expected value of the next round is $r^{PARL} [pW + (1 - p)L]$.

The relationship between constitutions and political reality is not an obvious one. Except for the United Kingdom and Israel, all countries have written, formally adopted constitutions. Yet these constitutions have had highly divergent roles in the actual political life of their countries. In the United States the same constitution has survived for two hundred years, during which time it has continually influenced political life, at least in the sense that major political conflicts, with one major exception, have been framed in terms of it. In Argentina, the constitution adopted in 1853 remained, on paper, in effect except for the brief period between 1949 and 1957. Yet in the past fifty years, political conflicts in Argentina have only half the time been processed according to its provisions. In France, the constitution has been changed several times since 1789; indeed, every major political upheaval has produced a new one. Yet while it was in force, each constitution did regulate the exercise of power and the pattern of succession. Finally, to fill the last cell of this fourfold table, in South Korea major constitutional reforms have occurred every three years and nine months since 1948, and no succession has conformed to the rules. A constitution that is long-lasting and observed, one that is long-lasting and ignored, some that are changed often and respected serially, and others that are modified frequently and remain irrelevant – historical experience is not very informative.

Indeed, I discovered, much to my surprise, that we do not have sufficiently reliable empirical knowledge to answer questions about institutional design. We have intuitions about the impact of presidentialism versus parliamentarism, we know the effects of alternative electoral systems, and we tend to believe that an independent judiciary is an important arbitrating force in the face of conflicts, but our current empirical knowledge leaves a broad margin for disagreements about institutional design. Is democracy in Poland more likely to be consolidated under a strong or a weak presidency? Under a plurality or under a system of proportional representation? Under a constitution that affirms the commitment to common values or under one that leaves them open? We just do not know enough to answer such questions when confronted with specific historical conditions.

The reason we cannot answer such questions in a reliable way is that the

---

Elementary algebra will then show that unless the tenure expected under parliamentarism is notably longer than under presidentialism, the loser has a greater incentive to stay in the democratic game under parliamentarism.

consolidation of democracy may be a joint effect of conditions and institutions. Institutions may have to fit conditions. Rousseau (1986: 1) may have been correct when, in the course of designing a constitution for Poland, he wrote, "One must know thoroughly the nation for which one is building; otherwise the final product, however excellent it may be in itself, will prove imperfect when it is acted upon – the more certainly if the nation be already formed, with its tastes, customs, prejudices, and failings too deeply rooted to be stifled by new plantings." And we have just not done enough empirical research to acquire a reliable knowledge of such joint effects.

Hence, I can venture only a rudimentary guess. Constitutions that are observed and last for a long time are those that reduce the stakes of political battles. Pretenders to office can expect to reach it; losers can expect to come back. Such constitutions, Napoleon is alleged to have said, should be "short and vague." They define the scope of government and establish rules of competition, leaving substantive outcomes open to the political interplay. Constitutions adopted to fortify transitory political advantage, constitutions that are nothing but pacts of domination among the most recent victors, are only as durable as the conditions that generated the last political victory. In turn, constitutions that allow everyone to introduce substantive demands, constitutions that ratify compromises by enshrining substantive commitments (of which the social rights chapter of the Weimar Constitution is the prototype) are often impossible to implement.[45]

To push this argument just one step farther, let me offer three – still excessively abstract – observations. First, it is worth noting that electoral majorities have been rare in the history of successful democracies; in the postwar period only about one election in fifteen has resulted in a majority of votes cast for one party. Hence, most democracies are ruled either by explicit coalitions among parties none of which can rule on its own or by minority governments based on implicit assurance of support. Second, successful democracies are those in which the institutions make it difficult to fortify a temporary advantage. Unless the increasing returns to power are institutionally mitigated, losers must fight the first time they lose, for waiting makes it less likely that they will ever succeed. Yet, third, governments must be able to govern, and this implies that they must be able to

---

[45] As Lula put it in a preelection interview, "If we put in practice the social rights chapter of the new constitution, we will make a revolution" (Luis Inacio Lula da Silva, interviewed in *Veja*, 29 November 1990, p. 4).

prevent some demands from reaching the public sphere and certainly that they cannot tolerate all important groups having veto power over public policy.

These observations add up to two negative rules. To be stable and effective, democratic institutions must not generate governments unresponsive to the changing relations of political forces, governments free from the obligation to consult and concert when they formulate policy, governments unconstrained to obey rules when they implement them. Yet they also must not paralyze decisions and their implementation. All interests must be represented in the making of policy, but none should be able unilaterally to block its formulation and implementation. Another way to formulate this conclusion is that a stable democracy requires that governments be strong enough to govern effectively but weak enough not to be able to govern against important interests.

If these observations are valid, democratic institutions must remain within narrow limits to be successful. And under some historical conditions there may be no space between the limits; consolidation of democracy is not always possible.

## Transitions to democracy

Self-enforcing democracy is not the only possible outcome of "transitions": strategic situations that arise when a dictatorship collapses.[46] A breakdown of an authoritarian regime may be reversed, or it may lead to a new dictatorship. And even if a democracy is established, it need not be self-sustaining; the democratic institutions may systematically generate outcomes that cause some politically important forces to subvert them. Hence, consolidated democracy is only one among the possible outcomes of the collapse of authoritarian regimes.

Given that under the current economic, political, and institutional conditions autonomous social forces struggle to impose on others a system that will fortify their political advantage, are there any institutions that will voluntarily be adopted that, once in place, will elicit decentralized compliance? When it is rational for the conflicting interests voluntarily to constrain their future ability to exploit political advantage by devolving

---

46 The term "transitions" is not a very fortunate label for these situations, since it suggests that the outcome is predetermined. Yet I decided to follow common usage in the immense body of literature on transitions to democracy.

some of their power to institutions? When will they conclude a "democratic pact" that engenders compliance and thus makes democracy self-enforcing?

We now confront nothing less than the classic problem of liberal political theory. Ever since the seventeenth century, political philosophers have been hunting for the secret of an alchemical transformation from the brutish chaos of conflict to the serene life of cooperation. Beginning with the Leviathan, proposals have been innumerable and, recently, increasingly optimistic. We are told that the problem of social order can be solved by conventions (Lewis 1969; Sugden 1986), by spontaneous evolution of cooperation (Taylor 1976; Axelrod 1984), by norms (Ullman-Margalit 1977; Axelrod 1986), by morals (Gauthier 1986), and by benevolent institutions (Schotter 1981).

The generic problem can be posed as follows. Given some strategic structure of interests classified by various mixes of conflict and coordination, the noncooperative solution to which has some normatively undesirable features, is there any device (the state, the plan, conventions, morals, norms, institutions, lotteries) that will be voluntarily adopted and that, once adopted, will evoke spontaneous (free and decentralized) compliance, that is, behaviors that support normative desiderata, such as collective (Pareto) rationality, some other welfare criteria, justice, fairness, equity, or equality? Note that the philosophers' quest is for devices that evoke spontaneous compliance, not for institutions that force compliance, even if they elicit behaviors that are normatively desirable.

This formulation is based on some assumptions that limit its usefulness.[47] The liberal point of departure – that hypothetical "individuals" confront the problem of cooperation in a state of nature – is not helpful for analyzing problems confronting real actors in concrete historical conditions.[48] The relevant actors are not abstract individuals but politi-

---

[47] One reason why the Hobbesian formulation is not very useful in our context is that for Hobbes the first reason for individuals to found a state is that it can defend them from invasion by foreigners. Only a secondary reason is that it can protect them from injuring one another (*Leviathan*, ch. 17). Although territorial conflicts flare up from time to time, the issue we are analyzing is not founding a state but organizing a state on territory already given. Hence, the Pareto superiority of having secure borders is not a major consideration in conflicts about institutions in transitions to democracy.

[48] The problem with game theory is that it combines a useful methodology with an ideologically derived and patently unreasonable ontology of "individuals" who in addition appear homogeneous in that they have available to them the same strategies and often the same payoffs. My biases on this topic are treated at length in Przeworski 1985. Note that

cal forces: previously constituted collective organizations, some categories of people who might become collectively organized if provoked, and individuals as voters. They enter conflicts in a context in which there are always preexisting conventions, norms, and institutions.

Yet, with these caveats, the role of the democratic pact is to effect just such an alchemical transformation. Pacts are (one-shot noncooperative[49]) equilibria in strategies that consist of altering the current conditions in such a way as to make decentralized voluntary compliance individually optimal. They are agreements to disagree. And the only way to change these conditions by agreement is to form new institutions.

Thus, solutions to the problem of democratization consist of institutions. Resources of political forces are given; so are their preferences and the conditions independent of everyone. The game is solved if a system of institutions that engenders spontaneous compliance is an equilibrium of the transition. The problem of establishing democracy is the following: Will political actors agree to a framework of democratic institutions that will evoke their compliance?

This question involves two separate issues.[50] The first is whether under given conditions there are any systems of democratic institutions that will evoke spontaneous decentralized compliance once they are established. Under some structures of interests, there may be no institutions that will stop important political forces from trying to subvert them once they are in place. The second is whether a self-enforcing system of democratic institutions will be established as a result of conflicts concerning the choice of institutions. For even if institutions could be found that would be self-enforcing once installed, they need not constitute the equilibrium of the

Kavka (1986: 148) is careful to define the state of nature as "a model of societies of real people dissolved by civil disorder or removal of the State."

[49] By which I mean only not externally enforced.

[50] These issues are collapsed in social contract theories. These theories pose the following question: What kind of political order would hypothetical individuals in the state of nature see as worth complying with? They differ with regard to the assumptions imposed on individuals. If individuals are placed behind a veil that prevents them from knowing anything about their welfare in the new social order, then the issue is why they would comply with this order once they were in it and knew how well off they were (Braybrooke 1976). If, in turn, individuals know their chances in the new order, then the question is why they will agree to one that they know will cause them to comply with outcomes that make them badly off. Say the military know that a democratic system will impose civilian control with which it would be best for them to comply; they may prefer their own dictatorship. Hence, the questions whether political forces will comply with a given institutional system once it is established and whether they will agree to establish it are distinct.

transitional situation when the chances of the particular political forces are very different under alternative institutional arrangements. Imagine that a group of people enters a casino that contains a roulette wheel, a poker table, a blackjack counter, and a crap stand. Is there a game that the players, given the resources they have, will continue to play even if they lose a few times in succession? And if there is, will the potential players agree which one to play?

These are the generic issues inherent in any transition to democracy.

## Appendix: Why do outcomes appear uncertain?

One characteristic feature of democracy is that outcomes appear in a particular way uncertain to all participants. It is as if all do what they think is best for them, and then some random device chooses the outcome; as if the results were decided by a throw of dice. Are they in fact? And if they are not, why do they appear as if they were? The purpose of this appendix is to clarify the origins and nature of the uncertainty generated by democracy.

Let us first try a less frivolous description of the way democracy operates. A few examples may help intuition.

Electoral competition is an obvious one. Parties look at the electorate, decide which issue positions will generate the most support, and choose those that maximize the probability of winning under that platform. On election day the result is read, and the parties receive the signal, more or less uniquely defined in each democracy, to form the government or go into opposition.

Proponents and opponents of public aid to private schools argue their case in front of a constitutional court. They cite the constitution if the law is on their side; the facts if it is not. The court deliberates and issues a verdict, which is now the legal status quo.

Banks are pressuring the legislature to bail them out of their past misdeeds. Everyone knows that universalistic appeals beat particularistic ones: Banks summon the specter of widows losing their lifesavings; politicians claiming to represent taxpayers evoke the perils of deficits. The legislature votes the bail-out, and the bureaucracy writes checks.

Note that in these illustrations there is no room for uncertainty. Given the resources of the participants and the institutional framework, the outcome is determined. Each actor can examine the distribution of resources, look up the rules, and determine who will lose or win what if they all go through the motions; that is, if they follow their best strategies. And yet the actors appear to behave as if they were not certain of the outcome.

The evidence that they do is twofold. If winning and losing are dichotomous, then those who expect to lose should simply do nothing, since there is nothing they can do: The court will decide against them because the other side has better arguments.[51] Hence, if they do compete, it must be because they are uncertain about the consequences of their actions. If payoffs are continuous, the eventual losers are compelled to go through the motions because otherwise they would do worse than they can do. Politicians must complain about government largesse even if they know that they will end up bailing out the banks, just in order not to lose votes. But I think there is much prima facie evidence that political actors are often uncertain about the outcome; everyone in a democracy has lived through at least one election-night drama. My favorite admission of surprise was the editorial in the right-wing Chilean daily *El Mercurio* the day after Salvador Allende won a plurality in the presidential election of 1970: "No one expected that an election via the secret, universal, bourgeois franchise could lead to the victory of a marxist candidate."

What, then, is the source of uncertainty inherent in democracy?

Let us examine a few card games. The first one is called LEN. Players come to the table and bid for the ace of spades. Whoever makes the highest bid gets his money back and collects the money on the table and a dollar from everyone who did not play. The rules are perfectly universalistic; everyone can play. But one player is richer than the others, and wealth uniquely determines the outcome.[52] Hence, there is no uncertainty here. This is why Lenin was correct to call his conception of democracy the dictatorship of the bourgeoisie.[53] Except for the certain winner, anyone who pays more than a dollar to enter this game is a dupe.

[51] For a dichotomous view of payoffs, see Riker 1962. This view was disputed by Stigler (1972).

[52] Think of (American) football. There are a field, a ball, and a set of rules. The rules are blind to the identity of the teams. Referees and umpires adjudicate impartially whether actions conform to the rules and administer specified penalties. But one team consists of 300-pound players, the other of 150-pound weaklings. The outcome is certain.

[53] "The bourgeois parliament, even the most democratic in the most democratic republic in which the property and the rule of the bourgeoisie are preserved, is a machine for the suppression of the toiling millions by small groups of exploiters. . . . As long as capitalist property exists universal suffrage is an instrument of the bourgeois state" ("The Letter to the Workers of Europe and America" [1919], Lenin 1959: 482). Lenin's most programmatic statement on this topic is "Theses on Bourgeois Democracy and Proletarian Dictatorship Presented to the First Congress of the Communist International," 4, March 1919.

Now let us play JON. Players bid for cards, face down. After all the cards have been bought, they look at what they have. The player who has the ace of spades wins, and payoffs are the same as before. In this game, if everyone plays as well as possible, the wealthiest player will buy the most cards and will have the best chance of getting the ace. If all the $N$ players are equally wealthy, their prior probabilities of winning are $\{1/N, 1/N, \ldots, 1/N\}$. In fact, the probabilities may be terribly unequal: The prior probability distribution may be as skewed as $\{(N - 1)/N, 1/N, 0, \ldots, 0\}$. But all money can buy is a better chance, because pure chance plays a role. Even a player who can afford only one card has one chance in fifty-two of pocketing the prize. Is this what democracy is like?

One obvious argument against this analogy is that democracies – at least modern ones – have no institutions that function as randomizing devices.[54] Parliaments, bureaucracies, and courts are supposed to deliberate and make decisions on justifiable grounds, not throw dice.

Note, however, that this is the explanation of uncertainty suggested by social choice theory: Collective preferences cycle incessantly, the time of reading them lacks particular justification, the outcome cannot be understood in terms of individual preferences. But the uncertainty implied by social choice theory is too radical; it permits no rational action. Social choice theory portrays democracy as if it were LOTTO: Actors decide whether to buy a ticket and wait for the winning numbers to appear on the screen. The outcome is fair, but this is its only justification. This is not enough to motivate participation in democracy; to participate, actors must see some relationship between what they do and what happens to them. If everyone believed the impossibility theorems, no one would participate. True, Elster (1989) has shown that there are some circumstances when collective rationality may call for a random decision: whenever the costs of deciding are greater than the difference the decision makes – for example, when a custody battle inflicts more damage on the child than landing with the less-qualified parent. But in general, a democracy in which people believed that outcomes were decided at random would be untenable.

Hence, I do not think that this is the way democracy is played. An element of pure chance does enter the democratic game, but only exogenously: The accidental death of a leader may radically alter the situation. But this is where the role of chance ends.

---

[54] There are instances in history of elections by chance and serious arguments in their favor. See Elster 1989.

Table 1.1

|  | | Column | |
|---|---|---|---|
|  | | King of hearts | Any other card |
| Row { Ace of spades<br>Any other card | | Nothing, All<br>Something, Something | All, Nothing<br>Something, Something |

Another reason outcomes can be uncertain is that actors do not know what to do. Some commentators on my earlier claim that democracy is inherently uncertain concluded that this assertion implies that individuals must be uncertain what to do.[55] Indeed, the Brazilians published one of my articles under the title "Ama a incerteza e seras democrático": "If You Like Uncertainty, You Will Be a Democrat."[56] Now, it may be true, as Manin (1987) argues, that democracy requires that citizens be willing to change their preferences. But they need not like uncertainty and need not be uncertain what to do.

Let NOR be a game in which actors do not know which strategies will produce the best outcomes, because these outcomes depend on simultaneous actions by others: there are no dominant strategies. The game is played as follows. Bids are made for cards, face down. Once all the cards have been bought, the players (two for the sake of simplicity, named Row and Column) play by each putting a card on the table face down and simultaneously turning over the cards. The payoffs are given by {first payoff to Row, second to Column}.[57]

Row does not know what to do. Playing the ace of spades is better than pulling any other card if Column plays any card other than the king of hearts; otherwise, it is worse. The same is true for Column. (Table 1.1.)

Some game theorists assert that the rational thing to do under the circumstances is to use a random device to choose one's actions. If a political

[55] Notably Lechner (1986) and Hirschman (1986). There are in fact two distinct reasons why actors may not know what to do. The one discussed in the text is that they do not know which course of action is best for them. But I have an impression that Hirschman and Manin (1987) have something else in mind, namely, that, educated by deliberation, actors are not certain whether they should act on their own current preferences or yield to the preferences of others. In the latter case, actors are uncertain about their own preferences rather than about courses of action.

[56] *Novos Estudos*, 1985.

[57] To limit the impact of resource inequality on the outcome, the Law of Fair Access ensures that the same player cannot have both the ace of spades and the king of hearts.

party does not know whether it can gain more votes moving to the left or to the right, because the outcome depends on where another party moves, it should decide by throwing an appropriately weighted coin. If banks do not know whether an argument about widows is more persuasive than one about its employees threatened with losing their jobs, they may decide by chance. In this case the outcome is uncertain because it emerges from probabilistically chosen strategies: The combination of strategies that has the property that no one would want to mix the strategies differently given what others can do is unique, but the outcomes are only probabilistically knowable.[58]

Lechner is right that NOR is not a plausible understanding of democracy, because democratic actors value order, an order that will indicate to them what to do. Disorder destabilizes democracies, argues Lechner, influenced by the trauma of the chaotic years of the Unidad Popular government in Chile. I agree, but I do not think that the uncertainty about outcomes entails either chaos at the institutional level or uncertainty about one's own actions.

The explanation of uncertainty that I find most persuasive has been offered by Aumann (1987). He has shown that if actors do not know something, if they are cognitively rational in the sense that they change their beliefs about the world as a function of information they get,[59] and if they act on these beliefs, then the strategies they choose independently will be distributed probabilistically, as if they had been chosen jointly using a random device.

What is it that actors do not know? One of the many powerful implications of Aumann's model is that they may not know all kinds of things, not only those that traditional game theory allowed them to be ignorant about, but also the strategies of other actors. Indeed, this is what actors do not know in Aumann's account. Each actor may know the unique outcome associated with each combination of strategies, and each may know what it

[58] This idea seems to be going out of fashion. See Aumann 1987 and Rubinstein 1988: 9; the latter says that "the naive interpretation of a mixed strategy, as an action which is conditioned on the outcome of a lottery executed by the player before playing the game, is intuitively ridiculous." In turn, a physically mixed strategy – mixing strategies in some proportion – would not lead to uncertainty.

[59] One important assumption underlying Aumann's model is the so-called Harsanyi doctrine, which asserts that the only source of knowledge is observation. Specifically, the assumption is that all actors have the same priors, so that if they attach different probabilities to crossing an intersection at any moment, it is only because what they have observed is different.

is best for others to do given what he or she does. Only the most minimalist assumption is required to generate uncertainty: that I am not sure how others see me. Leaders of a political party may know that if they keep the opponent's skeletons in the closet, it will be best for others to reciprocate, but if they are not sure whether opponents trust them not to cause scandals, uncertainty will ensue. The minimal assumption is that I am not sure that the opponents know my preferences or my character. If I allow that they may see me as moralistic rather than victory-oriented or as reckless, I cannot be sure what they will do.

Hence, the outcomes of the democratic process are not uncertain. They only appear to be uncertain to every participant. But "appears" should not be taken as an indication of remediable ignorance, as "false consciousness."[60] The appearance of uncertainty is necessarily generated by the system of decentralized decision making in which there is no way to be sure what others think about me. An omniscient observer could determine the unique outcome of each situation, but no participant can be an observer, because the observer's theory need not be universally shared by other participants. And if it is not shared, then she cannot be certain how others perceive her and hence what they will do. Note that the strategies are chosen independently and deterministically. Each actor decides independently what to do, and each actor knows what it is best to do at every moment. Yet the outcomes associated with these combinations are distributed probabilistically.

To highlight the distinguishing features of uncertainty inherent in democracy, consider a stylized model of authoritarian regimes (which I treat as synonymous with dictatorships, abandoning some important distinctions).[61]

---

[60] This lapse into marxist language is not accidental. Aumann's model provides microfoundations for Marx's theory of fetishized knowledge. Fetishized knowledge is simply local knowledge: the view of the system from the point of view of each agent. Individual agents exchanging under capitalism do gain or lose from exchanges: If I sell for more than I bought, I will gain and the buyer will lose labor values (but not necessarily utility). This is a valid local theory of the capitalist system; everyone operating within this system must act on the basis of this theory. Informed by marxist theoreticians, everyone may know that value is created only by labor and that when all values entering exchange are summed up, their sum is zero: Whatever I gained in exchange, someone else lost it. But this knowledge does not and cannot alter individual behavior within the system. A critique of capitalism is not sufficient to alter individual behavior.

[61] And distinctions there are. Just think of the Soviet Union, which was variously dubbed a totalitarian regime, an authoritarian one, a dictatorship of the proletariat, a dictatorship of a party, an autocracy (*samoderzhavie*), a state capitalist system, a nomenklatura, a bureaucracy,

One essential feature of authoritarian regimes is that someone has an effective capacity to prevent any outcome from occurring. As was said of Franco, "All the cards are in his hands, he does not *make* politics, he *is* politics" (cited in Carr and Fusi 1979: 1). That "someone" can be the ruler; an organization, such as the armed forces, the party, or the bureaucracy; or even a less easily identifiable ring of groups and individuals. I speak below of an authoritarian power apparatus and introduce distinctions only when they enlighten the problem at hand.[62] The power apparatus can act not only ex ante, but even ex post; that is, not only can it establish rules that prohibit actions that would lead to undesirable outcomes, but it can also overturn such outcomes even if they result from following its own rules. Here is an example drawn from Argentina. A minister of education appointed by the military government charges a group of experts with preparing a mathematics text for elementary schools. The textbook is prepared, and it is approved by the minister, published, and distributed. It then falls into the hands of the commandant of a local military zone, who orders that it be removed from the schools. Note that the text in question is not an underground pamphlet; it is a product of the authoritarian institutions themselves.[63] In contrast to a democracy, the set of possible outcomes cannot be deduced from the rules.[64] Under dictatorship, there is no distinction be-

and what not. My purpose is only to highlight what I see as the essential features of democracy, not to provide a classification of forms of government. Most important, my discussion collapses a distinction between what Montesquieu called despotism, where the will of the despot is the order of the day, and dictatorships that rule through laws (monarchy: rule by laws but not of law). For a discussion of various classifications of political regimes in history, see Bobbio 1989: 100–25.

[62] On the difficulties of identifying the centers of power under authoritarianism, see Przeworski 1982. A more systematic analysis is offered in Cardoso 1972.

[63] Note another aspect of this example: the absence of a clearly defined authority. There are no rules that give the commandant of a military zone the authority to act on primary-school textbooks. He has blanket power to act on anything. Another example: The Polish government decided in the early 1960s to rebuild the center of Warsaw. An architectural competition was announced, and the winning project was selected and approved by the government. But one of the secretaries of the Communist party decided that the proposed buildings would compete with a Stalinist monster that dominates the city and ordered their height reduced. He could have done anything else he wanted.

[64] This is not to say that retrospective action is not possible under democracy: The president may appoint a surgeon-general, who may charge a group of experts with preparing a report on AIDS; the report may be publicized; and the president may disclaim the report or even fire his appointee. But we know ex ante that the president can do all this; he has the right to repudiate, and he has the power to fire a member of his administration. He cannot repudiate, however, a ruling of the Supreme Court or fire a Justice, and we know that, too. What I am arguing is that under dictatorship we cannot know ex ante what the power apparatus can and cannot do, because the feasible outcomes are not entailed by any set of rules.

tween law and policy.[65] In this sense, dictatorships are arbitrary. Under democracy, an outcome of the democratic process can be overturned ex post if and only if it violates previously established and knowable rules; under dictatorship, the possible outcomes are not entailed by any set of rules.

Does this argument imply that democracies generate less uncertainty than dictatorships? I think this question cannot be answered, because the response depends on the point of view.[66] The difference is in the assumptions one must make to deduce the outcomes. In a dictatorship, they are deduced only from the preferences of one actor; in a democracy, from conflicting preferences and rules. Under a sufficiently capricious leader or a sufficiently divided power apparatus, the authoritarian regime may keep bewildering everyone with its twists and turns.[67] Indeed, under dictatorship the outcomes may be unpredictable: They can be predicted only by knowing the will of the dictator or the balance of forces among the conflicting factions. A democratic regime may, in contrast, yield highly predictable outcomes even when parties alternate in office. Hence, ex post an authoritarian regime may exhibit more variation of policies than a democratic one. But examine the situation ex ante. Under dictatorship, there is someone who is certain about the outcomes, and anyone who knows what the power apparatus wants also knows what will happen.[68] Under democracy, there is no such actor. Hence, the difference in uncertainty is conditional in the following sense: In an authoritarian system it is certain that political outcomes will not include those adverse to the will of the power apparatus, whereas in a democracy there is no group whose preferences and resources can predict outcomes with near certainty. Capitalists do not always win conflicts processed in a democratic manner,[69] and even one's current position in the political system does not guarantee

[65] This is the feature that Montesquieu saw as the fatal weakness of despotism.

[66] For a spirited statement of a subjectivist approach to game theory, see Rubinstein 1988. Rubinstein argues that if game theory is to make sense of the world around us, we should interpret games not as physical descriptions but as assumptions about the perceptions and reasoning procedures of the actors. Hence, what may be certain from the point of view of an observer may appear uncertain from the vantage point of each actor.

[67] Here is a Soviet view of the matter: Three men meet in a gulag. One asks another, "What are you here for?" "I was against Radek," he says. "And you?" "I was for Radek." They turn to the third man, thus far silent. "I am Radek," he says.

[68] Assuming, obviously, that nature does not throw dice.

[69] This is not an allusion to Marx, who argued in his writings on the 1848–51 period in France that universal suffrage represents a perpetual threat to capital. It is instead an allusion to Lenin, whose views were summarized above.

future victories. Incumbency may be an advantage, but incumbents do lose.

Hence, instrumental action under authoritarianism is limited to cases in which those actors who enjoy room for maneuver know that the power apparatus is indifferent to some outcomes. Party secretaries from particular localities may compete, for example, to get an investment provided for in the plan; producers' associations from different sectors may defend themselves against the lowering of tariffs on competing imports. Acting instrumentally makes sense for them only if they know that the power apparatus will not punish them for their actions and that it can tolerate the outcome they want. It would be irrational for anyone to act as if the outcome were to be determined by his or her actions under the existing institutional framework. Everyone has to try to anticipate the reaction of the power apparatus.[70]

To test these distinctions, consider the following example. After 1954, the Polish Communist regime regularly changed its agricultural policy. Whenever peasants stopped producing food for the cities, the party would tell them, "Enrich yourselves." And whenever peasants enriched themselves and their consumption began to appear ostentatious, the party would confiscate all the riches. Hence, the policy followed predictable cycles: Low productivity led to fiscal stimuli, visible inequality led to punitive taxation, and so on.[71] Now, we could imagine a similar dynamic under democracy: The Productivity party would campaign for fiscal stimuli; the Equality party would advocate taxing the rich peasants. When food was scarce, the Productivity party would win elections until peasants got too

---

[70] Yet note that authoritarian regimes systematically hide information about their true preferences. Their main concern is not to make it public that there are divisions within the power apparatus or even that any counterarguments were considered legitimate in the discussions inside the apparatus that led to a particular decision. What is communicated publicly is only "the line": a decision portrayed as unanimous and undisputable. Yet for any educated observer, the line is not credible information about the preferences of the rulers. I owe this observation to conversations with Tang Tsou.

The secrecy of the power apparatus sometimes reaches the grotesque. When Chernenko died, Soviet radio did not announce the fact for a day and a half; they let it be guessed by playing only solemn music on the radio. In the meantime, *Le Monde* announced the death of another member of the Politburo and reported the rumor that yet another had been ousted. The Soviet people did not know whether or not the dictator was still alive: Gabriel García Márquez's *The Autumn of the Patriarch* was performed in real life on the other side of the globe.

[71] Eventually, peasants did learn not to invest; workers were starved and threw party bureaucrats out. But it took forty years.

rich, whereupon the Equality party would be victorious. Ex post, therefore, the policy cycles, and the posterior probability that the tax rate is $t$ percent, may be identical in the two systems.

Ex ante, however, the uncertainty inherent in the two systems is different in three ways. First, the party changed the rules ex post: The central instrument of its policy was the *domiar,* a retroactive surtax. Income was earned by peasants when the tax rate was 40 percent; long after this income was earned and well after it was invested or consumed, it would be subjected to an additional tax. This can happen under democracy, but only according to established rules that permit retroactive taxation. Under dictatorship, it can happen despite the rules. Second, the timing and the amount of the confiscatory retribution was arbitrary in the sense defined above: It was not entailed by any set of rules. Under democracy, peasants may expect that when inequalities become conspicuous the tax rate will increase, but they can also expect that the rules will change only according to rules. Finally, under democracy, the new tax rate is determined jointly by the political actions of peasants and of other forces. Peasants can participate in determining the new tax rate; they can defend their interests. Given their reading of public opinion and their knowledge of the rules, they can attach prior probabilities to increases by any particular amount. Hence, they can calculate expected values and act upon them when deciding how much to invest. Under dictatorship, all they can do is to guess what the party will tolerate; if they cannot guess, they do not know when they will get hit and by how much.

None of the above implies that peasants will be better off under democracy. If the power apparatus wants to develop agricultural production and if it is willing to tolerate wealth, peasants will prosper. They will prosper even if other people starve and even if everyone else would prefer lower agricultural prices. Their interests are guaranteed by the will of the dictatorship; but this is all their interests depend upon. There is little they can do.[72]

Democracy is thus a system that generates the appearance of uncertainty because it is a system of decentralized strategic action in which knowledge is inescapably local. Dictators are observers because they do not have to consider what others think about them. If others guess incorrectly what the

---

[72] The NEP is the obvious example. Told by Lenin to enrich themselves, the Soviet *kulaks* waited for his death and the defeat of Bukharin to be massacred by Stalin.

dictator wants, he or she can correct the outcomes ex post. In turn, everyone who knows what the dictator wants can predict what will happen. Under democracy, no one is the dictator. Hence the appearance of uncertainty.

# 2. Transitions to democracy

## Introduction

The strategic problem of transition is to get to democracy without being either killed by those who have arms or starved by those who control productive resources. As this very formulation suggests, the path to democracy is mined. And the final destination depends on the path. In most countries where democracy has been established, it has turned out to be fragile. And in some countries, transitions have gotten stuck.

The central question concerning transitions is whether they lead to consolidated democracy, that is, a system in which the politically relevant forces subject their values and interests to the uncertain interplay of democratic institutions and comply with the outcomes of the democratic process. Democracy is consolidated when most conflicts are processed through democratic institutions, when nobody can control the outcomes ex post and the results are not predetermined ex ante, they matter within some predictable limits, and they evoke the compliance of the relevant political forces.

Note that a breakdown of an authoritarian regime may be reversed, as it was in Czechoslovakia in 1968, in Brazil in 1974, and in Poland in 1981, or it may lead to a new dictatorship, as in Iran and Romania. And even if the outcome is not the old or a new dictatorship, transitions can get stuck somewhere along the way in regimes that limit contestation or suffer from a threat of military intervention. Finally, even if democracy is established, it need not be consolidated. Under certain conditions, democratic institutions may systematically generate outcomes that cause some politically important forces to opt for authoritarianism. Hence, consolidated democracy is only one among the possible outcomes of breakdowns of authoritarian regimes.

To formulate the question for the analyses that follow, we need to examine the full range of possibilities inherent in different situations of transition

– moments when an authoritarian regime breaks down and democracy appears on the political agenda. Given the goals and resources of the particular political forces and the structure of conflicts they face, five outcomes are conceivable:

1. The structure of conflicts is such that no democratic institutions can last, and political forces end up fighting for a new dictatorship.

Conflicts over the political role of religion, race, or language are least likely to be resolvable by any set of institutions. Iran is perhaps the paradigmatic case here.

2. The structure of conflicts is such that no democratic institutions can last, yet political forces agree to democracy as a transitional solution.

The paradigmatic case of such situations is offered by O'Donnell's (1978b) analysis of Argentina between 1953 and 1976. Given the structure of the Argentine economy, where the main export goods are wage goods, democracy results in Argentina from coalitions between the urban bourgeoisie and the urban masses: the urban–urban alliance. Governments that result from this alliance overvalue the currency in order to direct consumption to the domestic market. After some time, this policy results in balance-of-payment crises and induces the urban bourgeoisie to ally itself with the landowning bourgeoisie, resulting in a bourgeois–bourgeois coalition. This coalition seeks to reduce popular consumption and needs authoritarianism to do so. But after a while the urban bourgeoisie finds itself without a market and shifts alliances again, this time back to democracy.

Examine this cycle at the moment when a dictatorship has just broken down. The pivotal actor – the urban bourgeoisie – faces the following choices: (a) to opt for a new dictatorship immediately; (b) to agree to democracy now and to shift alliances when a balance-of-payment crisis ensues; (c) to agree to democracy now and to continue supporting it in the future. Given the interests of the urban bourgeoisie and the structure of conflicts, the second strategy is optimal. Note that no myopia is involved here; the urban bourgeoisie knows that it will switch at some future moment. Democracy is simply the optimal transitional solution.

3. The structure of conflicts is such that some democratic institutions will be durable if adopted, but the conflicting political forces fight to establish a dictatorship.

This outcome may ensue when political forces have different preferences over the particular institutional frameworks; for example, over a unitary versus a federal system. One part of the country has a strong preference for a unitary system; other parts, for a federal one. What will happen under such conditions is not apparent – I shall return to it several times. Perhaps if any institutional framework is adopted temporarily, it will acquire the force of convention (Hardin 1987) and will last. But one conceivable outcome is open conflict, degenerating into civil war and dictatorship.

4. The structure of conflicts is such that some democratic institutions will be durable if adopted, but the conflicting political forces agree to an institutional framework that cannot last.

This outcome may seem perverse, but there are situations where it is to be expected. To anticipate what follows, imagine that a military regime is negotiating its way out of power. The forces represented by this regime prefer democracy with guarantees for their interests over the perpetuation of the dictatorship, but they fear democracy without guarantees more than the status quo, and they are capable of maintaining the dictatorship if the democratic opposition is not willing to adopt institutions that will constitute such a guarantee. The opposition then knows that unless it agrees to such institutions, the military will clamp down again. The result is democracy with guarantees. But if democratic institutions, once installed, erode the repressive power of the military, these institutions will not last. This situation does involve myopia or lack of knowledge. Recent events in Poland provide the paradigmatic case here.

5. Finally, and hopefully, the structure of conflicts is such that some democratic institutions will be durable if adopted, and they are.

The conditions under which these outcomes emerge and the paths that lead to them are the subject of this chapter. Liberalization of authoritarian regimes provides the prologue to the story and is first analyzed. Then follows a discussion of the way conflicts over the choice of institutions ensue in two different contexts: when the ancien régime extricates itself from power by negotiation, and when it falls apart, so that the problem of constituting the new democratic institutions remains entirely in the hands of proto-democratic forces. The last section is devoted to the interplay of institutions and ideologies.

The approach I use generates hypotheses of a comparative nature: hypotheses that specify the consequences of conflicts among actors endowed with particular interests and values operating under conditions independent of their will. These hypotheses should be tested by recourse to comparative evidence. And as the events in Eastern Europe unfold, we are for the first time on the verge of having enough cases to test them systematically, perhaps even statistically. I only suggest, not test, such hypotheses here.

## Liberalization

A common feature of dictatorships, whatever mix of inducements and constraints they use, is that they cannot and do not tolerate independent organizations.[1] The reason is that as long as no collective alternatives are available, individual attitudes toward the regime matter little for its stability.[2] Even Weber (1968: I, 214) observed that "people may submit from individual weakness and helplessness because there is no acceptable alternative." What is threatening to authoritarian regimes is not the breakdown of legitimacy but the organization of counterhegemony: collective projects

[1] Obviously, not all dictatorships are the same. Some tolerate no autonomous organizations of any kind; even the Animal Protection Society is organized from above and is a part of the Association of Associations, which is a part of the Front of National Unity, run out of the Ministry of Order. Other dictatorships are more selective; they ban unions and parties but tolerate stamp collectors' societies, churches, or producers' associations. But no dictatorship permits autonomous organization of political forces.

[2] This is why explanations of regime breakdown in terms of legitimacy are either tautological or false. If by a loss of legitimacy we understand the appearance of collectively organized alternatives, they are tautological in that the fact that these alternatives are collectively organized means that the regime has broken down. If we see legitimacy in terms of individual attitudes, in Lamounier's (1979: 13) terms as "acquiescence motivated by subjective agreement with given norms and values," they are false. Some authoritarian regimes have been illegitimate since their inception, and they have been around for forty years.

It is hard to evaluate how much attitude change occurs before and how much as a result of liberalization. In Spain, 35 percent of respondents supported a democratic representative system, as opposed to one-man rule, in 1966; 60 percent in 1974; and 78 percent in May 1976. In 1971, 12 percent thought political parties beneficial; by 1973, 37 percent thought they should exist, and this proportion rose to 56 percent by April 1975, fell to 41 percent by January 1976, and rose again to 67 percent by May 1975 (López-Pintor 1980). In Hungary in 1985, 88 percent of respondents declared confidence in the national leadership (57.3 percent "fully"), 81 percent in the parliament, 66 percent in the party, and 62 percent in trade unions (Bruszt 1988). In Poland, where organized opposition had functioned openly since 1976 and was repressed in 1981, confidence in the Communist (PUWP) party declined slowly from 66.2 percent in June 1985 to 53.1 percent in July 1987 and precipitously to 26.6 percent during the wave of strikes of August 1988; increased again to 38.6 percent by November 1988; and fell again to 26.0 percent on the eve of the Magdalenka talks in January 1989. During the same period, confidence in the opposition increased from 20.5 percent in 1985 to 26.2 percent in August 1988 to 45.9 percent by January 1989 (Ostrowski 1989).

for an alternative future.[3] Only when collective alternatives are available does political choice become available to isolated individuals.[4] This is why authoritarian regimes abhor independent organizations; they either incorporate them under centralized control or repress them by force.[5] This is why they are so afraid of words, even if these words convey what everyone knows anyway, for it is the fact of uttering them, not their content, that has the mobilizing potential.

How does it happen, then, that at some moment a group inside the authoritarian power establishment decides to tolerate an autonomous organization in the civil society? At one point the Spanish regime stopped repressing the Commissiones Obreras; General Pinochet allowed the re-emergence of political parties; in July 1986, General Jaruzelski passed an amnesty law for political activities that did not include a recidivism clause, thus signaling a de facto legalization of the opposition; Egon Krenz accepted the existence of the embryonic Nueue Forum. Such moments signal

[3] The Gramscian inspiration of these hypotheses is obvious, but Gramsci's framework, with its duality of coercion and consent, is not sufficiently specific institutionally to serve as a guide to the problem at hand. In particular, Gramsci failed to distinguish concessions given by someone who controls the political system from realizations of interests achieved through open-ended, even if limited, competition.

[4] Demonstration effects play an important role in transitions to democracy. Here is a Brazilian joke, dating to the twilight of the dictatorship: In a crowded Rio bus, a man slaps the face of an officer standing next to him. Another man does the same. From the back of the bus, a *mulatinho* pushes his way through and administers a third slap. The bus stops and is surrounded by the police. The first man is asked, "Why did you hit the officer on the face?" "He offended the honor of my daughter; I had to react" is the answer. The second man is interrogated: "He offended the honor of my niece; I had to react." Finally, the question is directed to the *mulatinho*. "When I saw them hitting the officer, I thought the dictatorship had fallen," he explains.

As someone observed, the breakdown of the communist monopoly of power took ten years in Poland, ten months in Hungary, ten weeks in East Germany, and ten days in Czechoslovakia. The events in Poland and Hungary demonstrated to East Germans the possibility of this breakdown; the spectacle of the crumbling wall signaled to individual Czechs the feasibility of regime transformation.

[5] A Soviet samizdat, *Chronicle-Express* (no. 16, 17 November 1987), made public a document of the Komsomol entitled "To Strengthen the Work in the Autonomous Youth Associations." This document observes that "the recent extension of democracy resulted in the appearance of a growing number of autonomous socio-political youth associations. . . . The range of their interests is extremely broad, from international information, ecology and protection of historical monuments, to a shameful speculation on not yet surpassed difficulties of the reconstruction." The document goes on to distinguish good and bad associations. In the case of the good ones, Komsomol organizations should extend their cooperation and should send their "best militants to play the role of commissars." In the case of the less good ones, their leaders should be bribed, or "should be offered in private concrete ways of realizing their capacities." Finally, the document goes on, if this strategy fails, the Komsomol should be prepared "to create its own alternative association."

fissures in the authoritarian power bloc and suggest to the civil society that at least some forms of autonomous organization will not be repressed. They mark the onset of liberalization.[6]

Explanations of such decisions fall into two categories: from above and from below. To some extent, these explanations reflect real differences. Hungary, for example, is generally viewed as an almost pure case of divisions in the authoritarian power bloc. In the words of Karoly Grosz, "the party was shattered not by its opponents but – paradoxically – by the leadership."[7] East Germany represents the other extreme: There were no indications of a split in the power bloc until hundreds of thousands of people had occupied the streets of Leipzig. Yet a striking aspect of the case-study literature is that often different causes are cited to explain the same event. With regard to Brazil, for example, Cardoso (1979) saw the *distensão* as a result of a long-standing division within the military; Lamounier (1979), as a consequence of popular mobilization. Indeed, the top-down and bottom-up models often compete to explain liberalization.[8]

The reason for these analytical difficulties is that the model that simply distinguishes the two directions is too crude. Short of a real revolution – a mass uprising that leads to the disintegration of the apparatus of repression[9] – decisions to liberalize combine elements from above and from below. For even in those cases where divisions in the authoritarian regime became visible well before any popular mobilization, the question is why the regime cracked at a particular moment. And part of the answer is always that the Liberalizers in the regime saw the possibility of an alliance with some forces that up to then had remained unorganized, which implies

[6] I am using the terminology of O'Donnell (1979: 8), according to whom "liberalization consists of measures which, although entailing a significant opening of the previous bureaucratic authoritarian regime (such as effective judicial guarantees of some individual rights or introduction of parliamentary forms not based on free electoral competition), remain short of what could be called political democracy."

[7] Interview with Karoly Grosz, former first secretary of the Hungarian (Socialist Workers') Communist party, in *Przegląd Tygodniowy*, no. 51 (403), Warsaw, 22 December 1989, p. 15.

[8] Even Hungary and Poland are not exempt from alternative interpretations: Szelenyi (1989) emphasized the from-below aspects of the Hungarian transition, and Comisso (1989) countered that Szelenyi was neglecting the from-above elements. Walicki (1990) went against the standard interpretations of the Polish transition, which assign the crucial role to Solidarity, by arguing that it was an effect of an agreement between two elites. Wiatr (1989), perhaps even more provocatively, described it as a pact between the army and the church.

[9] Even Romania does not represent the case of a true revolution. There seems to be much we still do not know about the background of these tragic events, but note that the Romanian army survived the destruction of the Ceausescu regime with its command structure intact.

that there was some force in the civil society with which to ally. Conversely, in the cases in which mass mobilization antedated visible splits in the regime, the question remains why the regime decided not to repress it by force. Again, part of the answer is that the regime was divided between Liberalizers and Hardliners. Liberalization is a result of an interaction between splits in the authoritarian regime and autonomous organization of the civil society. Popular mobilization signals to the potential Liberalizers the possibility of an alliance that could change the relations of forces within the power bloc to their advantage; visible splits in the power bloc indicate to the civil society that political space may have been opened for autonomous organization. Hence, popular mobilization and splits in the regime feed on each other.

Whether a visible split or popular mobilization occurs first, the logic of liberalization is the same. What is different is its pace. Popular mobilization dictates the rhythm of transformation, since it forces the regime to decide whether to repress, coopt, or devolve power. Yet whether liberalization lasts years, months, or days, the regime and the opposition face the same sequence of choices.

Projects of liberalization launched by forces from within the authoritarian power establishment are invariably intended as controlled openings of political space. They typically result from divisions in the authoritarian bloc sparked by various signals that portend an imminent crisis of some sorts, including signs of popular unrest. The project of Liberalizers is to relax social tension and to strengthen their position in the power bloc by broadening the social base of the regime: to allow some autonomous organization of the civil society and to incorporate the new groups into the authoritarian institutions.[10] In the light of this project, liberalization is to be continually contingent on the compatibility of its outcomes with the interests or values of the authoritarian bloc. Thus, liberalization is referred to as an "opening" (*apertura*), "decompression" (*dis-*

---

[10] According to Carr and Fusi (1979: 179), in Spain "the political class was divided by struggle between *aperturistas* – those who believed that the regime must be 'opened' in order to survive by winning a wider support, usually called 'participation' – and *immobilistas*." The former first secretary of the Polish United Workers' (Communist) party, Edward Gierek, revealed in a recent interview (Rolicki 1990: 146) that in the late seventies he "intended to introduce to the Seym [Parliament] a significant group of 25 percent of Catholic deputies. It would have permitted us . . . ," Gierek continued, "to broaden the political base of the authorities."

*tensão*), "renewal" (*odnowa*), or "reconstruction" (*perestroika* – "re-modeling," as of a house). These are terms with strong connotations of limits to reform.

Yet liberalization is inherently unstable. What normally happens is what Ilya Ehrenburg called in 1954 "the thaw" (*ottepel*): a melting of the ice-berg of civil society that overflows the dams of the authoritarian regime. Once repression lessens, for whatever reason, the first reaction is an outburst of autonomous organization in the civil society. Student associations, unions, and proto-parties are formed almost overnight. In Brazil, lawyers, journalists, and students organized first, followed by the *comunidades de base*. In Poland, ten million people joined Solidarność within a few weeks of September 1980. Even organizations founded and controlled by the regime declared themselves independent: not only professional associations but even the Tourism and Sightseeing Society and the Stamp Collectors' Association. According to a story by K. S. Karol (*Le Nouvel Observateur*, no. 1200, Paris, 6 November 1987), the first autonomous group established in Gorbachev's Soviet Union may have been the Spartakists, meaning, obviously, fans of the Moscow soccer club Spartak. By 1987, there were already thirty thousand independent groups and they held a national congress. By the end of 1989, sixty thousand autonomous groups, clubs, associations, circles, and federations were probing the limits of the political space (*Pravda*, 10 December 1989).[11]

The pace of mobilization of the civil society is different in different regimes, depending on whether the authoritarian equilibrium rests mainly on lies, fear, or economic prosperity. The equilibrium of lies is the least stable. In regimes of ritualized speech, where everyone goes through the motions of uttering words they do not believe and do not expect anyone else to believe, fresh words are subversive. Once the king is announced to be naked, the equilibrium is destroyed instantaneously. In Romania, a few people started shouting anti-Ceausescu slogans during the demonstration organized to welcome his return from Iran, and the regime fell a few days later. In regimes based on fear, where words are permitted as long as they do not enter the public sphere – post-Stalinist Poland and post-1982 Mex-

---

[11] A careful study of popular mobilization in Spain, focusing on unions, is Maravall 1981.
One does not know to what extent these estimates can be trusted, but here are some numbers concerning Bulgaria: On 13 November 1989, the subhead in the *New York Times* was "Bulgarians Are Passive"; on 28 December, the independent union Podkrepa was said by the *New York Times* to have 5,000 members; on 16 January 1990, Paris *Liberation* reported that Podkrepa had 100,000 members.

ico provide good cases – dissent can smolder for a long time before it erupts into flames. The crucial factor in breaking individual isolation is the safety of numbers. Poles discovered the strength of the opposition when the Pope's visit in June 1979 brought two million people into the streets; in Bulgaria, the first autonomous demonstration, on 17 November 1989, grew out of one organized by Mladenov's new government in his support; the same occurred in Romania when Ceausescu returned from Iran; in East Germany, the mass movement was released when trains carrying refugees began crossing from Czechoslovakia to West Germany. Finally, regimes based on a tacit exchange of material prosperity for passive acquiescence – the "goulash communism" of Kadar in Hungary, the Gierek period in Poland, or the pre-1982 PRI regime in Mexico – are vulnerable primarily to economic crises. Hence, the time lag between the opening and popular mobilization varies from regime to regime.

At some time the civil society mobilizes, and new organizations form, declare themselves independent of the regime, proclaim their goals, interests, and projects. But the regime has centralized, noncompetitive institutions that incorporate only those groups that accept its direction and that control the outcomes of any political process ex post. Thus, on the one hand, autonomous organizations emerge in the civil society; on the other hand, there are no institutions where these organizations can present their views and negotiate their interests. Because of this *décalage* between the autonomous organization of the civil society and the closed character of state institutions, the only place where the newly organized groups can eventually struggle for their values and interests is the streets. Inevitably, the struggle assumes a mass character.[12]

Once that happens, liberalization can no longer continue. The tear gas

---

[12] The Brazilian experience does not contradict this general proposition. It is true that in Brazil the struggle for democracy did not reach the streets until the Direitas, ja! campaign of 1984, but the reason, I think, is that the *distencão* of 1974 was immediately transformed into electoral competition. The institutional framework to channel opposition was available. The project of liberalization got into trouble anyway because of the unexpected electoral success of the MDB.

Similarly, liberalization in the Soviet Union did not lead to mass demonstrations in the Russian part of the country, I think for two reasons. First, popular mobilization was in fact encouraged by Gorbachev, who attempted to develop a traditional Russian coalition of the tsar and the people against the bureaucracy. (See explicit statements to this effect in his *Perestroika*.) Second, the Supreme Soviet was transformed overnight into a fairly contestatory institution, which witnessed sharp confrontations and passed laws with small majorities. Hence, the institutional framework was transformed de facto to correspond to its status de jure.

that shrouds the streets stings the eyes of Liberalizers; the eruption of mass movements, the unrest and disorder, constitute evidence that the policy of liberalization has failed. Since liberalization is always intended as a process controlled from above, the emergence of autonomous movements constitutes the proof that liberalization is not, or at least is no longer, a viable project. Street demonstrations are the demonstration that the most sacrosanct of authoritarian values, order itself, has been violated. Mass eruptions undermine the position of Liberalizers in the authoritarian bloc.

In China, student demonstrations forced the Liberalizers to beat a retreat and cost them the leadership of the party. Repression increased again. In South Korea, however, similar demonstrations led to a break in the regime and transformed Liberalizers into democratizers. These indeed are the alternatives: either to incorporate the few groups that can be incorporated and to repress everyone else, returning to the authoritarian stasis, or to open the political agenda to the problem of institutions, that is, of democracy.[13] Liberalizations are either reversed, leading to grim periods euphemistically termed normalization,[14] or continue to democratization.

The perplexing fact is that so many authoritarian politicians believe that they will succeed where others have failed, and they go on to fail. The Brazilian case is classic. As Smith (1987: 207) observed, "The difference between liberalization and democratization was clear for Golbery: If implemented properly, careful doses of liberalization could substitute for genuine democratization, thereby maintaining the political exclusion of subaltern groups and preempting meaningful demands for real reform of the economic model."[15] In Poland, the Jaruzelski regime came as close as one

[13] The Polish events of 1955–7 are a classic case of liberalization that ended up in normalization. After a period of autonomous organization, workers' councils were incorporated into the regime, while the student movement was repressed. In Brazil, the failed liberalization attempt of 1974 was followed during 1975–7 by a mixture of intensified repression and welfare measures. See Andrade 1980. For some reason, several Brazilian writers found it surprising that the liberalization project did not quite work the way it was intended, and they went on to distinguish "the project" from "the process" (Diniz 1986). They must not know Perez's third law of decompression: "Things always get out of hand."

[14] These were best summarized by Milan Kundera: "A man is vomiting in Wenceslaus Square. A passerby approaches. 'Do not worry. I understand you,' he says." (I do not remember from which novel this story comes.)

[15] A fascinating document outlining plans for liberalization is the speech given by General Golbery do Couto e Silva in 1980 (Golbery 1981). Karoly Grosz summarized his earlier stance as follows: "My position was the following; Let us move forward, with courage but also prudence, so that the nation will understand us and follow us. . . . I thought that a single party, having lost its two radical wings, would be able to overcome the difficulties" (see n. 7).

can to squaring the circle. The strategy was to create democratic institutions, such as the Administrative Court, the Constitutional Tribunal, self-management councils and independent unions, the Consultative Council to the Government, and an Office of the Ombudsman – and to retain power.[16] Even in cases in which liberalization occurred only under the intense pressure of mass demonstrations (East Germany and Czechoslovakia), the first project of the liberalizing leadership was to suck the dissent into the authoritarian system: Krenz encouraged "the people" to share their grievances with the party and promised that the "authorities" would listen, Vladyslav Adamec hand-picked some noncommunists for his first cabinet, and both hoped that the mobilization would be diffused by these measures. Yet all erred in their expectations, and all were eventually forced to accept democratization. Why?

Examine the situation from the point of view of proto-Liberalizers at the moment when the choice of opening the regime appears on the horizon. The proto-Liberalizers can maintain their present position in the power bloc, and then the result is the status quo, denoted in Figure 2.1 as SDIC (status quo dictatorship). Or they can decide to issue signals that they are willing to tolerate some autonomous organization outside the power bloc: to open. If the organized forces in the civil society decide to enter into the new organizational forms created by the regime, typically some Front of National Unity, and no further autonomous mobilization occurs, the result is BDIC (broadened dictatorship); and the liberalization strategy is successful. If the civil society continues to organize autonomously, Liberalizers face the choice of going back to the fold and agreeing to repress popular mobilization or of continuing on to TRANSITION to democracy. Repression, however, may be ineffective: If it succeeds, the outcome is NDIC (narrower dictatorship) in which the Liberalizers find themselves at the mercy of the executors of repression; if it fails, the outcome is an INSURRECTION. Assume that Liberalizers attach the probability $r$ to successful repression.

Note immediately that the process of liberalization can be launched only if some groups in the authoritarian regime prefer broader dictatorship to the status quo. Liberalizers prefer BDIC to SDIC because broadening the social

---

[16] A nice statement of this strategy is an article by Leszek Gontarski entitled "Are We Afraid of Democracy?" ("Czy boimy się demokracji?"), *Życie Warszawy*, no. 291, Warsaw, 12–13 December 1987, p. 3.

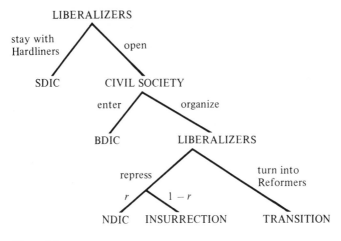

Figure 2.1

base strengthens the regime as a whole and because groups that enter the regime constitute natural allies for Liberalizers vis-à-vis Hardliners. INSURRECTION is the worst outcome for everyone in the regime.

Now, if everyone knows everything and everyone knows the same, then the only possible outcomes of this game are either the status quo or broadened dictatorship; liberalization occurs only when it will be successful. Suppose that the preferences of Liberalizers are BDIC > SDIC > TRANSITION > NDIC > INSURRECTION. Then Liberalizers will know that if the society organizes, they will have to turn into Reformers. So does the civil society. Hence, if Liberalizers open, society organizes. But Liberalizers prefer SDIC to TRANSITION. Hence, they never open. In turn, suppose that the preferences of Liberalizers are BDIC > SDIC > NDIC > TRANSITION > INSURRECTION and that Liberalizers attach a high probability to the success of repression. Then Liberalizers know that they will choose repression if society organizes. So does the civil society. Since for the society BDIC > NDIC, civil society enters knowing that Liberalizers will opt for repression if they organize. And since for Liberalizers BDIC > SDIC, they open. The outcome is thus BDIC.

How then can the process ever arrive at TRANSITION? I see two possible ways, both relying on someone's mistaken assumptions.

(1) Suppose Liberalizers are in fact proto-democratizers; that is, their

preferences are BDIC > TRANSITION > SDIC > NDIC > INSURRECTION.[17] Yet Liberalizers have to reveal their preferences strategically, given that Hardliners in the regime would never accede to liberalization if they knew that Liberalizers were prepared to go all the way. Hence, Liberalizers announce that they prefer BDIC > SDIC > NDIC > TRANSITION, and Hardliners believe them.

Now, suppose that the decision to open depends on the consent of Hardliners. If Liberalizers propose to open, Hardliners decide to agree, in which case the rest of the game ensues, or not to permit the opening, in which case the outcome is the status quo. Now, assume that (a) Hardliners prefer NDIC to SDIC and that (b) Hardliners believe that the society mistakenly believes that Liberalizers are in fact proto-democratizers. Then Hardliners analyze the situation as follows: If they agree to open, the society, believing that Liberalizers will not opt for repression, will organize. Yet Liberalizers prefer the outcome expected as a consequence of repression. Hence, Hardliners think the result of opening will be NDIC. They agree to open. But given the true preferences of the Liberalizers, the outcome is TRANSITION.

This explanation assumes that Liberalizers know all along what they are doing and deliberately mislead Hardliners while sending correct signals to the society. It is hard to evaluate the plausibility of this scenario, precisely because under it Liberalizers are forced to reveal their preferences strategically. We have to decide whether Liberalizers are sincere when they claim that they want only to invigorate the regime by broadening its base.[18] Given their public statements, either they are very good liars or this is not a plausible story.

(2) Suppose that the preferences of Liberalizers are BDIC > SDIC > NDIC > TRANSITION > INSURRECTION and their prior estimate of successful repression is high, which implies that the outcome will be BDIC. Hardliners play no role in this story; perhaps the regime is not divided or the Liberalizers control the weapons. Liberalizers open, expecting the society to

[17] Or perhaps Liberalizers are even democratizers in sheep's clothing, with TRANSITION > BDIC > SDIC > NDIC > INSURRECTION.

[18] O'Donnell (1979: 13) noted with regard to the liberalizations initiated by Lanusse (1971–3) in Argentina and by Geisel (1975–9) in Brazil that in each case they threatened that they would "be obliged" to stop the process if things went too far. But they were too committed to stop; a reversal of liberalization would have been a victory for hardliners over the "*blandos.*"

enter. But the society has a lower estimate of successful repression and believes that Liberalizers have the same estimate. Hence, society organizes. Once Liberalizers observe that the society is continuing to organize, they downgrade their estimate of successful repression to the point where they prefer TRANSITION to the outcome expected under repression. Hence, civil society organizes, and Liberalizers update their beliefs about the effectiveness of repression as they watch the streets.

These assumptions seem plausible. As the eighty-two-year-old head of the East German security apparatus, Erich Mielke, is alleged to have said to Honecker, "Erich, we can't beat up hundreds of thousands of people" – a statement I interpret as a technical, not a moral, admonition (*New York Times*, 19 November 1989, p. 15). If popular mobilization increases in spite of beatings and jailings, the regime revises downward its beliefs about the effectiveness of shooting. Moreover, at one moment the stakes become enormous. Not enlisting in the repression is an act of treason, for which a Romanian general was forced to "commit suicide" as Ceausescu's last act in power;[19] and joining in repression that fails landed Prague's party secretary in jail just a couple of weeks later. Under such conditions, jumping ship seems as good a way to save one's skin as shooting.[20]

These two explanations assume that preferences are fixed and that actors are rational, even if ill informed. But two more explanations are plausible.

One is sociological. As the organization of the civil society crystallizes, its leadership becomes known, and personal contacts become established, the Liberalizers learn that the opposition is not as threatening as they had thought. Here is General Jaruzelski, interviewed when he had become the elected president, by Adam Michnik, now editor-in-chief of the pro-

---

[19] From what we know thus far, it appears that the minister of defense, the minister of interior, and the chief of the secret police did not comply with Ceausescu's initial order to arm their forces. When harangued by Ceausescu during the last meeting of the Political Bureau, the last two made a sufficiently convincing show of obeisance and survived, only to try to change sides a few days later. For the minutes of this meeting, see Jean-Paul Mari, "La dernière colère de Ceausescu," *Le Nouvel Observateur,* 11 January 1990, pp. 42–45.

[20] See Przeworski 1986c, for a more formal treatment of such situations.

A comment is needed here on the theory of collective action. The main weakness of Olson's (1965) view is his assumption of a "pre-strategic" status quo: In his theory, individuals have a choice between doing nothing or acting to bring about a public good. But, as Sartre (1960) observed, there are situations in which the choice is only between acting for or acting against. When the royal troops were searching for arms in the houses along the street leading to the Bastille, the inhabitants who were hiding them had only the choice of finding themselves in the Bastille or destroying it. Under these conditions, the "collective action problem" is not a prisoner's dilemma.

Solidarity daily newspaper, on the eighth anniversary of the repression of 1981; "Gradually our view of the world was changing. Today we see it differently. But we had to arrive there, we had to bump our head. All of us had to. In any case, why look far? For several years you passed in my eyes, and not only mine, as a particularly demonic personage."[21] Negotiations show that the opposition is willing to listen and to make concessions; personal contacts bring rapprochement among individuals. Gradually, transition appears as less of a chasm, and repression seems simply uncivilized. Liberalizers change their preferences endogenously as a result of bargaining with the opposition.

The second explanation is psychological. Liberalizers may not be rational. Rational actors form their beliefs based on the information they receive and act upon their desires given these beliefs. Indeed, if they are truly rational, they use beliefs to temper desires. Irrational actors let their desires affect their beliefs and screen out undesirable information. Suppose that the regime has no choice but to open. Foreign pressure, economic and political strangulation, may leave no choice but to liberalize. Nicaragua is a clear case here. Popular mobilization may be uncontainable, as it was in Poland. Under such conditions, the Liberalizers are likely to persuade themselves that the opening will be successful, even that they will win competitive elections if they proceed all the way to democracy.

If any of these hypotheses are true, the spectacle of Liberalizers who venture into an unfeasible project and turn coats in mid course becomes intelligible. Either Liberalizers were in fact ready to proceed to democracy to begin with but had to hide their true intentions, or they discovered in mid course that repression is unlikely to succeed, or they found that they did not have as much to lose as they had thought at the beginning, or they had no choice and were just putting a good face on it.

But liberalization does not always lead to transition, as the tragic events of Tiananmen Square have reminded us. When will the outcome of liberalization be repression and a narrower dictatorship in which Liberalizers are eliminated? We already know that this outcome is not possible if

---

[21] "Z generałem Jaruzelskim o stanie wojennym," *Gazeta,* Warsaw, 18 December 1989, pp. 5–6. General Kiszczak, in turn, remarked that "agents of the MSW [Ministry of Interior, i.e., the police] were gradually getting used to the perspective of coexistence with the opposition, of the inevitability of the Polish compromise. Had they not been prepared, today there might have been resistance and tension" (Przewrót niewykonywalny," interview with General Czesław Kiszczak, *Gazeta,* Warsaw, 11 September 1989, p. 4).

everyone knows everything and all know the same. Suppose that (1) Liberalizers want only to broaden the regime, (2) Liberalizers believe that the
society knows that they prefer BDIC to TRANSITION and that they are ready
to repress if need be, and (3) the society mistakenly believes that Liberalizers are in fact democratizers or that they will not opt for repression
because they believe it to be ineffective. Then Liberalizers open, expecting
the society to enter; the society believes that if it continues to organize,
Liberalizers will opt for transition, but Liberalizers opt for repression.

Hence, liberalization – an opening that results in the broadening of the
social base of the regime without changing its structure – is not a feasible
project unless everyone has full and accurate knowledge about everybody
else's preferences and the probability of successful repression. Some mis-
perceptions lead liberalization to transition; others, to repression. The perennial tragedy of Liberalizers was described by Marx as early as 1851:
They want democracy that will keep them in power, and they are stung
when it turns against them. They try to hold on as long as they can, but at
some point they must decide whether to go backward to authoritarian
restoration or forward to democratic emancipation.

## Democratization

*Introduction*

The problem that thrusts itself to the center of the political agenda once a
dictatorship breaks down is whether any institutions that will allow open-
ended, even if limited, contestation will be accepted by the relevant political forces. And as soon as these institutions are in place, the question arises
whether they will evoke spontaneous compliance; that is, whether, willing
to subject their interests to the uncertainty of competition and to comply
with its outcomes, they will absorb the relevant political forces as participants.

To organize the analysis, note that the conflicts inherent in transitions to
democracy often occur on two fronts: between the opponents and defenders
of the authoritarian regime about democracy and among the proto-
democratic actors against one another for the best chance under democracy.
The image of the campaign for democracy as a struggle of the society
against the state is a useful fiction during the first period of transition, as a
unifying slogan of the forces opposed to the current authoritarian regime.

But societies are divided in many ways, and the very essence of democracy is the competition among political forces with conflicting interests. This situation creates a dilemma: to bring about democracy, anti-authoritarian forces must unite against authoritarianism, but to be victorious under democracy, they must compete with each other. Hence, the struggle for democracy always takes place on two fronts: against the authoritarian regime for democracy and against one's allies for the best place under democracy.

Thus, even if they sometimes coincide temporally, it is useful to focus separately on the two different aspects of democratization: extrication from the authoritarian regime and the constitution of a democratic one. The relative importance of extrication and constitution depends on the place within the authoritarian regime of those political forces that control the apparatus of repression, most often the armed forces.[22] Wherever the military remains cohesive in defense of the regime, elements of extrication dominate the process of transition. Chile and Poland are the paradigmatic cases of extrication, but extrication also overshadowed the transitions in Spain, Brazil, Uruguay, South Korea, and Bulgaria. In contrast, wherever military cohesion disintegrated because of a failed foreign adventure – Greece, Portugal, and Argentina – and in regimes where the military were effectively subjected to civilian control – all the other Eastern European countries – the process of constituting a new regime was less affected by elements of extrication.

### Extrication

Since extrication has been extensively studied, I proceed schematically. First, let me follow O'Donnell (1979) and O'Donnell and Schmitter (1986) in distinguishing four political actors: Hardliners and Reformers (who may or may not have been Liberalizers) inside the authoritarian bloc and Moderates and Radicals in the opposition. Hardliners tend to be found in the repressive cores of the authoritarian bloc: the police, the legal bureaucracy, censors, among journalists, and so on. Reformers tend to be recruited from among politicians of the regime and from some groups outside the state

---

[22] These need not be monolithic. Note that, as a legacy of the Stalin era, in Eastern Europe there have been two organized forces of repression: the armed forces for external defense under the control of the Ministry of Defense, and the army for internal order under the control of the Ministry of Interior. The autonomy of the secret police varied from country to country and period to period.

apparatus: sectors of the bourgeoisie under capitalism, and some economic managers under socialism.[23] Moderates and Radicals may but need not represent different interests. They may be distinguished only by risk aversion. Moderates may be those who fear Hardliners, not necessarily those who have less radical goals.[24]

Extrication can result only from understandings between Reformers and Moderates. Extrication is possible if (1) an agreement can be reached between Reformers and Moderates to establish institutions under which the social forces they represent would have a significant political presence in the democratic system, (2) Reformers can deliver the consent of Hardliners or neutralize them, and (3) Moderates can control Radicals.

The last two conditions are logically prior, since they determine the set of possible solutions for Reformers and Moderates. Whatever agreement they reach, it must induce Hardliners to go along with Reformers and dissuade Radicals from mobilizing for a more profound transformation. When can these conditions be satisfied?

If the armed forces control extrication, they must either opt for reforms or be cajoled into cooperation, or at least passivity, by Reformers. Moderates must pay the price. But if Reformers are a viable interlocutor for Moderates only when they can control or deliver the armed forces, Moder-

---

[23] The attitudes of the bourgeoisie toward authoritarian regimes belie facile generalizations. The reason is the following. The bourgeoisie has three ways of defending its interests: (1) Under democracy, it can organize itself as a party and compete; (2) under any regime, it can organize itself as a pressure group and use privileged channels of access to the state; (3) under any regime, decentralized pursuit of profit constitutes a constraint on the actions of the state directed against its interests ("structural dependence of the state on capital" – see Przeworski and Wallerstein 1988). Now, contrary to Marx, the last constraint may turn out to be insufficient to protect the bourgeoisie from the state. In fact, several military regimes in Latin America did enormous damage to some sectors of the bourgeoisie: Martínez de Hoz destroyed one-half of Argentine firms, and the Brazilian military built a state sector that competed with private firms. This is why by 1978 the leading sectors of the Paulista bourgeoisie saw the military regime as a threat. Thus, at least in Brazil, the anti-authoritarian posture arose from economic liberalism. (For interpretations of this posture, see Bresser Pereira 1978 and Cardoso 1983.) In turn, in countries where popular mobilization is feeble, the bourgeoisie can compete quite well under democratic conditions. This seems to be the case in Ecuador, where the autonomy of the technobureaucrats – the style rather than the substance of economic policy making, according to Conaghan (1983) – turned the bourgeoisie against the military government and where the bourgeoisie did not fear electoral competition.

Similarly, in the socialist countries some factory managers saw relatively early the possibility of converting their political power into economic power (Hankiss 1989) and supported democratization.

[24] In fact, in Poland in 1981 moderates were those who perceived Soviet intervention as imminent; radicals, those who saw it as unlikely.

Table 2.1

|  |  | Moderates ally with | |
| --- | --- | --- | --- |
|  |  | Radicals | Reformers |
| Reformers ally with | Hardliners | Authoritarian regime survives in old form: 2,1 | Authoritarian regime holds, with concessions: 4,2 |
|  | Moderates | Democracy without guarantees: 1,4 | Democracy with guarantees: 3,3 |

ates have no political importance unless they can restrain Radicals. Moderate gentlemen in cravats may lead civilized negotiations in government palaces, but if streets are filled with crowds or factories are occupied by workers calling for the necks of their interlocutors, their moderation is irrelevant. Hence, Moderates must either deliver terms tolerable to Radicals or, if they cannot obtain such terms from Reformers, they must leave enough power in the hands of the apparatus of repression to intimidate Radicals. On the one hand, Moderates need Radicals to be able to put pressure on Reformers; on the other, Moderates fear that Radicals will not consent to the deal they work out with Reformers. No wonder the feasible set is often empty.

When can an agreement that satisfies all these constraints be reached? Reformers face a strategic choice of remaining in an authoritarian alliance with Hardliners or seeking a democratic alliance with Moderates. Moderates, in turn, can seek all-out destruction of the political forces organized under the authoritarian regime by allying with Radicals, or they can seek an accommodation by negotiating with Reformers. Suppose the structure of the situation is as in Table 2.1.[25]

If Reformers ally with Hardliners and Moderates with Radicals, two opposing coalitions are formed, and they fight it out. If Reformers ally with Moderates and Moderates with Reformers, the outcome is democracy with guarantees. The off-diagonal outcomes should be read as follows: When Moderates ally with Radicals and Reformers with Moderates, Re-

[25] The first number in each cell represents the value of this outcome to Reformers; the second number, to Moderates (4 is better than 3, and so on). These numbers are not interpersonally comparable; they only rank the alternatives. Hence, Moderates may be miserable under their second-worst option, while Reformers may be quite happy with theirs.

formers are accepting the democracy without guarantees that results from the Radical–Moderate coalition. When Reformers ally with Hardliners and Moderates with Reformers, Moderates are accepting liberalization. They are entering in the sense used above.

Under such conditions, Reformers have a dominant strategy, namely, always to ally with Hardliners. If Moderates ally with Radicals, the opposition is defeated and the authoritarian bloc survives intact, which is better for Reformers than democracy brought about by a coalition of Moderates and Radicals that offers no guarantees. If Moderates seek an alliance with Reformers, some concessions are made, to the cost of Hardliners. These concessions are better for Reformers than democracy even with guarantees. Hence, potential Reformers are always better off defending the authoritarian regime in alliance with Hardliners.

The defining feature of this situation is that Reformers have no political strength of their own and thus no prospect of being politically successful under democracy. Without special guarantees, they will do very badly under democracy, and even with guarantees they are still better off under the protection of their authoritarian allies. This was the case of Poland in 1980–1.[26] Any solution had to satisfy two conditions: (1) The opposition insisted on the principle of open electoral competition, and (2) the party wanted to have a guarantee that it could win the electoral competition. The opposition was willing to have the party win; it did not demand a chance to win but only to compete. The party did not object to elections but wanted to have a good chance of winning.[27] But in clandestine polls, the party was running at about 3 percent in voting intentions. No way was found to overcome this impediment. If the party had been getting 35 percent, it would have been child's play to invent an electoral system that would be competitive and give it a good chance of winning. But not at 3 percent. No

[26] The Polish situation was analyzed in game theoretic terms by Stefan Nowak in *Polityka*, Warsaw, September 1981.

[27] This general posture was put forth rather directly by Jakub Berman, number-two man in Poland during the Stalinist period, in a 1981 interview. Referring to the postwar election, Berman said: "To whom were we supposed to yield power? Perhaps Mikołajczyk [leader of the Peasant party]? Or perhaps those standing even farther to the right of Mikołajczyk? Or who the hell knows who else? You will tell me immediately that this would represent respect for democracy. So what? Who needs such democracy! Now, by the way, we cannot have free elections either, even less now than ten or twenty years ago, because we would lose. There is no doubt about this. So what is the sense of such elections? Unless we would want to show ourselves to be such super-democrats, such gentlemen, that we would take top hats off our heads, bow down and say: 'Be welcome, we are retiring, take power for yourself'" (interview in Torańska 1985: 290).

Table 2.2

|  |  | *Moderates* ally with | |
|---|---|---|---|
|  |  | Radicals | Reformers |
| *Reformers* ally with | Hardliners | Authoritarian regime survives in old form: 2,1 | Authoritarian regime holds, with concessions: 3,2 |
|  | Moderates | Democracy without guarantees: 1,4 | Democracy with guarantees: 4,3 |

institutions existed to satisfy the constraints imposed by the interests and outside opportunities of the conflicting political forces.[28] Under such conditions, Reformers could not venture into a democratic alliance with Moderates.

Suppose that Reformers do have sufficient political strength to be able to compete under democratic conditions if they are given institutional guarantees. Is this sufficient for them to opt for democracy? Consider Table 2.2. Here Reformers have political weight independent of Hardliners: They can get some support under competitive conditions, and they prefer democracy with guarantees over other alternatives. Yet the outcome for Reformers depends on the actions of Moderates. If Moderates opt for guarantees, Reformers are better off under democracy, but if Moderates ally with Radicals, Reformers lose.[29] And Moderates prefer democracy without guarantees. Examine this structure of conflict in the extensive form; that is, assume that first Reformers decide what to do, anticipating the reaction of Moderates (see Figure 2.2). Reformers analyze the situation as follows: If they ally with Hardliners, the result will be the status quo, which is the second-best outcome. They would be better off under democracy with guarantees. But if they decide to negotiate with Moderates, the latter will opt for an alliance with Radicals, which will result in the worst outcome for Reformers. Hence, Reformers stay with the regime.

[28] The same strategic situation was solved in March 1989 by a stroke of genius. Someone suggested creating an upper chamber of the parliament and having completely free elections to this chamber while guaranteeing the Communist party and its allies a majority in the lower house and hence the right to form the government.
[29] In this game there is no equilibrium in pure strategies.

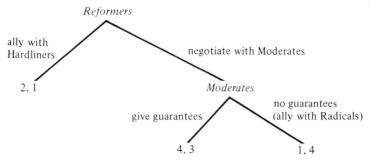

Figure 2.2

Will not democracy come about nevertheless, as a result of repetitions of this situation?[30] Imagine everyone knows that this strategic situation is almost certain to be repeated forever. Moderates know that if they respond to the opening by embracing the demands of Radicals, Reformers will ally with Hardliners next time around. Hence, the payoff to Moderates from defecting on the first round will be {4, 1, 1, . . . } or another mixture of 4s and 1s, depending on the punishment strategy chosen by Reformers.[31] But if Moderates decide to give guarantees on the first round, Reformers will respond in kind, and the payoff to Moderates will be {3,3,3, . . . }. It is easy to see that there are many Reformers' punishment strategies that should persuade Moderates to cooperate. Hence, if the original situation is to be repeated, democracy can evolve spontaneously.

But I do not think that situations in which regime change is at stake are repeatable. These are unique situations; something cracks in the authoritarian power apparatus; a group begins to feel that perhaps it would prefer to share power with consent rather than monopolize it by force, decides to make a move, and turns to eventual partners outside the regime in quest of assurances about its role under democracy. Once Reformers decide to make a move, *alea iacta est* – they cannot go back to the status quo. Payoffs for the future change as a result of actions chosen now. To go back is to admit the failure of the strategy of democratic opening and to

[30] The paragraphs that follow result from a heated discussion with Jon Elster, who, as always, forced me to decide what I really think.

[31] Tit for tat, the strategy people tend to choose in experimental situations, does maximize overtime payoff, but it is not a strategy for perfect equilibrium. In turn, there are a very large number of strategies that support the cooperative outcome. On this and many other technicalities involved here, see the excellent textbook by Rasmusen 1989.

meet with the wrath of Hardliners. Reformers who decide to go back almost never survive their failure; they are playing for broke.[32] This does not mean that an opening may not be tried again in the future by new Reformers; this is what did happen in South Korea and in Poland. But these are new forces, facing new circumstances. And if the Reformers' strategy is successful and democracy is institutionalized, the payoffs change as well. The devolution of power to democratic institutions is irreversible even if democracy can be subverted anew.[33]

Does this argument imply that democracy is never established as an equilibrium but can only result from a normative commitment to democracy? No; it is sufficient to tinker with the payoffs to see that there can exist unique situations in which the equilibrium outcome is democracy. There are two possibilities. One is that Radicals will accept democracy with guarantees; the other, that Moderates will continue to be protected by the existence of autonomous armed forces.

The first possibility – that Radicals will cease being radical – is not so farfetched as it may first appear. Until democracy is established, forces that seek profound political or economic transformation have no alternative to channeling their actions into streets and factories; there are no political institutions where their demands will not meet with violent repression. Yet once a competitive democratic framework is established because of an agreement between Moderates and Reformers, Radicals find that they too can play the game, participate. They tend to be wary of democratic institutions, distrustful of their chances, and skeptical that their victories will ever be tolerated. Yet the attraction of an open-ended democratic interplay is irresistible, and Radicals find that to abstain is to forsake popular support. As the history of Socialist parties in Western Europe demonstrates, all

[32] I say "almost" because of Brazil, where the architects of the failed "decompression" of 1974 succeeded in regrouping and trying again.

[33] This is why I do not think that evolutionary theories of institutions (Schotter 1981, 1986) can explain transitions to democracy.

Some technical issues are involved here. The results concerning the emergence of cooperation in repeated games govern only those situations that are repeated exactly; specifically, with the same payoffs. To the best of my knowledge, we know little about games in which component subgames change somewhat from one round to the next. Benhabib and Radner (1988) analyzed a labor–capital game in which payoffs change and discovered that if they change greatly from one subgame to the next, the equilibrium is noncooperative; if they change somewhat, the path of the equilibria moves monotonically to cooperative equilibrium, which reigns once the game becomes stationary. This result makes intuitive sense, so the relevant question is how much payoffs change from one situation to the next. My argument is that, at least for the Reformers, they change drastically.

political forces face the alternatives of joining or vanishing, and, except for the Anarchists, who persevered in resisting "the siren song of elections," they all joined (see Przeworski 1985: ch. 1).

If Radicals refuse to participate in the institutions forged by Moderates and Reformers, Moderates' interests may still be such that they prefer a democracy in which the forces in the civil society represented by Reformers have a significant presence to one that is dominated by Radicals.[34] Under such conditions, the payoffs in the game tree above will be interchanged: Moderates will prefer democracy with guarantees for Reformers to an alliance with Radicals. What this often means is that some sectors associated with the authoritarian regime continue to enjoy the protection of the armed forces. If Reformers have some political strength of their own and if Moderates prefer an institutional arrangement in which the armed forces remain autonomous as a counterbalance to the demands of Radicals, then Reformers have little to fear from democracy. Under such conditions, the equilibrium outcome will be democracy, but a democracy in which the armed forces will remain free of civilian control and will exercise tutelage over the democratic process.[35]

But why would Moderates tolerate military autonomy? Why would they consent to military tutelage that restricts the possible range of democratic outcomes, at times humiliates civilian politicians, and introduces a source of instability into the democratic system?[36]

Except in Poland, the communist systems of Eastern Europe produced civilian regimes. The military and most of the forces of order were subject to minute political control, which extended even to operational matters.[37] Hence, it should not be surprising that in conflicts over the leading role of

[34] In Figure 2.2, let the payoff to Moderates in a democracy with guarantees be 4, with no 3.

[35] I realize that the game is in fact more complicated than my analysis suggests, since I take the behavior of Hardliners as parametric. Yet Hardliners may, for example, provoke Radicals in order to undermine the agreement between Moderates and Reformers. In many cases of transition, there emerge shadowy groups that appear to be Radicals but may be Provocateurs: GRAPO in Spain provides one illustration; the Tablada affair in Argentina another.

[36] In October 1987, the Brazilian government raised military pay by more than 100 percent overnight in reaction to a takeover of a city hall by a small military unit stationed in a provincial town – this after the minister of finance had publicly committed himself not to do it.

[37] The secret police are a different matter. Conflicts between the secret police and Communist parties have punctuated much of the political life of communist regimes. The secret police are the group that had the most to lose from the dismantling of communism, and they were the target of popular ire in several countries.

the Communist parties, the armed forces in all Eastern European countries placed themselves squarely on the side of those who wanted to abolish the communist monopoly on power. "The army wants to serve not a party but the nation" – this has been the generals' paradigmatic declaration. From a Latin American perspective, this noble sentiment sounds ominous: not a pledge to democratic values but an assertion of independence.

In most Latin American countries, the military have preserved their autonomy and have continued to exercise tutelage over the political system, not only in countries where the transition to democracy was a result of negotiations, but even in Argentina, where the armed forces suffered a humiliating external defeat. The specter of military intervention is a permanent constraint on the political process, and the eventual reaction of the military is a consideration that permeates everyday political life in the new democracies. The Argentine experience is particularly poignant, since the impunity enjoyed by kidnappers, torturers, and murderers has a profoundly demoralizing effect on all political life. Among the recent transitions to democracy, Spain and Greece are the only countries where democratic governments succeeded in establishing effective civilian control over the military and freed themselves from this tutelage.

One obvious answer is that Moderates fear that any attempt to impose civilian control will immediately provoke exactly what it is intended to eliminate: military intervention. The strategic calculus involved must be the following. First, the probability of an immediate coup after any attempt to establish civilian control must be seen as higher than when the military are left alone. Hence, even if civilian control, once established, would greatly reduce the likelihood of military intervention, the probability that the coup will ever occur is lower without civilian control. Consider Table 2.3. The probability that the military will step in now or in the future if they continue to exercise tutelage over the political system is 68 percent, while the probability that they will undertake a coup if the government seeks to impose civilian control is 80.2 percent.[38]

This is not the end of the difficulty, for not all coups are the same. One argument for punishing violations of human rights is that the effect of

---

[38] Let $p$ be the probability of an immediate coup under tutelage, and $t$ the probability of an eventual coup in the same case. Let $q$ be the probability of an immediate coup if the government imposes civilian control, and $c$ the probability of an eventual coup. Then the total probability of a coup under tutelage is $p + (1 - p)t$, and under attempted civilian control it is $q + (1 - q)c$.

Table 2.3

| | Probability that a coup will occur | |
| --- | --- | --- |
| | Immediately | Eventually but not now |
| With tutelage | 0.20 | 0.60 |
| With civilian control | 0.80 | 0.01 |

punishment is dissuasive: The military will think twice before stepping in again because they know that once out of power they will be punished. That may be true, but if this argument is valid, it also implies that if the military are not deterred by the threat of punishment from stepping in, it will be less likely to give up power because of this threat. Thus, imposition of civilian control may lower the probability of a coup but increase the conditional probability that, once it occurs, the coup will be highly repressive, a *golpe duro*.

Thus, if a government is intent on not provoking a coup and not risking repression, it may swallow its moral outrage and its democratic ideals and accept the limits set by military tutelage.[39] But I suspect that this reasoning is not sufficient to explain the behavior of civilian politicians vis-à-vis the military. There are two reasons why democratic politicians may not want to dismantle the threat from the military even if they could.

First, Fontana (1984: 121) observed that in 1981 the Argentine political parties feared that if the threat from the military was removed, a new wave of popular mobilization would push them, as in 1973, farther to the left than they wanted: They feared radicals. To paraphrase an expression Ernest Bevin once used about the Labour party, they "did not want to be put in the position of having to listen to their own people." If the military can be counted on to repress popular mobilizations, their tutelage is a bulwark for established political parties.

Second, the problem in many countries with a long tradition of military

[39] In an 1987 article entitled "La política militar del gobierno constitucional argentino," Fontana stresses that in 1983 the government did not have a good picture of the situation in the armed forces, that it believed erroneously that the military would purify itself if given a chance, and that it repeatedly underestimated the solidarity among military generations. All of this may be true, but what strikes me is that the article fails to demonstrate that the government had any military policy.

intervention is the absence of institutional models through which civilian control over the military can be exercised.[40] Through the chain of command, the military are responsible directly to the president rather than to parliamentary committees and civilian bureaus that supervise particular aspects of their conduct. Without such an apparatus of civilian control, the choice faced by democratic governments may be one of either tolerating military autonomy or destroying the military altogether.[41] And here, I suspect, nationalism plays a role: No president can afford to commit himself or herself to actions that will undermine the ability of the nation to defend itself. Perhaps when the choice of strategy vis-à-vis the military appears to be one of leaving it intact or dismantling it altogether, the perpetuation of military domination turns out to be a lesser evil for nationalistic politicians.

The issue of civilian control over the military is thus not only whether it is prudent to attempt it but also who wants to have it.[42] Military tutelage may be preferred by some civilian political forces as a protection from demands for greater representation, to ward off pressure from those who seek a social as well as a political revolution.[43]

[40] This observation is due to José Murilo de Carvalho.

[41] For example, Delich (1984: 135) presents as follows the choice available to the Argentine democratic government. Since the atrocities committed by the military constituted acts sanctioned by the military as an institution, under written orders and under control by the military command, the democratic government could only either condemn the armed forces as a whole or forget the whole matter.

[42] This is how in October 1987 José Murilo de Carvalho (1987: 18) characterized the attitudes of the Brazilian political forces in the Constituent Assembly: "It is more difficult to visualize a surge of solid political will to construct the hegemony of civil power. As we have seen, such a will certainly does not exist in the political action of the actual occupant of the presidency of the Republic, and it does not manifest itself in an unambivalent way in the majority party, the PMDB. It is not even necessary to say that there are no traces of such will in the PFL, the PTB, etc. Whoever observes the political scene in the new Republic has the impression that military tutelage is something normal and that it should continue to be exercised."

It should not be surprising, therefore, that the *Latin American Weekly Report* of 15 September 1988 (WR–88–36) could report, under the title "Brazil's Military Gain Quietly What Pinochet Demands Loudly," that "as some Brazilian military men have readily admitted in private, whereas elsewhere civilians have worried how much autonomy they could or should grant the military, in Brazil the military have carefully dosed [prescribed] the autonomy of the civilians."

[43] José Antonio Cheibub (personal communication) offered the following criticism of this hypothesis. "The explanation based on the elite's fear of popular mobilization is not good for two reasons. First, because leaders of countries that face a problem of civilian control over the military learned (or should have learned) that the protection the military offers (from one perspective) is also a threat (from another perspective). In other words, their job as politicians is also threatened by the very tutelage they want to maintain to protect them from popular

Extrications thus leave institutional traces. Just note the price extorted by Pinochet for his consent to free elections: (1) permanent office for the current commanders in chief of the armed forces and the police, (2) protection of the "prestige of members of the military and the police," (3) an "energetic struggle against terrorism," (4) respect for the opinions of a national security council to be formed of four military representatives and four civilians, (5) maintenance of the amnesty covering political crimes committed between 1973 and 1978, (6) abstention by the political authorities from intervening in the definition and application of defense policies, including not modifying the powers of military courts, the command structure, and the military budget and not interfering in the promotion of generals (normally a presidential prerogative), (7) the right to name nine members to the Senate, (8) autonomy of the central bank, the president of which was chosen by the military, (9) acceptance of privatizations conducted during the last months of the military regime without investigation of how they were conducted, and (10) automatic allocation of 20 percent of copper revenues to the military budget. When the armed forces themselves are the Reformers and the resistance comes from bureaucrats, the situation is simpler, even if at moments dramatic.[44] Yet note that in Poland, where the impetus for reforms came from the head of the armed forces, the regime also succeeded in exacting several guarantees: (1) The Communist party was guaranteed 35 percent of the seats in the more important house of the parliament (Sejm), and its then allies were given another 30 percent: in principle, ample support to form a government; (2) it was understood that the opposition would not block the election of General Jaruzelski as president; and (3) matters of external defense and internal order were left under the control of communists.

Hence, the optimal strategy of extrication is inconsistent. The forces pushing for democracy must be prudent ex ante, and they would like to be resolute ex post. But decisions made ex ante create conditions that are hard to reverse ex post, since they preserve the power of forces associated with

mobilization. . . . Second, it seems to me that this explanation may be . . . transformed into an argument that assumes the political elite in those countries to be inherently conservative; that it always prefers the risk of a military coup to a greater representativeness of the regime."

[44] The program of political reforms proposed by General Jaruzelski at the party plenum in January 1989 failed to win a majority. At that moment, the general (who was the commander in chief), the minister of defense, and the minister of interior (both also generals) offered their resignations and walked out of the meeting. Only then did the Central Committee deem desirable the turn toward negotiations with the opposition.

the ancien régime. Ex post the democratic forces regret their prudence, but ex ante they have no choice but to be prudent.[45]

Yet the conditions created by transitions negotiated with the ancien régime are not irreversible. The essential feature of democracy is that nothing is decided definitively. If sovereignty resides with the people, the people can decide to undermine all the guarantees reached by politicians around a negotiating table. Even the most institutionalized guarantees give at best a high degree of assurance, never certainty.[46] True, in Chile, South Korea, and Pakistan attempts to modify the constitutions left as the authoritarian legacy have thus far been abortive, and in Uruguay a referendum failed to reverse the auto-amnesty declared by the military. In Poland, the initial agreement concluded in April 1989 unraveled immediately as a result of the elections of June 1989, and its remains were gradually destroyed. Transition by extrication generates incentives for the democratic forces to remove the guarantees left as the authoritarian legacy. Hence, it leaves an institutional legacy that is inherently unstable.

## Constitution

Suppose the aspect of extrication is absent: The armed forces have fallen apart, as in Greece and East Germany, or they support the transition to democracy, as they did in a number of Eastern European countries. A self-

[45] Since democracy has been consolidated in a number of countries, some North American intellectuals now advise us that the protagonists in the struggles against authoritarianism should have been more radical in pushing for social and economic transformation. For a fantasy of this kind, see Cumings 1989.

[46] Moreover, this entire analysis assumes more knowledge than the protagonists normally have or can have. In Poland, everyone miscalculated at several points: The party got so little electoral support in the first round of elections in June 1989 that the legitimacy of the negotiated deal was undermined, the heretofore loyal allies of the communists decided to venture out on their own, and the whole carefully designed plan of transition unraveled. The opposition had to make last-minute additional concessions to keep the reformers in the game. I suspect that if the party had known what would happen, it would not have agreed to elections; if the opposition had anticipated what happened, it would not have made the concessions.

Party strategists cited all kinds of reasons why Solidarity would do badly in the elections of June 1989. An eminent reformer assured me that party candidates would win a majority in the elections to the Senate. (In fact, they received 15.8 percent of the vote; see Ostrowski 1989.) But the other side was equally surprised. When asked whether political developments followed his plan, Wałęsa responded: "My project was different from what happened. With regard to politics, I wanted to stop at the conquests of the round table: make a pause and occupy ourselves with the economy and the society. But, by a stroke of bad luck, we won the elections" (interview in *Le Figaro*, Paris, 26 September 1989, p. 4).

enforcing democracy will be established if the conflicting political forces agree to an institutional framework that permits open, albeit limited, contestation and when this framework engenders continued compliance. The question is thus twofold: (1) What institutions will be selected? (2) Will they be self-enforcing?

Note first that all transitions to democracy are negotiated: some with representatives of the old regime and some only among the pro-democratic forces seeking to form a new system. Negotiations are not always needed to extricate the society from the authoritarian regime, but they are necessary to constitute democratic institutions. Democracy cannot be dictated; it emerges from bargaining.

A model of such bargaining can easily be constructed in the same vein in which we analyzed extrication. It has the following structure: Conflicts concern institutions. Each political force opts for the institutional framework that will best further its values, projects, or interests. Depending on the relation of forces, including the ability of the particular actors to impose nondemocratic solutions, either some democratic institutional framework is established or the struggle for a dictatorship ensues. This model implies hypotheses that relate the relations of force and objective conditions to the institutional results. In particular, different institutional frameworks are explained in terms of the conditions under which transitions occur.

Before developing this model, let me first flesh out the issues involved in institutional choice. Groups in conflict over the choice of democratic institutions confront three generic problems: substance versus procedure, agreement versus competition, and majoritarianism versus constitutionalism. To what extent should social and economic outcomes be left open-ended, and to what extent should some of them be guaranteed and protected regardless of the outcomes of the competitive interplay?[47] Which decisions should be made by agreement, and which should be subject to competition? Must some institutions, such as constitutional tribunals, armed forces, or heads of state, stand as arbiters above the competitive process, or should they all be subject to periodic electoral verdicts? Finally,

---

[47] On the tension between procedural and substantive aspects of constitutions, see Casper 1989. Among recent experiences, the Spanish constitution of 1977 came nearest to a classic liberal constitution that specifies only the rules of the game and says almost nothing about outcomes (except in the matter of private property), while the Brazilian constitution of 1988 went to the other extreme and listed detailed social and economic rights.

to what extent and by what means should the society bind itself to prevent some future transformations?[48] These are the central issues inherent in conflicts about institutions.

The institutional solutions required are specific and elaborate. A classic case of successful negotiations is the Swedish reforms of 1905–7.[49] The following issues were negotiated and resolved: (1) whether to extend the franchise and to whom, (2) whether the suffrage reform should include the upper or only the lower house, (3) whether seats should be allocated to single-member districts or multimember constituencies with proportional representation, (4) if single-member districts were to be retained, whether the victor should be the first past the post or the winner of a run-off election, and (5) whether the executive should continue to be responsible to the Crown rather than to the Rikstag.[50]

The reason agreement is problematic is that institutions have distributional consequences. If the choice of institutions were just a matter of efficiency, it would evoke no controversy; no one would have reason to fear a system that makes someone better off at no cost to anyone else. But given the distribution of economic, political and ideological resources, institutions do affect the degree and manner in which particular interests and values can be advanced. Hence, preferences concerning institutions differ.

What, then, can we expect to happen under different conditions? Two conditions are salient: whether the relation of forces is known to the participants when the institutional framework is being adopted and, if yes, whether this relation is uneven or balanced. These conditions determine what kinds of institutions are adopted and whether these institutions will be stable. Three hypotheses emerge from this reasoning: (1) If the relation of

[48] On this topic, see essays in Elster and Slagstad 1988.

[49] See Rustow 1955 and Verney 1959.

[50] The list of institutional issues that were the subject of discussion during the American and French constitutional processes two hundred years ago includes (1) universal versus restricted suffrage, (2) direct versus indirect elections, (3) integral versus phased renewal of deputies, (4) unicameralism versus bicameralism, (5) secret versus public voting, (6) parliamentarism versus presidentialism, (7) fixed-calendar elections versus governmental discretion about the timing of elections, (8) a reeligible versus a nonreeligible executive, (9) inviolability of deputies, (10) executive veto, (11) a responsible executive, liable to dismissal, (12) the right of dissolution, (13) legislative power to initiate and repeal laws, (14) legislative monopoly over the power of the purse, (15) an independent judiciary, (16) trial by jury, open to the public, (17) a ban on retroactive laws, (18) absolute freedom of the press, (19) freedom of religion, (20) institutional barriers between the army and the police, and (21) territorial decentralization of decision-making power. This list is Stephen Holmes's. See Hardin, Holmes, and Przeworski 1988.

forces is known ex ante to be uneven, the institutions ratify this relation and are stable only as long as the original conditions prevail; (2) if the relation of forces is known ex ante to be balanced, anything can happen: prolonged civil war, agreement to institutions that cannot work, or agreement to an institutional framework that eventually assumes the force of convention; (3) if the relation of forces is unknown ex ante, the institutions will comprise extensive checks and balances and will last in the face of a variety of conditions. These hypotheses are discussed in turn.

*The relation of forces is known and uneven.* When the relation of forces is known and uneven, the institutions are custom-made for a particular person, party, or alliance. Geddes (1990) has shown that new constitutions have been adopted in Latin America whenever a new party system has emerged from the authoritarian period. The features of the new institutions she analyzed were designed to consolidate the new relations of forces.

The origins and role of such institutions were best described by Hayward (1983: 1), writing, not accidentally, about France: "Because Frenchmen expected regimes to be short-lived – indeed their Constitutions were often dismissed as periodical literature – little authority was attached to the Constitution itself at any one time. The current document was regarded as a treaty provisionally settling the allocation of power to suit the victors in a political struggle. Far from being a basic and neutral document, it was seen as only a partisan procedural device setting out the formal conditions according to which the government was entitled to rule."

In Poland, the constitution of 1921 designed a weak presidency because Marshal Piłsudski's opponents knew he would be elected president. Piłsudski refused to run under these conditions and assumed power as the result of a coup d'état in May 1926. Nine years later, a new constitution was crafted to ratify his effective power. He died a year later, and it turned out that there was no one able to step into his shoes. In France, the constitution of the Fifth Republic was crafted specifically for General de Gaulle, but it survived the test of *cohabitation* when a Socialist president coexisted with a parliamentary majority of the Right.

It is reasonable to expect that constitutions that ratify present relations of forces will be only as durable as these relations. The case of the Chilean constitution of 1925 provides an excellent illustration (the following is based on Stanton 1990). This constitution was not generally accepted until 1932, when a side agreement was made to leave in the hands of landlords control over the votes of peasants and to maintain indefinitely the over-representation of rural districts. In effect, therefore, the constitution that had emerged by 1932 was a cartel of the urban sectors and the *latifundistas,* designed to keep the prices of agricultural products low by allowing landowners to depress rural wages. The barriers to entry created by this pact eroded only during the 1960s when Christian Democrats came to office and sought the support of the peasants. By 1968, the system had collapsed, and democracy was subverted in 1973. Note that the institutions in question did last for forty-one years. But from the beginning they were designed in such a way that they could not survive one specific change of conditions: the effective enfranchisement of the rural masses.

*The relation of forces is known and balanced.* This is by far the most complex set of circumstances. Suppose that the conflicting political forces have strong preferences over alternative ways of organizing the political life of the society. One part of a country may strongly prefer a unitary form of government, while another has a strong preference for a federal system. Some groups may think that their interests will be best protected under a parliamentary system, and others insist on a presidential one.[51] One alliance of forces insists on the separation of church and state; another calls for a state religion. Imagine generically that one alliance of forces, called Row, would find democracy more advantageous under institutional system A, while the other, Column, feels threatened by this system and prefers B. They do not agree. (Table 2.4.)

This situation has no equilibrium in pure strategies, and one possible outcome is civil war. This was the case in Argentina between 1810 and 1862; two attempts to write the constitution failed, and a stable situation was reached only after the province of Buenos Aires was defeated in a war (Saguir 1990). This may very well be the current situation in the Soviet Union, where nationalist, federalist, and unitary forces conflict without any apparent solution.

Yet prospects of a prolonged conflict, of a civil war lasting perhaps for generations, are forbidding. Hence, political forces may be led to adopt some institutional framework, any framework, just as a temporizing solu-

[51] In a recent survey of 418 members of Brazil's elite, 71 percent of respondents wanted to see a parliamentary system adopted, among them 80 percent of politicians and journalists, 60 percent of union leaders, and 45 percent of the military (*Latin American Weekly Report,* 90–26, 12 July 1990, p. 5).

Table 2.4

|  | | Column | |
|---|---|---|---|
|  | | A | B |
| Row | A | Best, So-so | Terrible, Terrible |
|  | B | Terrible, Terrible | So-so, Best |

tion.[52] As Rustow (1970) observed, when none of the parties can impose its solution unilaterally, "this prolonged standoff leads the parties concerned to seek a suboptimal compromise solution."

Indeed, this is what did occur in several countries: Conflicts about institutions were quickly terminated. In Brazil, a new constitution was adopted, with full knowledge that it could not be observed, explicitly to reduce the intensity of conflict by promising to satisfy all kinds of demands in the future. In Argentina, the constitution of 1853 was reinstated, though this constitution had never worked before and there was no reason to think it would work now.[53]

Why are such temporizing solutions attractive? One reason is the belief of the political actors that institutions matter little, not enough to be worth the risk of continuing conflict. Indeed, trust in the causal power of institutions seems to be a distinctive feature of the political culture of the United States, where politicians and scholars alike believe that institutions cause people to behave differently than they would otherwise and where they attribute political stability to the genius of the founders. Outside the Anglo-Saxon world, institutions are seen as much less effective; a renowned Brazilian scholar and politician once remarked that "one does not stop a coup d'état by an article of the constitution."[54] In Hungary, a referendum

[52] Kavka (1986: 185) describes the choice of constitutions as a case of "impure coordination": No agreement is disastrous for both parties, but each party prefers a different one. He argues that under such conditions the parties will first agree to agree and then decide on what. I am not sure, however, how this is to be done.

[53] Between 1854 and 1983, the average proportion of the constitutional term served by Argentine presidents was 52 percent: 72 percent up to 1930, and 37 percent during the recent period (see de Pablo 1990: 113). The constitution of 1853 provided for a nine-month period between the election and the inauguration. The reason was that electors needed time to travel to Buenos Aires, and this is how long it took. This provision remained when the constitution was reinstated, and the first democratic transfer of power, between Raúl Alfonsín and Carlos Menem, was already unconstitutional: They agreed that the country could not tolerate a lame-duck government for such a long period and transferred power early.

[54] Fernando Henrique Cardoso, interviewed in Veja, 9 September 1987.

on the mode of electing the president brought to the polls only 14 percent of the electorate. Hence, while some institutional framework is required to coordinate political strategies, it matters little what this framework happens to be, for it will not be binding anyway.

Moreover, even if politicians do suspect that institutions matter, they know that they cannot accurately predict the consequences of alternative institutional frameworks. European conservatives called for compulsory voting, thinking that it was their own electorate that was abstaining, and they fought against female suffrage, expecting that this vote would benefit their adversaries; and they were wrong in both cases.

Neither skepticism about the importance nor lack of knowledge about the effects of institutions should be exaggerated. Politicians do know that and know how electoral systems influence the distribution of seats; they know that it matters who supervises the intelligence services; they are sensitive to regulations concerning the financing of political parties. History is replete with evidence of conflicts over institutions: conflicts in which protagonists acted on their belief about the importance of minute institutional arrangements. Hence, it is important to specify the hypothesis implied by the arguments above precisely: In my view, protagonists agree to terminate conflicts over institutions because they fear that a continuation of conflict may lead to a civil war that will be both collectively and individually threatening. The pressure to stabilize the situation is tremendous, since governance must somehow continue. Chaos is the worst alternative for all. And under such conditions, political actors calculate that whatever difference in their welfare could result from a more favorable institutional framework is not worth the risk inherent in continued conflict.

But how can they terminate conflict? They must establish some institutional framework, but which framework can they adopt if no institutions constitute an equilibrium solution? The only way out is to look for what Schelling called the focal points: solutions that are readily available and are not seen as self-serving. And the search for foci naturally leads to national traditions if these are available, or to foreign examples if they are not. This is why Argentines went back to the constitution of 1853, and Spaniards relied to a large extent on the West German system.[55] Indeed, several voices in Poland suggested that the country should just take any old West-

---

[55] Herrero de Miñon (1979) argues that the Spanish constitution was not "a servile copy" of one or several foreign models. He does provide evidence, however, that foreign examples, particularly the West German, loomed large in a number of key provisions.

ern European constitution and be done with it.[56] Since any order is better than disorder, any order is established.

This brings us to the question whether these institutional solutions are likely to last. In the light of game theory, coordination solutions are unstable when the situation involves conflict. But the question is not a simple one. Hardin (1987) argued that coordination points acquire causal power once they are adopted: Some institutions are around because they have been around for a long time. Change is costly.[57]

Hardin's theory finds strong support in the observation made by Dahl (1990) that, except in Uruguay, democracy has never been internally subverted in any country in which it has survived for twenty years.[58] Yet the theory of "contract by convention" is too strong: It may explain why the U.S. constitution has held, but it offers no understanding of why a constitution would ever fail or why so many have proved to be short-lived or irrelevant.

The reason temporizing solutions may not survive for twenty years is the following. Suppose that when the original confrontation occurs, any arrangement is superior for the relevant political forces to continued conflicts. Yet the system adopted as a temporary expedient favors the chances of some groups over others. Two mechanisms now set in. First, the losing alliance knows that its chances of winning under this system are lower than under an alternative system. This expectation is fulfilled, and this alliance loses one or more consecutive times. Hence, the ex post situation is not the same as the ex ante: If it had happened to win, in spite of its smaller chance, the calculus would have been different. Second, actors learn about their future chances when they observe current outcomes. The losers update downward their expectations concerning the system of institutions and may find the risk of reopening the conflict about institutions less forbidding than before.[59]

---

[56] This proposal has a tradition of its own. As early as the end of the eighteenth century, Poles turned to Rousseau to draft a constitution for the country.

[57] In Hardin's (1987: 17) words, "once we have settled on a constitutional arrangement, it is not likely to be in the interest of some of us then to try to renege on the arrangement. Our interests will be better served by living with the arrangement." And "The Constitution of 1787 worked in the end because enough of the relevant people worked within its confines long enough to get it established in everyone's expectations that there was no point in not working within its confines" (p. 23). Kavka (1986) makes a similar point.

[58] Democracy is defined here as a system in which there are free elections, the government is responsible to the elected parliament or president, and – a condition that strongly restricts the number of cases – a majority of the population has the right to vote.

[59] The difference between my views and those of Hardin (1987) and Kavka (1986) probably stems from our respective understandings of payoffs under democracy, which they treat as

If this argument is valid, then temporizing solutions may turn out to be exactly that. They were adopted because continued struggle was seen as too dangerous. But if they generate outcomes that hurt, the affected political forces will naturally be tempted to try to avoid the costs involved in competing under democratic rules or at least to improve their future chances in this competition. Hence, political forces that can pursue alternatives will do so.

*The relation of forces is not known.* Suppose a country emerges from a long period of authoritarian rule and no one knows what the relation of forces will be. The timing of constitution writing is then important. If the constitution is put off until elections and other events clarify this relation, we are back to the situations discussed above: The focus may turn out to be unequal and institutions will be designed to ratify the current advantage, or they may turn out to be balanced, with all the possibilities this situation implies. The relative timing of presidential elections, parliamentary elections, and constitution writing was the subject of intense conflict in Poland, and the decision was to hold presidential elections before the constitution was written. Yet suppose that the constitution is written first, as it was in Greece, or that elections are held and are highly uninstructive, as they were in Spain.

If everyone is behind the Rawlsian veil, that is, if they know little about their political strength under the eventual democratic institutions, all opt for a maximin solution: institutions that introduce checks and balances and maximize the political influence of minorities, or, equivalently, make policy highly insensitive to fluctuations in public opinion. Each of the conflicting political forces will seek institutions that provide guarantees against temporary political adversity, against unfavorable tides of opinion, against contrary shifts of alliances.[60] In Sweden, Liberals and Social Dem-

certain once a particular set of institutions is adopted and I consider as uncertain with known probabilities. Even in the simple model developed in the preceding chapter, the probability required to stay in the game after losing once, $p^*(1)$, is higher than the probability required ex ante to opt for democracy, $p^*(0)$; in fact, $p^*(1) = p^*(0)/r$, where $r < 1$. In addition, if actors update their beliefs on observing outcomes, then there is another reason why $p^*|L > p^*(0)$. Hence, there may be an actor that accepts democracy ex ante but seeks to subvert it having lost on one round, two rounds, etc.

[60] Several instances of veil-of-ignorance reasoning can be found in the Constitutional Convention of 1789. According to Madison's notes, for instance, George Mason made the following argument: "We ought to attend to the right of every class of people. He had often wondered at the indifference of the superior classes of society to this dictate of humanity & policy, considering that however affluent their circumstances, or elevated their situations, might be, the course of a few years, not only might but certainly would distribute their

ocrats were willing to provide the guarantees required by Conservatives; as the Conservative spokesman, Bishop Gottfrid Billing, put it, he would rather have "stronger guarantees and a further extension of the suffrage than weaker guarantees and a lesser extension" (cited in Rustow 1955: 59).

Hence, constitutions that are written when the relation of forces are still unclear are likely to counteract increasing returns to power, provide insurance to the eventual losers, and reduce the stakes of competition. They are more likely to induce the losers to comply with the outcomes and more likely to induce them to participate. They are more likely, therefore, to be stable across a wide range of historical conditions.

The tentative conclusions, to be tested against systematic evidence, are thus the following. Institutions adopted when the relation of forces is unknown or unclear are most likely to last across a variety of conditions. Institutions adopted as temporizing solutions when the relation of forces is known to be balanced and different groups have strong preferences over alternative solutions may acquire the force of convention if they happen to survive for a sufficient period, but they are not likely to last long enough. Finally, institutions that ratify a transitory advantage are likely to be as durable as the conditions that generate them.

## Contestation

There is one additional aspect to consider. Following O'Donnell and Schmitter, we need to make a distinction between democratization of the state and of the regime. The first process concerns institutions; the second, the relations between state institutions and the civil society.[61]

Each of the forces struggling against authoritarianism must also consider its future position under democracy. They must all stand united against dictatorship, but they must divide against each other.[62] If they divide too

posteriority through the lowest classes of Society. Every selfish motive therefore, every family attachment, ought to recommend such a system of policy as would provide no less carefully for the rights and happiness of the lowest than that of the highest orders of Citizens" (Farrand 1966: I, 49). I owe this quotation to Jon Elster.

[61] According to O'Donnell and Schmitter (1986: IV, 73), a regime is "the ensemble of patterns, explicit or not, that determines the forms and channels of access to principal government positions, the characteristics of the actors who are admitted and excluded from such access, and the resources and strategies that they can use to gain access."

[62] Thus, negotiations about the shape of the negotiating table are not just petty squabbling. The regime in place has good reason to fear a two-sided division, since this arrangement unites the opposition. The Polish solution was to make the table round. The Hungarian way was to make it triangular, but octagonal solutions were entertained.

early, the outcome is likely to repeat the experience of South Korea, where the rivalry between two anti-authoritarian presidential candidates – rivalry that was personal but also regional and economic – permitted electoral victory for the candidate associated with dictatorship.[63] If they do not divide at all, the new regime will be a mirror image of the old one: not representative, not competitive. This is the danger facing several Eastern European countries: that the revolution will end up being only anticommunist, not democratic.[64]

The same dilemma appears in modified form after democratic institutions are in place. The classic problem of any opposition under democracy is how much to oppose and by what means. If the opposition does not oppose – does not present alternatives and struggle energetically for them – then the representative power of political institutions – their capacity to mobilize and to incorporate – is weak.[65] Democracy is anemic. But if the opposition does oppose vigorously, democracy may be threatened. Particularly under difficult economic conditions, intransigent opposition may create an ungovernable situation. If every time a party loses an election or every time a government adopts an unpopular policy, the opposition

---

[63] Note that the democratic opposition could not unite in Spain until the death of Franco. The main issue was the participation of communists (see Carr and Fusi 1979). The Chilean opposition experienced the same difficulty.

[64] The situation in several Eastern European countries is particularly complicated, because any new party of the Left would have to include some former communists, but an alliance with them would be the kiss of death. In Poland, some groups in the anticommunist coalition deliberately tried to provoke a Left–Right split precisely because they knew the electoral consequences for any group that was cast as the Left. (See the editorial in *Tygodnik Solidarność*, Warsaw, 22 December 1989.) In turn, those painted as the Left were forced to respond that there were no real divisions within the coalition and no reason to split and form multiple political parties.

Note that in Brazil it took five years before the PMDB divided into its ideological currents. Established originally to provide window dressing for the authoritarian regime, the MDB was the only cover for legal opposition activity, and as such it became an umbrella for all kinds of political forces. Everyone was certain that this artificial creature would break up into its natural parts the day political parties could legally exist, and it briefly did when the right wing broke off as the Partido Popular. But the separation did not last long, and in its new incarnation the PMDB turned into the largest party in the country, developed local machines, and continued to win elections until 1989.

[65] Since a particular view of representation underlies the argument that follows, let me recall how I see a representative regime. A representative system is one in which (1) there exist autonomous organizations, (2) they are stratified internally into leaders and followers, (3) leaders have the capacity to (a) invoke collective identities, (b) control the strategic behavior of followers, and (c) sanction defections, (4) leaders are representatives, that is, participate in representative institutions, and (5) representation makes a difference for the well-being of their followers. Organized political forces participate in democratic institutions if they believe that actions channeled through these institutions affect their welfare.

launches a general strike, democratic institutions may be weakened and the conditions created for the military to step in.

Perhaps the clearest place to observe this dilemma is in the Peronist movement in Argentina. The "Renovadores" wanted to become an electoral party and to reduce their tactics to electoral and parliamentary struggle, while the orthodox wing wanted to remain a "movement" and to struggle for "social justice" by all possible means. Thus, Ubaldini did not think that losing elections should prevent the CGT from undertaking general strikes, while Peronist deputies in the Congress absented themselves whenever they thought they would lose, thus undermining the quorum.

One solution to this dilemma is political pacts: agreements among leaders of political parties (or proto-parties) to (1) divide government offices among themselves independent of election results, (2) fix basic policy orientations, and (3) exclude and, if need be, repress outsiders.[66] Such pacts have a long tradition in Italy, Spain, and Uruguay of what used to be called *transformismo*. The 1958 Venezuelan pact of Punto Fijo is the model for such agreements. According to this pact, three parties would divide government posts, pursuing policies committed to development goals under private property and excluding communists from the political system. This pact has been highly successful in organizing democratic alterations in office.

The ostensible purpose of such pacts is to protect embryonic democratic institutions by reducing the level of conflict about policies and personnel. Whereas institutional pacts establish the rules of the game and leave the rest to competition, these are substantive pacts intended to remove major policy issues from the competitive process. Such pacts are offered as necessary to protect the democratic institutions from pressures to which they cannot respond. But note that such pacts are feasible only if the partners extract private benefits from democracy; and note that they can extract such rents only by excluding outsiders from the competition.[67] The danger inherent in such substantive pacts is that they will become cartels of incumbents against contenders, cartels that restrict competition, bar access, and distribute the benefits of political power among the insiders.

[66] Wiatr (1983, 1989) proposed a similar arrangement for Poland under the name of contractual democracy.

[67] In the language of the preceding chapter, such pacts cannot be bargains, since there is no third party to enforce them. If they are to be stable, they must constitute equilibria. But an agreement to limit competition is an equilibrium only if it effectively dissuades outsiders from entry. The source of rents is monopoly.

Democracy would then turn into a private project of leaders of some political parties and corporatist associations, an oligopoly in which leaders of some organizations collude to prevent outsiders from entering.

Entrepreneurial profits may be an inevitable private reward to those who undertake the democratic project. Moreover, democratic institutions may be unable to process all the important conflicts that divide a society; vide the deliberate exclusion of religious issues from the United States constitutional process. All democratic systems create some barriers to entry – electoral politics is perhaps the most protected industry in the United States. Yet if democracy is to be consolidated, the role of competition should be to dissipate such profits rather than to turn them into permanent rents. One should not forget that the success of the Pacto de Punto Fijo cost Venezuela the largest guerrilla movement in Latin America. Exclusion requires coercion and destabilizes democratic institutions.[68]

This analysis of political pacts has been couched in the economist's language of rents to be derived from collusion. Yet fear of divisions is motivated not only by the specter of authoritarian restoration and not only by the self-interested behavior of politicians. It is inherent in democracy for ideological reasons.

One reason stems from the rationalist origins of the democratic theory. The theory of democracy that developed during the eighteenth century saw the democratic process as one of rational deliberation that leads to unanimity and converges to a presumed general interest. If the citizenry is homogeneous or if its interests are harmonious, then there is one and only one interest that is both general and rational. In this view of the world, all divisions are divisions of opinion; there is no room for conflicts that cannot be reconciled by rational discussion. The role of the political process is epistemological: It constitutes a search for truth. And the status of consensus is moral: It represents an embodiment of the general interest. The

---

[68] The main difficulty with this hypothesis comes from the United States, where the barriers to entry have been formidable, where the representative power of political parties is minimal, and where economic inequality is high by comparative standards – all that in the face of relatively low levels of political repression. One might be tempted to make sense of this anomaly by making the claim some Brazilians (Andrade 1980; Moisés 1986) make with regard to their country, namely, that their civil society is weak, which I take to mean unable to organize to push its way into the representative system. But the civil society in the United States appears extremely strong, at least if we believe various measures of political participation other than voting. My hunch is that the role of repression in the United States has been historically greater than standard interpretations allow for, but I know no systematic evidence to that effect.

superiority of democracy consists precisely in its rationality. Hence, both Rousseau and Madison feared interests, passions, and the "factions" to which they give rise; both saw democracy as a mechanism to reach an agreement, to discover the common good.

Given these ideological origins, persistent differences of opinion, passionate conflicts of interest, procedural wranglings are often seen as obstacles to rationality. "If we could only agree" is the perennial dream of those appalled by the clamor of party politics, even if most politicians mean "If you would only agree with me" when they call for rational discussion. Consensus has a higher moral status than decisions by numbers or by rules. Hence, the striving to resolve conflicts by agreement, by ceremoniously celebrated pacts, is ubiquitous whenever political conflicts seem to get out of hand, whenever they appear to threaten democratic institutions.

An even more powerful impetus to unanimity is present in countries that have entrenched traditions of organicist views of the nation, often inspired by Catholicism.[69] If the nation is organism, it is not a body that can breed divisions and conflicts. Its unity is organic, that is, given by existing ties. The nation is "a live social organism, having a spiritual specificity derived from racial and historical bases" (Dmowski 1989: 71).[70] Those who do not partake in the national spirit can only be those who do not belong: alien to the body of the nation. And if the nation is an organism, it is not a body that can tolerate alien elements.[71] Individualism and dissent are manifestations of not belonging.

As O'Donnell (1989) has shown, the notion of an organic unity of interests leads each of the political forces to strive for a monopoly in representing the "national interest." Political forces do not see themselves as parties representing particular interests and particular views against representatives of other interests and projects. Since the nation is one body with one will, each of the political forces aspires to become the one and

---

[69] The paragraphs that follow result from several conversations with Guillermo O'Donnell about our native countries, Argentina and Poland.

[70] Roman Dmowski was the spiritual and political leader of Polish National Democrats before 1939. The eighth edition of Dmowski's seminal essay, *Myśli nowoczesnego polaka*, written originally in 1903, was published in Poland in 1989.

[71] This organicist language is notorious in Argentina; see several examples in O'Donnell 1989. I remember a speech by the head of the army under Alfonsín in 1988: "We are the immunological system which protects the nation from the virus of subversion" (*Pagina 12*, Buenos Aires, September 1988). In the recent abortion debate in the Polish parliament, Senator Kaczyński, the leader of the pro-Wałęsa party, declared that "all good Poles are against abortion" and those who support it "are a bad part of the nation" (*Libération*, 1 October 1990, p. 19).

only representative of the nation, to cloak itself in the mantle of *el movimiento nacional*. And since there are no conflicts to be resolved by competition under rules, democracy serves only as an opportunity to struggle for a monopoly in representing the national interest.

Catholic–nationalist ideology is alive in many countries; indeed, this is the ideology that motivated many, though by no means all, Eastern European dissidents in their struggle against communism. Many were caught between their opposition to communism and their opposition to the nationalist–religious ideology that was the only effective political force against communism.[72] In spite of Vaclav Havel's eloquent eulogies to the subversive power of truth, the spiritual force that provided the lasting source of opposition to communism was not a yearning for liberty (as distinguished from independence from the Soviet Union), but religion and nationalism; indeed, the historically specific amalgam of the two.[73] The resurgence of the political power of the church,[74] the flare-up of nationalist ideologies and of ethnic conflicts, and a burst of antisemitism constitute symptoms of the vitality of organicist ideologies in Eastern Europe.

Hence, the striving for consensus is motivated not only by considerations of self-interest. Democracy calls for a particular form of suspension of belief: the certainty that one outcome is best for all, rational. Decisions by numbers or by rules do not have prima facie rationality. The everyday life of democratic politics is not a spectacle that inspires awe: an endless

[72] The most revealing, and most poignant, document of the tension this dilemma engendered is the memoirs of Jacek Kuroń, *Wiara i Wina: Do i od komunizmu* (1990).

[73] Havel, in my view, confuses the subversive role of truth in regimes of ritualized speech with the commitment to free speech by those who uttered their truths in the struggle against these regimes. To say "We are a nation, with our own culture" under communism was to speak against Soviet domination; to say it in a democracy may mean that those who reject this culture have no right to speak. One should not forget that, except in Bohemia, the political culture that was suppressed by communists in the aftermath of World War II was a nationalist–religious–authoritarian amalgam that gave rise to several dictatorships during the interwar period. This culture was frozen under communist rule; it had no chance to evolve in the direction of democracy, as it did in France, Italy, and Finland. And this is to a large extent the culture that was defrosted in the autumn of 1989.

[74] It is a commonplace to emphasize the power of the Catholic Church in Poland. Yet this is a puzzling phenomenon. While the church is indeed politically most influential, as a moral force it is ineffective. Birth control is practiced in Poland, abortions are exceedingly frequent, divorce rates are high, alcoholism is rampant, crime has been growing alarmingly – the impact of the church on everyday moral behavior is hard to detect. And situations in which the church has political but not moral power naturally lead it to an authoritarian posture: What it cannot do by persuasion, it does by compulsion. Divorce was made more difficult by causing divorce proceedings to take place in higher courts; religious instruction in preschools, elementary schools, and high schools was introduced by a decree issued during the summer vacation by the minister of education; and abortion was criminalized.

squabble among petty ambitions, rhetoric designed to hide and mislead, shady connections between power and money, laws that make no pretense of justice, policies that reinforce privilege. This experience is particularly painful for people who had to idealize democracy in the struggle against authoritarian oppression, people for whom democracy was the paradise forbidden. When paradise turns into everyday life, disenchantment sets in. Hence the temptation to make everything transparent in one swoop, to stop the bickering, to replace politics with administration, anarchy with discipline, to do the rational – the authoritarian temptation.

## Conclusions

This entire analysis is less conclusive than one might wish. Let me just summarize the major hypotheses.

First, whenever the ancien régime negotiates its way out of power, the optimal strategy of democratization is inconsistent: It requires compromises ex ante, resolution ex post. Transitions by extrication leave institutional traces: most important, the autonomy of the armed forces. These traces can be effaced, but transitions are more problematic and longer in countries where they result from negotiated agreements with the old regime. The transition was longer in Brazil than in Argentina; longer in Poland than in Czechoslovakia. And wherever the armed forces have remained independent of civilian control, the military question is a permanent source of instability for democratic institutions.

Second, it seems that the choice of institutions during recent cases of transition has been to a large extent haphazard, dominated by the understandable desire to terminate fundamental conflicts as quickly as possible. And there are reasons to believe that institutions adopted as temporizing solutions will turn out to be precisely that. Hence, the new democracies are likely to experience continued conflict over the basic institutions; the political forces that suffer defeat as a result of the interplay of these institutions will repeatedly bring the institutional framework back to the political agenda.

Finally, we should not be seduced by the democratic rhetoric of some forces that successfully joined in opposition to particular authoritarian regimes. Not all anti-authoritarian movements are pro-democratic; some join under the slogan of democracy only as a step toward devouring both their authoritarian opponents[75] and their allies in the struggle against the old authoritarian regime. The search for consensus is often not more than a guise for a new authoritarian temptation. For many, democracy represents disorder, chaos, anarchy. As Marx noted almost 150 years ago, the party that defends dictatorship is the Party of Order.[76] And fear of the unknown is not limited to the forces associated with the ancien régime.

Democracy is the realm of the indeterminate; the future is not written. Conflicts of values and of interests are inherent in all societies. Democracy is needed precisely because we cannot agree. Democracy is only a system for processing conflicts without killing one another; it is a system in which there are differences, conflicts, winners and losers. Conflicts are absent only in authoritarian systems. No country in which a party wins 60 percent of the vote twice in a row is a democracy.

As everyone agrees, the eventual survival of the new democracies will depend to a large extent on their economic performance. And since many among them emerged in the midst of an unprecedented economic crisis, economic factors work against their survival. But before we can analyze the interplay of political and economic conditions, we need to examine the choices inherent in the economic systems.

## Appendix: Approaches to the study of transitions

The approach used above is one among several possible. And since methods do affect conclusions, it may be helpful to place it among alternative perspectives. My intent is not to review the different bodies of literature employing the particular approaches, but simply to highlight the central logic of the alternatives.

The final question in studies of transitions to democracy concerns the

[75] Should former members of the nomenklatura be deprived of political rights without individual due process? Should they be purged from the bureaucracy? In all Eastern European countries, calls for a purge enjoy widespread popular support. Yet are such purges consistent with the rule of law? As Adam Michnik recently put it in a speech with an almost Danton-esque tone, "When we deprive others of political rights, we are taking them away from ourselves" (Vienna Seminar on Democratization in Eastern Europe, June 1990). The best treatment of this issue I have found is Bence 1990.

[76] To cite our contemporaries, Milos Jakes, the hardline first secretary of the Czechoslovak Communist party, accused the organizers of the demonstrations in Prague of "seeking to create chaos and anarchy" (*New York Times,* 21 November 1989). So did Erich Honecker. So did several of Gorbachev's opponents at the February 1990 Plenum of the Soviet Central Committee.

modalities of the system that emerges as the end state. Does the process end in a democracy or in a dictatorship, new or old? Is the new democracy a stable one? Which institutions constitute it? Is the new system effective in generating substantive outcomes? Is it conducive to individual freedom and social justice? These are the kinds of questions we seek to answer in studying transitions.

To stylize the analysis, let me refer to the system that emerges as the end state of transition by its Brazilian term, *Nova República,* the "new republic." Studies of transition attempt to explain the features of the new republic.

The point of departure is the authoritarian status quo that precedes it, *l'ancien régime, and perhaps even the social conditions that gave rise to this authoritarian system, l'ancienne société.*[77] Hence, transition proceeds from the ancien régime to the new republic.

Now, one approach, probably dominant until the late 1970s, was to correlate the features of the point of departure and the point of arrival. This approach is generally known as macrohistorical comparative sociology, and the seminal works include Moore (1965) and Lipset and Rokkan (1967). The method characteristic of this approach is to associate inductively outcomes, such as democracy or fascism, with initial conditions, such as an agrarian class structure. In this formulation the outcome is uniquely determined by conditions, and history goes on without anyone ever doing anything.

This approach lost much of its popularity when the possibility of democratization appeared on the historical horizon, first in Southern Europe and then in the Southern Cone of Latin America. The reason was, I believe, primarily political. The perspective was simply too deterministic to orient the activities of political actors who could not help believing that the success of democratization might depend on their strategies and those of their opponents rather than being given once and for all by past conditions.[78] It made little sense to Brazilians to believe that all their efforts were for naught because of the agrarian class structure of their country; it appeared ludicrous to Spanish democrats in 1975 that the future of their country had been decided once and for all by the relative timing of industrialization and universal male suffrage. The macrohistorical approach was

---

[77] Philippe Schmitter drew my attention to these social factors.

[78] I remember how struck I was that Barrington Moore's work was not even mentioned during the first meeting of the O'Donnell–Schmitter democratization project in 1979.

unappealing even to those scholar-activists who resisted the intellectual assumptions of the micro perspective because it condemned them to political impotence.

As events developed, so did scholarly reflection about them. The first set of questions concerned the impact of various features of the ancien régime on the modalities of transition. Transitions were variously classified into "modes." In particular, the collapse of the authoritarian regime was distinguished from – the term was Spanish for good reasons – a *"ruptura pactada,"* a negotiated break. A perusal of the voluminous literature on this topic demonstrates, in my view, that these studies bore little fruit: It turned out to be hard to find common factors that triggered liberalization in different countries. Some authoritarian regimes collapsed after long periods of economic prosperity; some, after they experienced acute economic crises.[79] Some regimes were vulnerable to foreign pressure; others used such pressure successfully to close ranks under nationalistic slogans. The problem these studies encounter – and the rush of writings on Eastern Europe provides new illustrations – is that it is easier to explain ex post why a particular regime "had to" fall than to predict when it would fall. Social science is just not very good at sorting out underlying structural causes and precipitating conditions. And while explanations in terms of structural conditions are satisfying ex post, they are useless ex ante, since even a small mistake about the timing of collapse often costs human lives. The Franco regime was still executing people in 1975, one year before it was all over.

The O'Donnell–Schmitter (1986) approach was to focus on the strategies of different actors and explain the outcomes as a result of these strategies. Perhaps the reason for adopting this approach was that many participants in their project were protagonists in the struggles for democracy and needed to understand the consequences of alternative courses of action. Yet while this approach focused on strategic analysis, it shied away from adopting a formalistic, ahistorical approach inherent in the abstract theory of games. Given that the macrolanguage of classes, their alliances, and "pacts of domination" was the dominant vocabulary of the time, the result was an intuitive micro approach often couched in macro language. The main conclusion of the O'Donnell–Schmitter approach was that

---

[79] My intuition is that finer analysis may still show that economic factors operate in a uniform way: Liberalization occurs when an economic crisis follows a long period of growth. Perhaps there were just not enough cases to substantiate results derived inductively.

modalities of transition determine the features of the new regime; specifically, that unless the armed forces collapse, successful transition can be brought about only as a result of negotiations, of pacts. The political implication was that pro-democratic forces must be prudent; they must be prepared to offer concessions in exchange for democracy. And the corollary was that the democracy that results from the *ruptura pactada* is inevitably conservative economically and socially.

Once democracy had been established in several countries, these conclusions drew the accusation that they were unduly conservative. Such retrospective evaluations are easy to support, particularly for observers tucked safely away within the walls of North American academia. Indeed, for many protagonists, the central political issue at the time was whether their struggle should be simultaneously for political and economic transformation or only be about political issues. Should it be for democracy and socialism simultaneously, or should democracy be striven for as a goal in itself? And the answer given in their political practice by most of the forces that turned out to be historically relevant was resolutely that democracy was an autonomous value, worth the economic and social compromises that successful strategies to bring it about engendered. This was the simple lesson drawn from the bestiality of the military regimes in Argentina, Chile, and Uruguay; anything was better than the mass murder and torture that these regimes perpetuated.

Indeed, the relevant question in retrospect seems not political but empirical: Is it true that modalities of transition determine the final outcome? As my analysis indicates, transition by extrication does leave institutional traces, specifically when it places democracy under the tutelage of an autonomous military. Yet, first, these traces can be gradually wiped away. In Spain, successive democratic governments were effective in gradually removing the remnants of Francismo and in placing the military under civilian control; in Poland, the evolving relations of forces eliminated most of the relics of the Magdalenka pact. Second, I find surprisingly little evidence that the features of the "new republic" do in fact correspond either to traits of the ancien régime or to modalities of transition. This is perhaps an inadequacy of my analysis – we are only now beginning to have enough cases to engage in systematic empirical studies. Yet I can think of at least two reasons why the new democracies should be more alike than the conditions that brought them about.

First, timing matters. The fact that recent transitions to democracy occurred as a wave also means that they happened under the same ideological and political conditions in the world. Moreover, contagion plays a role. Co-temporality induces homogeneity: The new democracies learn from the established ones and from one another.

Second, our cultural repertoire of political institutions is limited. In spite of minute variations, the institutional models of democracy are very few. Democracies are systems that have presidential, parliamentary, or mixed governments; recourse to periodic elections that ratify agreements among politicians; vertical organization of interests; and almost no institutional mechanisms for direct control over the bureaucracy by citizens. Certainly, there are important differences among types of democracy, but there are not as many types as the variety of conditions under which transitions occur.

Thus, where one is going matters as much as where one is coming from. The transitions we analyze are from authoritarianism, and the features of the anciens régimes do shape their modalities and their directions. But the transitions are also to democracy, and the destination makes the paths converge.

# 3. Capitalism and socialism

## Introduction

"We could feed everyone," my daughter remarked confidently at the dinner table. Could we?

What she meant is that "we," humankind, have the technological and organizational capacity to produce in the immediate future enough to satisfy the basic needs of everyone on earth. Yet we do not. Instead, we pay cultivators not to plant, winegrowers to refine their harvest into poisonous liquids, sheep breeders not to raise female lambs. We take what farmers do produce and build mountains of butter the size of ski runs. And we do all this while millions starve.

The absurdity is apparent. Yet we have learned to live with it. Indeed, we distribute prizes to people who refer to this world as rational under constraints that are not of our making. And under such constraints, it is; if there is nothing better that can be done, doing as well as we can is rational. But are these constraints not of our making?

The question goes all the way back to the industrial revolution (Elster 1975). But my generation is the last that can reasonably place faith, and commitment, in the particular blueprint that congealed in Europe between 1848 and 1891: "rational administration of things to satisfy human needs," socialism. Today, as market-oriented reforms sweep the countries that have experienced "socialism on earth," this vision is no longer credible.

A good economic system would produce as much as possible of what people want[1] in ways that minimize the use of natural resources and labor while providing a minimum of material welfare for everyone. As we have known them, neither capitalism nor socialism has done it very well. Whence the questions: Is the social organization of our economic systems

[1] I assume that people know or are able to reflect upon what they need. Hence, I understand needs as subjectively defined and equivalent to preferences over all produced goods, leisure, and effort.

the reason we underutilize the productive potential? Does the failure of socialism invalidate the socialist critique of the irrationality of capitalism? Can either system be reformed to ensure material welfare for everyone?

To study these questions, I begin by stating definitions and clarifying the logical structure of the problem. Then I review various critiques of capitalism and of socialism. These critiques concern (1) blueprints, (2) the feasibility of these blueprints, and (3) realities, and (4) the reformability of the realities. The conclusion returns to the central questions.

## Methodological preliminaries

By "capitalism" I mean any economic system in which (1) the optimal division of labor is so advanced that most people produce for the needs of others, (2) the means of production and the capacity to work are owned privately, and (3) there are markets in both. By "socialism" I mean any system in which (1) the division of labor is equally advanced, (2) the means of production are owned publicly, and (3) most productive resources, at least other than labor services, are allocated by centralized command. Other ways of organizing economic systems, including "market socialism," enter the discussion at one point, but unless otherwise noted I use the term "socialism" as synonymous with centralized command over resource allocation.

Before plunging into the subject, we need some criteria for valid inferences. Both champions of capitalism and advocates of socialism often cite deficiencies in one system as arguments in favor of the other. The misery and oppression widespread under capitalism are used to buttress the case for socialism; the blunders of central planning serve to bolster arguments for capitalism. Yet such conclusions do not follow unless several conditions hold (Dunn 1984: ch. 1). At the least, whatever is wrong with capitalism (socialism) must be repairable under socialism (capitalism). If something is wrong with one system because it is wrong with all conceivable systems, little of interest follows. Instead of enumerating conditions, however, it may be worth reflecting first why comparisons of capitalism and socialism are so fraught with difficulty.

### Endogenous preferences

Preferences over economic systems can be endogenous. Examine Table 3.1, in which preference IJ is to be read "An individual who lives under I

Table 3.1. *Preferences over economic systems*

|  |  | Prefers | |
| --- | --- | --- | --- |
|  |  | Capitalism | Socialism |
| Person under { | Capitalism | CC | CS |
|  | Socialism | SC | SS |

prefers J."[2] Let us call the combination of preferences CC and SS "conservative" and the combination of SC with CS "revolutionary." Both the conservative and revolutionary preferences are endogenous.

Now, proponents of both systems have at times argued that conservative preferences can be disregarded. The claim goes as follows: (1) People living under I prefer I to J only because they do not know J any better. (2) If they lived under J, they would prefer J to I. (3) Therefore, the preference for I under I (or J under J) is not "authentic," "valid," or "independent." People who prefer socialism under socialism are brainwashed, say psychological studies financed by the U.S. Department of Defense. A transitional dictatorship is justified because people need "reeducation" was the communist counterpart.[3] Yet the very symmetry of this argument defeats it.

The same symmetry works against revolutionary preferences. Though the legitimacy of capitalism has increased all over the world during the past few years,[4] many intellectuals and poor people continue to see socialism as a superior economic system. In turn, most groups other than unskilled workers and party bureaucrats in the East opt for capitalism. As in Sławomir Mrożek's play, with such preferences we would tango from one system to another in every generation.

Endogenous preferences cannot serve as a basis for transsystem judgments.[5]

[2] A similar table appears in Elster 1986.

[3] Marxist literature, particularly of the 1960s and 1970s, is full of arguments about "unauthentic needs." In these stories, people living under capitalism prefer it only because capitalism creates artificial consumption needs and satisfies these needs. If people were allowed to have truly human rather than these alienated needs, they would prefer socialism.

[4] See Weffort 1989 for observations on Brazil, Moatti 1989 for a comparison of the attitudes of young and older people in France, and Kalyvas 1989 for a review of UK data concerning attitudes toward nationalization.

[5] Jon Elster pointed out to me that such comparisons would be valid if we were willing to make interpersonal utility comparisons or to admit counterfactual arguments about the same individuals living in different systems. These are, however, heroic assumptions.

## Blueprints and realities

To people who suffer, alternatives appear as hopes. They tend to compare the reality of their system with blueprints of the alternative: economies rationally planned to satisfy their needs or markets that open opportunity and guarantee efficiency. And while all of us know our own life conditions, most of us perceive other systems only at second hand. I suspect that if preferences are revolutionary, it is often because we tend to compare the reality of our system with the blueprint of the other.

By a "blueprint" I mean the model of a system that grants its proponents all the assumptions. Yet one argument against a blueprint may be that it is not feasible. For example, proponents of capitalism may admit that blueprint socialism is superior to blueprint capitalism but argue that some assumptions underlying the socialist model are unrealistic. Since arguments about feasibility involve counterfactuals, they may be irresolvable. But since we do make judgments about it, I shall use the term "feasible blueprint" as the model of a system that is based only on assumptions that are granted by reasonable opponents.[6]

Now, if blueprints are superior to any reality, then their comparison with reality always leads to endogenous preferences; this much is obvious. Moreover, if both blueprints and realities enter the choice set, preferences can get truly contorted: I wonder how many leftist intellectuals prefer the socialist blueprint over the capitalist blueprint over capitalist reality over socialist reality. Yet it would be unrealistic to demand that comparisons juxtapose only blueprints with blueprints and realities with realities. We are political beings, and judgments about blueprints affect evaluations of realities.[7]

[6] Operationally, this is perhaps not a different definition from the one used by Alec Nove (1983: 11), for whom "feasible socialism" is one that is "conceivable within the lifespan of one generation . . . without making extreme, utopian, or far-fetched assumptions."

[7] Buchanan (1985: 44–5) presents an argument for making welfare comparisons of realities on the basis of evaluating blueprints. He ascribes this argument to David Friedman and calls it the "some theory is better than no theory argument." It goes as follows: "Suppose you wish to fire a cannon at a distant target. You have had an elementary physics course which includes a theory of the trajectory of an ideal projectile – the path which a point mass will traverse in a vacuum in a uniform gravitational field. Of course the cannon ball is not a point mass (it has extension), and the path it follows will not be in a vacuum. . . . But nonetheless it surely would be more reasonable to aim the cannon at the angle arrived at by calculating according to the ideal theory than to choose an angle at random! Similarly, our best show at efficiency is to choose a system for which there is a theory capable of generating an efficiency theorem – rather than one for which there is no such theory." But I wonder whether this

In particular, one standard that enters our evaluations is the best practice of each system. Reality, as we know, comes in infinite variations and gradations, and there are major differences among capitalist as well as socialist countries. The reason Sweden is so important in discussions of economic systems is that for many people it represents a live demonstration of capitalism at its best. A Peruvian may reasonably rank the socialist blueprint over the capitalist one, Sweden over the best incarnation of "socialism on earth," and Cuba over Peru.

### Class bases of preferences

Note that thus far we have examined only the preferences of abstract individuals: "people living under. . ." Yet individual preferences may run along lines of self-interest; therefore, class. In fact, the little evidence we do have indicates that poor people and intellectuals in the capitalist South and poor people and bureaucrats in the socialist East are more likely to opt for socialism, while other groups under both systems are more likely to opt for capitalism.[8] Hence, it may be true that preferences follow self-interest; they are class-based and exogenous with regard to the economic systems under which people live.

Even if everyone agrees that a good economic system produces as much as possible of what people need in the most efficient way, this criterion is not sufficient to choose a distribution. Efficiency is compatible with many distributions of welfare. Some additional criteria are necessary, and as we shall see below, the crux of all controversies about the rationality of economic systems is whether the first criterion is compatible with various candidates for the second.[9]

At the moment, what matters is that particular combinations of these criteria affect differentially the welfare of individuals with different endowments. If they are self-interested, people who have little chance to earn a high income under capitalism prefer socialism; people whose earning potential is restrained under socialism prefer capitalism. Hence, preferences about economic systems have class bases.

---

argument would be equally convincing if it was dubbed the William Tell argument. The difficulty is that the second-best may be terrible: One cannot infer the ordering of second-bests from the ordering of first-bests.

[8] See Kolarska-Bobinska 1988 for survey evidence concerning Poland, Bruszt 1988 concerning Hungary, and Zaslavskaya 1988 for an analysis of the Soviet Union.

[9] The classic book on this topic is Dobb 1969.

# Capitalism and socialism

Does the failure of socialism invalidate the socialist critique of the irrationality of capitalism? I try to answer this question in terms of blueprints, their feasibility, and real experiences.

## Blueprints

Socialist critiques of capitalism are frequently quaint, often incoherent, and at times bizarre. They bear the imprint of the nineteenth century; the very notion that any decentralized social system can function in an orderly way still baffles the imagination of many socialist critics of capitalism.[10] And they are frightfully ignorant; they dispose of arguments for capitalism with a wave of a hand. Yet I am persuaded that the central marxist argument for the irrationality of capitalism is both fundamental and valid.

To formulate these critiques in a modern way, we need to reconstruct the capitalist blueprint, that is, remember, the model of capitalism that grants its proponents all the assumptions except feasibility. This blueprint was developed during the last years of Marx's life by Walras (1874) and Edgeworth (1881) and was then reformulated by Pareto (1927), Pigou (1932), and others. The model is simple: Individuals know that they need, they have endowments, and they exchange and engage in production whenever they want. In equilibrium no one wants to do anything else given what others have done or will do; or, equivalently, the expectations under which individual agents act are all fulfilled. Moreover, in equilibrium all markets clear. Hence, the prices at which individuals exchange reflect their preferences and relative scarcities; these prices inform individuals about the opportunities they forsake. As a result, resources are allocated in such a way that all gains from trade are exhausted, no one can be better off without someone else being worse off, and the resulting distribution of welfare would not be altered under a unanimity rule. These are three equivalent definitions of collective rationality (optimality in Pareto's sense).[11]

---

[10] Durkheim recalled somewhere that what motivated him as a sociologist was the puzzlement that he could open the back door of his apartment every morning at 5:30 and find a bottle of milk waiting there, and he did not even know the milkman. Socialists were, and many continue to be, convinced that the bottle could not be there without the central planner ensuring that it would be. But, it turned out, under central planning there is a shortage of either milk or bottles.

[11] Buchanan (1985: ch. 2) offers a good nontechnical summary of this blueprint. Campbell 1987 is a technical textbook.

Reasonable marxist critiques of this model all converge on the assertion that capitalism generates waste.[12] Yet they evoke several alternative reasons: (1) the "anarchy" of capitalist production, (2) the "contradiction" between individual and collective rationality, and (3) the "contradiction" between forces of production and relations of production. Moreover, the "waste" involved in each of these explanations is different: Anarchy causes waste of existing endowments and even of commodities already produced, while the waste caused by the two kinds of contradictions is of opportunities.[13] My view is that the first of these critiques is valid but that it concerns feasibility, not the blueprint, and that the second critique fails to draw some important distinctions and is misdirected once these are made, whereas the third is directed against the blueprint, is valid, and is important.

The anarchy critique concerns (1) the efficiency of the competitive equilibrium and (2) the feasibility of costless adjustment to a state in which the expectations under which individual agents make their decisions are simultaneously fulfilled.[14] Both are complicated issues.

First, in the light of recent developments in neoclassical theory, labor and capital are underutilized, and final goods markets do not clear in equilibrium because employers, lenders, and consumers must pay rents to ensure that employees, borrowers, and sellers will deliver goods and services of the contracted quality.[15] The reason is the impossibility of organizing a "complete market," that is, a market that will specify claims contingent on every possible state of nature (Arrow 1964). And, as Stiglitz has shown, under such conditions the equilibrium allocation will not be efficient: If employees, borrowers, or sellers behaved in the best interest of

---

[12] Other criticisms are (1) that competition is based on envy and (2) that capitalist production is oriented toward profit, not toward use or enjoyment. Note that I am concerned only with critiques of the irrationality of capitalism, not of injustice (about which more below).

[13] In Schumpeter's language, this is a difference between static and dynamic inefficiency.

[14] An exceptionally clear statement of this critique is offered by O'Neill (1989: 209): "Information that is relevant to economic actors, in order that they be able to coordinate their activities, is not communicated, and . . . no mechanism exists to achieve the mutual adjustment of plans. The market *in virtue of its competitive nature* blocks the communication of information and fails to coordinate plans for economic action."

[15] This paragraph reflects one of my many debts to Zhiyuan Cui.

Note that economists tend to use the term "equilibrium" in a confusing way. Because until recently they were persuaded that markets always clear, they use this term in the intuitive sense of balance. They speak of "disequilibrium" when markets do not clear. But a disequilibrium is an equilibrium in the mathematical sense: It is a state that will not be altered unless exogenous conditions change. It is just an equilibrium in which markets do not clear.

their principals, someone could gain without anyone losing.[16] Capitalism is thus inefficient even in competitive equilibrium. One way to see this is to perceive that if employees worked to the best of their ability, they would not require costly supervision to exert the same amount of effort.[17]

Second, even if the competitive equilibrium is efficient, as the capitalist blueprint maintains, a costless adjustment to this equilibrium may be unfeasible either because decentralized economies are never in equilibrium or because the adjustment is gradual. Marx himself seems to have wavered about the first point, and he firmly adhered to the second. On the first point, he asserted that capitalist markets do sometimes clear, but only by accident.[18] And he developed an elaborate theory of "crises" of overproduction and underconsumption that became the mainstay of the economic theory of his followers. In these crises, capital and labor lie idle, and the final goods markets do not clear. Hence, the waste is of the already available factors of production and commodities.

The neoclassical theory never succeeded in specifying how adjustment occurs. As Fischer (1989: 36) states in an authoritative summary of the current state of knowledge, "the very power and elegance of equilibrium analysis often obscures the fact that it rests on a very uncertain foundation. We have no similarly elegant theory of what happens *out* of equilibrium, of how agents behave when their plans are frustrated. As a result, we have no rigorous basis for believing that equilibria can be achieved or maintained if disturbed." To prove convergence, models must rely either on a prompt of a centralized "auctioneer" or on assumptions that are patently unreason-

---

[16] "With an incomplete set of markets, the marginal rate of substitution of different individuals between different stages of nature will differ; farmers [or producers in general], in choosing their production technique, look only at the price distribution and their own marginal rates of substitution, which may differ markedly from those of other farmers and consumers. When they all do this, equilibrium which results may not be Pareto efficient; there is some alternative choice of technique and redistribution of income which could make all individuals better off" (Newbery and Stiglitz 1981: 209).

[17] This implication is particularly emphasized by Bowles (1985). I return to it below.

[18] Marx emphasized that under capitalism the act of sale and the act of purchase are not the same because of the intermediation of money. Therefore, supply and demand need not coincide, not just for any particular commodity but for all commodities. Marx seems to have believed at times that voluntary decentralized exchanges do lead economies to a market-clearing equilibrium (1967: I, 355–6), but in other passages he suggested that, "owing to the spontaneous nature of this [capitalist] production, a balance is in itself an accident" (1967: II, 494–5). Hence, Marx believed that capitalism generates situations where markets do not clear: disproportionality crises, overproduction crises, underconsumption crises. These analyses allowed socialists to speak routinely of the anarchy and chaos of capitalist production expressing themselves in crises.

able or inconsistent. Yet introducing an auctioneer violates, as Hahn (1989: 64) notes, the very assumption that information is decentralized. Hence, neoclassical models lead to all the wonderful Pareto properties only because they ignore adjustment problems. In turn, Austrian models, which assume that trades are consummated out of equilibrium, cannot substantiate the Pareto conclusions.[19]

Hence, the anarchy critique seems vindicated by the recent developments of economic theory. Yet whether this critique establishes the irrationality of capitalism depends on whether the anarchy characteristic of capitalist markets can be remedied by some alternative economic organization. And since I doubt it can be, I do not see this critique as crucial.

The claim that under capitalism individually rational actions lead to collective irrationality confuses two situations, is false about the first one, and is misdirected concerning the second. Marx thought that competition forces individual firms to invest in such a way that the uniform, which means also their own, rate of profit falls.[20] This argument has been shown to be false. In general, if consumption is rival and there are no externalities, no increasing returns to scale, and no myopia, then there is no conflict between individual and collective rationality; the allocation of welfare resulting from unrestricted exchange among individual agents is collectively rational in the sense cited above. Only if any of these assumptions are violated does individual rationality diverge from collective rationality.

In real economies, these assumptions are violated; about this much, no one disagrees. But all that this implies is that any reasonable blueprint of capitalism must have some way of coping with situations under which individual and social rates of return diverge, and in the aftermath of Pigou all such blueprints do treat this situation. One way is to introduce corrective fiscal intervention; another is to reassign property rights. Hence, even under capitalism, markets may do only what they do well, and the state may have to step in where markets fail. As Arrow (1971: 137) put it,

---

[19] Heiner Ganssman made me sensitive to this point.

[20] Somehow for Marx it was obvious that since market allocation follows individual self-interest rather than social interest, any allocation resulting from decentralized actions must be collectively irrational. Moreover, competition is the mechanism responsible for the collective suboptimality; competition works in ways no individual understands, behind economic agents' backs. Hence, the outcomes of competition are unknowable. And hence the leap to the conclusion that they are also collectively undesirable. This was a leap, not an argument: No deductive framework existed in which this argument could be couched.

"when the market fails to achieve an optimal state, society will, to some extent at least, recognize the gap, and nonmarket social institutions will arise attempting to bridge it." This observation gives comfort to many marxists, who gleefully observe that capitalism cannot exist without state intervention. But in fact it dulls the marxist critique: Capitalism is not any less, or more, capable than socialism of handling all the situations in which social rates of return diverge from private ones.[21]

Having cleared away the underbrush, we arrive at the claim that capitalism leads to systematic underutilization of productive potential. Since the contradiction between the relations of production and the forces of production is the subject of an enormous literature, most of which recently has concerned G. A. Cohen's magisterial reconstruction of Marx's theory of history, and since the point I want to make is quite narrow, I shy away from discussing other conceptualizations of this contradiction.

My version of this argument asserts that capitalism is irrational because it cannot access some technically feasible distributions of welfare. We may have technological and organizational means to feed everyone on earth, and we may want to feed everyone, and yet we may be still be unable to do it under capitalism. Here is the argument.

Imagine an economy in which there are two agents, $P$ and $W$. If output does not depend on rates of return to the endowments controlled by these agents, then under a given state of technology all distributions of welfare that sum up to this level of output are accessible. These distributions are represented by the line with a slope of $-1$ in Figure 3.1. A perfectly egalitarian distribution lies at the intersection, $E$, of this outer possibility frontier with the line that parts from the origin at 45 degrees.

But under capitalism, output does depend on the rate of return to endowments. If capitalists receive the entire return from capital and workers the entire return from labor, then resources will be efficiently allocated, and the distribution of income will reflect the marginal productivity of the two factors; this is point $M$. But if either capitalists or workers receive less than the entire return, that is, if the distribution of income diverges from the competitive market, they will withdraw capital or labor, and resources will be underutilized.

Under capitalism, endowments – capital and labor power – are privately

---

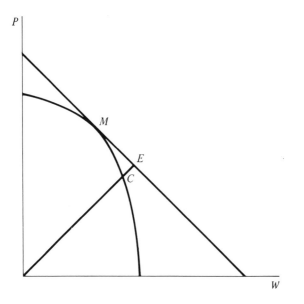

Figure 3.1

owned, and the agents who decide whether and how to utilize them are self-interested. Private property implies that owners have the right to withdraw their endowments from productive use if they do not expect to receive an adequate rate of return. As Aumann and Kurz (1977: 1139) put it, "every agent can, if he wishes, destroy part or all of his endowment." Suppose that wage earners have the power to raise wages above the competitive level or that the government taxes profits and transfers the income to wage earners in such a way as to equalize welfare, reaching a point on the 45-degree line. Then profit takers will undersupply their endowments, and the outcome will be point C on the inner (capitalist) possibility frontier. Point E is unreachable under capitalism. Indeed, no point other than M on the outer frontier can be reached.[22]

Hence, when the final distribution of welfare diverges from the allocation that would be generated by competitive markets, the possibility frontier falls faster than at the rate of −1. The profit takers will utilize their resources fully if and only if they receive all the return above marginal

[22] This is not an argument for egalitarianism. Point E, where incomes are equally distributed between two agents, is used only as an illustration. The argument is general.

product of the wage earners. Otherwise they will undersupply their endowments, resources will be underutilized, and capitalism will lead to an inefficient, – that is, collectively irrational – allocation.

Suppose that instead of wasting the already produced food, we distribute it to the poor. Then the price of food would fall, farmers would be getting a lower rate of return, and they would produce less. Moreover, some people who produce food for themselves would find it more profitable to do something else and get free food. Or suppose we pay farmers to produce, support farm prices out of taxes, and distribute food to the poor. But then the rate of return would fall throughout the economy, and the output of other commodities would decline. In fact, we do some of both, out of compassion or other motivations. But under capitalism we do it at the cost of reducing output below its potential level.[23]

Hence, capitalism is irrational in the sense that under this system we cannot use the full productive potential without rewarding those who control the productive endowments. Even if we grant the capitalist blueprint all the assumptions, we discover that technically possible distributions of welfare are inaccessible under the capitalist system.[24] As Elson (1988: 18) nicely put it, under capitalism "choice in the small does not provide choice in the large": Individuals can choose, but the society as a whole cannot.

But why juxtapose individuals and society? Is not choice by "the society" the same as choice by the competing individuals? The warrant for claiming that capitalism is irrational stems from the fact that individuals are simultaneously market agents and citizens. The allocation of resources that they prefer as citizens does not in general coincide with that at which they arrive via the market. Capitalism is a system in which scarce resources are owned privately. Yet under capitalism property is institutionally distinct from authority. As a result, there are two mechanisms by which resources can be allocated to uses and distributed among households: the market and

[23] Here are two economists speaking about the world food situation: "It is increasingly apparent that failure to choose and pursue . . . optimal growth strategy has led to a pessimistic view of prospects for reducing food deprivation through growth and it has turned attention, unproductively, to direct welfare-oriented approaches which seem likely to have adverse effects on efforts to achieve rapid and broadly-based development" (Mellor and Johnston 1984: 533.)

[24] An equivalent way of making the same point is that without externally enforced long-term contracts, joint exploitation of assets leads to inefficient outcomes. Specifically, when both capitalists and workers can affect the distribution of consumption, the rate of investment will be lower than it would have been had only one class of agents received all the return (beyond the next best opportunity or subsistence). The seminal formulation was Lancaster 1973; see Levhari and Mirman 1980 and Przeworski and Wallerstein 1982.

the state. The market is a mechanism in which individuals cast votes for allocation with the resources they own and in which these resources are always distributed unequally; the state is a system that allocates resources it does not own, with rights distributed differently from the market outcome. The two mechanisms lead to the same outcome only by a fluke.

Democracy in the political realm exacerbates this divergence by equalizing the right to influence the allocation of resources. Indeed, distributions of consumption caused by the market and those collectively preferred by citizens must differ, since democracy offers those who are poor, oppressed, or otherwise miserable as a consequence of the initial distribution of endowments an opportunity to find redress via the state.

Hence, if "the people" (in its eighteenth-century singular) is sovereign, it prefers an allocation and distribution of resources that differs from the market outcome. It is this preference that cannot be reached when endowments are owned privately and allocated in a decentralized way. Even when individuals express as citizens their collective preference for a particular allocation and when all the material conditions are present to implement this preference, the democratically chosen allocation is unreachable under capitalism.[25]

Does this critique of capitalism imply that the outer possibility frontier would under socialism be accessible if resources were rationally allocated to satisfy human needs? Could we reach point E, a full utilization of the productive potential and an egalitarian distribution of welfare? I can think of no critiques of the socialist blueprint that would deny this possibility. If

---

[25] This conception of the irrationality of capitalism is subject to a twofold criticism. First, as Alessandro Pizzorno (personal communication) pointed out, it is not capitalism that is irrational according to this definition, but a combination of capitalism with an autonomous state. Second, this conception is vulnerable to social choice problems: According to Joshua Cohen's reformulation of my definition, an economic system is irrational if "it blocks access to an allocation that is in the set of allocations that could be agreed to by equal citizens" (personal communication). Yet the latter allocation may not exist or may be collectively suboptimal (by McKelvey's theorem). In other words, if rationality of economic systems is defined as full utilization of the productive potential, it need not be the collective preference of sovereign citizens; if it is defined as the implementation of the collective preference, it need not consist of a full utilization of productive resources.

My response is the following. First, capitalism in which the state has no power to allocate, or at least indirectly to influence the allocation of privately owned resources (via taxes, regulations, etc.), is inconceivable, in spite of the calls for constitutional self-restraint. Since competition cannot be organized without regulation by the state, the possibility that the state may opt for an allocation different from the competitive allocation is entailed by the blueprint for capitalism. Second, even if people may not opt for the full utilization of productive potential, they may also opt for it, and if they do, they will be unable to realize this preference under capitalism.

individuals truthfully revealed their needs and their productive potential, if they exerted effort independently of reward, if planners behaved as perfect agents and could solve problems of optimal allocation, then socialism would generate all the wonderful effects its proponents advertise.[26] But all that this says is that reasonable critiques of socialism are not directed at its blueprint but at the feasibility of this blueprint and its real incarnations.

*Feasibility*

Debates about feasibility are more heated, for they are inevitably less conclusive. Once the assumptions are granted, discussions about blueprints call only for making logical deductions. But verdicts about feasibility call for judgments. Hence, they leave more room for disagreements.

Socialist lines of attack on the feasibility of the capitalist blueprint are three: (1) There can be no capitalism without state intervention, (2) capitalism can never, or only at great cost, reach the equilibria for which its proponents claim all the virtues, and (3) capitalism is self-destructive because it necessarily leads to monopoly. I discussed the first point above: I think it can be dismissed with a "So what?" The second point seems valid: The idea that markets permanently reside in competitive equilibria is difficult to fathom; the claim that adjustments involve waste is highly plausible. Finally, the argument that competitive markets are self-destructive is obviously true to some extent, but the extent is not obvious.[27]

If I treat these claims in a perfunctory manner, it is not because I consider them unimportant, but only because they seem to contribute little to the central question. If the capitalist blueprint is unfeasible, capitalism may be incapable of fulfilling even the promise it does offer. But the force

[26] Or if we could design institutions that would implement in a decentralized way the notion of public ownership suggested by Roemer (1989a and b).

[27] One version of this argument, dating back to Engels, goes as follows: Most decisions made under capitalism these days are in fact intra-firm rather than market decisions, and the intra-firm decision making is the same as planned socialist allocation, only on an incomplete scale. Hence, capitalism has been largely "socialized" by virtue of its own dynamics, and all that is left is to complete this process. This is Ernest Mandel's central argument for socialism: Capitalism has historically shown itself to be unfeasible. See the discussion in several issues of the *New Left Review:* Mandel 1986; Nove 1987; Mandel 1988; Auerbach, Desai, and Shamsavari 1988; Elson 1988.

My view is that the intra-firm decisions of large capitalist firms are not like socialist planning and that the crucial difference is not one of internal organization. True, Poland in the 1970s was an economy the size of General Motors. But General Motors used market prices to make decisions, and it laid off workers as a function of demand. Poland did not.

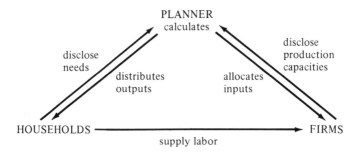

Figure 3.2

of the socialist critique of capitalism, in my view, is directed against its blueprint, its most ideal conceivable realization. Socialists would reject capitalism even if this system realized its fullest potential. Hence, arguments against the feasibility of a permanent competitive equilibrium play a secondary role in the socialist critique.[28]

Arguments concerning feasibility are, in turn, damaging to socialism. Let me first restate the socialist blueprint.

Households have needs. Firms have the capacity to produce objects that satisfy needs. The planner learns about the needs of households and the production capacities of firms and calculates how to allocate resources among firms and how to distribute the output among households in order to satisfy needs to the extent possible given the resources (Figure 3.2). The result is rational administration of things to satisfy needs.

Critiques of the feasibility of socialism fall into two categories: (1) Even with truthful information, the planner would be incapable of handling it because of the sheer complexity of the problem. (2) If individuals are self-interested, the planner cannot learn about the true needs of households and the true capacities of firms; moreover, the planner does not act to promote the general welfare.

The "socialist calculation debate" has a history of its own. I will not

---

[28]Suppose that capitalism became "organized," à la Hilferding and successfully avoided periodic crises. Then there would be no anarchy: no static inefficiency. But dynamic efficiency could be reached only if the distribution of welfare followed at each time the initial distribution of resources: All attempts to alter the distribution of consumption and leisure would generate deadweight losses. Hence, capitalism would still be irrational even though its proponents were granted all the assumptions. This is why I think that static waste is less important for the socialist critique of capitalism – but I am not certain about this point.

summarize it here. The claim that planners will necessarily be defeated by the sheer complexity of the problem has a different meaning in the neo-classical framework and in the Austrian approach.[29] And even if the planner's problem can be resolved in principle, the task facing planners is enormous. Soviet economists envisaged a couple of years ago that under the reformed price system, between 1,500 and 2,000 prices of basic products would be fixed by Gosplan, another 20,000 to 30,000 prices would be administered by specialized agencies, and the remaining prices would be determined by contracts between suppliers and users (Petrakov and Yassine 1988). It is hard to imagine how so many prices could be gotten right even with the use of Lange tâtonnement and computers.[30]

Even if the planner is able to solve the calculation problem, the case for the feasibility of socialism hinges on the assumption that once individuals – as households, firms, and planners — become co-proprietors of productive wealth, they act spontaneously in ways that support the collective welfare.[31] Specifically, households truthfully reveal to the planner their

[29] In the Taylor–Lange–Lerner model, the planner can start with any random set of prices, observe which markets do not clear, correct prices, and arrive at equilibrium. This is possible because, in their neoclassical approach, there exists a set of prices that clears the market, and the market converges to this set of prices. But we know now that tâtonnement leads to equilibrium only under either unreasonable or very special assumptions. In the Austrian school, price movements occur because trades are actually consummated. Hence, the planner can never centralize the private knowledge that makes prices change. At least this is the claim of followers of Hayek, who claim that Lange misunderstood the Austrian objections to socialism. On Austrian views, see Lavoie 1985, Kirzner 1988, and Shapiro 1989.

[30] I am aware that this is a subjective judgment, and I am not sure how disagreements about the feasibility of socialist calculation can be resolved. Nove, for example, believes that "it is inconceivable to 'mathematicise' the complexities of current operational production-and-supply planning and thereby secure a more efficient operation of the centralised system" (1983: 105). He emphasizes that no planning system, no matter how technologically advanced, can handle variety. Yet I wonder: Is the Soviet economy more complex than the worldwide airline reservation system?

[31] I deliberately formulate this assumption in agnostic language. The standard way of putting it is to say that individuals would become altruistic, that they would be guided by solidarity, or that they would cooperate. Yet if in "altruism" we understand a utility function that takes as its argument the consumption or the welfare of others, there can be all kinds of strategic problems, including collective irrationality in an altruistic society. See Collard 1978. Indeed, it is not even apparent that altruistic individuals will reveal their preferences truthfully. The same is true of solidarity: How are individual agents to know which behavior is solidaristic in particular circumstances? If a manager of the plant I supply asks me to divert input from another firm and give it to her, because otherwise she will be unable to fulfill the plan, should I do it? "Cooperation," in turn, is a truly muddled term. In game theory, cooperation sometimes means communication, sometimes external enforcement of offers, sometimes coalitions, sometimes a joint choice of strategies, and, in prisoner's dilemma situations, any strategy that supports Pareto-optimal outcomes. In colloquial language, cooperation connotes "lending a hand": reciprocal help.

needs and firms their productive capacities, while planners act as perfect agents for the public.

None of these assumptions have worked in actual socialist systems. This may not be a decisive argument, for it is easy to claim that the non-democratic nature of economic decision making in the socialist countries subverted the very notion of social ownership.[32] But it is obvious that this notion ignores the problem of free riders. "The property of all people (state property), the master form of social property," as the canonical Soviet phrase had it, is no one's property. In a path-breaking analysis, Butenko (1988: ch. 5) pointed out that individual direct producers are not owners of the means of production but only co-owners by virtue of their membership in the organization that administers the common property. This fact has several consequences. For one, stealing from oneself is individually rational, since the part privately appropriated (or not performed) is larger than the individual's share of the common loss. For another, in an analysis reminiscent of Karl Korsch, Butenko shows that nationalization of the means of production is not a sufficient condition for socialization of those means, since the relationship between the role of individuals as co-producers and their role as co-owners involves the entire economic and political system.

First, if individuals continue to be self-interested even when they jointly own the productive wealth, households overreport their needs. True, the planner need not rely on revealed preferences to decide what to produce and how to distribute. In a poor country, the urgency of some needs is apparent to any observer. The planner can rely on some theory of needs to decide that minimal calorie consumption should first be assured to everyone, followed by shelter, medical attention, education, and so on. Or the

---

[32] When Bukharin criticized the project of the First Five-Year Plan in an article published in *Pravda* (30 September 1928), the Political Bureau of the Soviet Communist party immediately drew the conclusion that "issues like this should first be discussed in a narrower group of party officials" (Wilk 1988: 78–9).

We do not know whether individual agents would reveal their preferences and capabilities truthfully if the planning process were democratic. In Poland in the mid sixties, a project of the plan prepared by the Planning Office was subjected to discussion at all levels, all the way down to sections of factories. Several million people participated. The aggregate output that emerged from this massive consultation was higher than in the original proposal, although the share of consumption in the national product was also somewhat higher. Most of the corrections were of a rationalizing kind: Workers offered to produce more than originally demanded of them if they were assured of the requisite inputs. The party decided, however, to override the parameters of the corrected plan, because it considered the rate of investment insufficient. To the best of my knowledge, this experiment was never repeated. See Ostrowski and Przeworski 1965.

planner can rely on anonymous surveys of households and act on the aggregated answers. This was the original intuition behind physical planning. These methods will not work, however, once needs become more differentiated. And if the planner relies on revealed preferences, households have an incentive to misrepresent their needs.[33]

Second, firms have powerful incentives to hide some of their productive capacities. If firms are rewarded and punished depending on whether they complete the tasks set by the planner, they need to protect themselves from exogenous events that might make it impossible to utilize their true capacities fully. If firms know that the planner sets tasks as a function of past performance, they have an incentive to underperform.

Third, individuals may shirk in production.[34] Finally, if planners are self-interested and if they do not compete,[35] they behave as bureaucrats do, that is, in Nove's favorite quotation from Trotsky, "they never forget themselves when they have something to distribute."

Following the seminal article by Hurwicz (1973), there have been several attempts to invent a mechanism that will provide the planner with true information even if individuals are self-interested and their knowledge is private.[36] Yet all such mechanisms are either too complex to be practicable or violate one of the assumptions.[37] Hence, at least thus far, arguments for

[33] See an unusually clear formulation by Roemer (1989b).

[34] This seems to me the weakest argument against socialism. First, the little evidence we have indicates that workers work at least as hard under socialism as under capitalism, if not harder. Second, we are still far from a consensus as to why they work hard under capitalism.

[35] One could think of a system in which planning would be democratic in the sense that political parties offer competing plans (Castoriadis 1979). For example, their campaigns could propose rates of time preference (or rates of investment); the platform corresponding to the median preference would win, and this would be the plan to be detailed by the winning party. The difficulties with this proposal are the same as with any electoral platform: Only rudimentary plans could be understood by the general public, and social choice problems would raise their ugly head. Nove (1983: 179) focuses on the complexity of the issue, arguing that "no means can be devised to 'democratise' this process [planning], unless it is seriously thought that the allocation of 10 tonnes of metal, 1,000 metres of cloth or of electric components should be voted on." Beck (1978) shows that social choice concerning rates of time preference would cycle if suboptimal plans were allowed on the agenda.

[36] The notion of mechanisms can be defined with the aid of game theory. Suppose the central planner seeks to maximize some utilitarian welfare function. If the planner knew the utility functions of all households and the production function of all firms, then the solution to the planner's problem would be some vector $y^*(x)$ of final consumption goods and leisure, where $x$ is a vector of inputs. An economic mechanism implements the planner's solution if it constitutes a decentralized game the solution to which is the allocation $y^*(x)$ when information about utility and production functions is private.

[37] John Roemer argues that the assumptions and the pessimistic conclusions of the implementation theory are too strong, since this theory assumes that the planner knows nothing. In fact, planners need not know the features of particular individuals; it may be sufficient that

the feasibility of socialism must rest on the assumption that socialization of the means of production causes individuals to adopt socialist preferences; and this assumption is unrealistic. Since collective ownership does create free-rider problems, the hope that it will alter preferences is tenuous. The fact is that the only practicable mechanism we know today by which people can inform each other about their needs and their capacities is the price mechanism, and this mechanism works only when individuals experience the consequences of their decisions in terms of their material welfare. Hence, socialism is unfeasible.

One could argue that it is unreasonable to derive this conclusion from a judgment about the "first-best" of the socialist system. Suppose that households exaggerate their needs somewhat, firms hide some productive capacities, workers goof off from time to time, and planners take care of their own needs before the needs of others. Even if socialism on earth does not quite match the blueprint, does it necessarily imply that it is not feasible?

The problem is that the second-best of socialism is not a stable state. The planner allocates inputs and issues directives that are supposed to ensure that the goals are fulfilled. But if the plan is inconsistent (some firms cannot fulfill their tasks given the inputs they receive) or if anything unexpected happens exogenously or if any firm deviates from the plan, some firms find themselves without the necessary inputs, and the entire plan unravels. Hence, plans formulated in physical quantities are always subverted.[38] And plans formulated in terms of indicators require weights, that is, prices. This is why socialist economies are not in fact planned.[39] They work only because the originally planned allocations are continually corrected ex post by firms that seek the necessary inputs on their own and by the planner that tries to regain control over the allocation process.[40]

they know the statistical distribution of traits. Yet thus far he cannot find a decentralized mechanism that will be institutionally practicable and will not violate one of the axioms he sees as desirable features of any decentralized implementation of public ownership. See his recent series of papers, in particular "Decentralization, Duplicity, and Minimal Equity" (1989b).

[38] As Asselain (1984: 35) observed, "all the main failures in the functioning of Soviet-type economies can be attributed to the violation of the fundamental principle of the centralised model: the absolute primacy of centralised objectives."

[39] See Zaleski 1984 for extensive empirical evidence. Zaleski concludes (p. 615) that "the existence of one central plan, coherent and perfect, which would be apportioned and then executed at all levels, is in fact but a myth. In every command economy [économie dirigée], we find ourselves in the presence of an innumerable quantity of plans, in perpetual evolution, which are definitely coordinated only ex post, after they are put in train."

[40] See Roland 1989 for a review of these ex-post equilibrating mechanisms.

Planning is thus best seen as a continuous game between the planner and the firms. And this game does not converge to a stable allocation even if there are no exogenous events and no technological change. The planner observes that firms have found a way to get around the plan and reacts by issuing directives that close this loophole. In turn, firms trying to secure the necessary inputs find other ways to escape from the planner's control. The planner issues more directives, firms find new ways, and so on. Hence, the planning system becomes progressively more complex even if the economy remains the same. And at some point firms find themselves in a situation in which they cannot behave according to the plan – the total system of directives and allocations – even if they want to.

When planners are misinformed and self-interested and producers shirk, output may be inferior to capitalism's at any distribution of welfare. Socialist output may lie inside possible capitalist production: Under socialism we may be unable to feed everyone because we cannot produce enough.

*Realities*

Whether the socialist or the capitalist model has been more successful in practice is impossible to tell. The discrepancies in accounting conventions and in weights according to which different outputs are aggregated, the startling disparities in the use of inputs, the differences in starting positions and in comparative advantage render judgments almost meaningless. Detailed comparisons of particular aspects of economic performance and material welfare generate verdicts that depend on the dimension and the period under consideration.[41] There are not even good grounds to argue that, while capitalist economies are more efficient, socialist systems are superior in providing job security, equality, and material security. On the one hand, over the long term the aggregate rates of growth of the socialist countries have matched those of the most rapidly developing capitalist economies. On the other hand, there is accumulating evidence about income inequality in the Soviet Union and Eastern Europe and growing testimony about the deterioration of social welfare services.[42]

---

[41] For a recent review of such studies and a comprehensive collection of statistics, see Bideleux 1985.

[42] Income inequality in the Soviet Union and Hungary is somewhat less than in developed capitalist countries but probably not much different from Sweden's or Japan's. On the Soviet Union, see Bergson 1984; on Hungary, Kornai 1986; on Poland, Wnuk-Lipiński 1989.

A Soviet economist has just revealed that the labor share (of the gross national product) in the Soviet Union is 37 percent: well below that in developed capitalist countries and about the

Given that the systematic evidence does not support any, even the most tentative, verdict, the consensus that the socialist model has simply failed is baffling. And this consensus is widespread. Nationalization of the means of production no longer animates socialist movements in the West or even in the capitalist South, while in several Eastern European countries central planning has fallen into utter disrepute. The feeling of deprivation is acute; but the experience of misery is not peculiar to socialist countries. It is striking that whereas in Brazil people see their deprivation as a result of injustice, in Poland survey respondents attribute their deprivation to the irrationality of the socialist system.[43]

One explanation of this puzzle may be that the available numbers systematically overvalue socialist performance. The input–output structure of socialist economies is inefficient; they use 1.8 times more energy and more than twice the amount of steel as capitalist countries to produce a unit of output.[44] Illustrations of irrationality abound: One-half of the agricultural output of the Soviet Union is said to be lost before it reaches the consumer market; in the winter children enjoy sledding down mountains of fertilizer that surround railway stations waiting to be trucked to farms; the value of goods that no one wants to take home at a zero price from Czech stores is equivalent to the economy's growth over two years; the ratio of input to output inventories in Hungarian factories is five times higher than in the West; and the like. Indicators of welfare are equally bewildering: Socialist countries tend to have more doctors per capita, higher high-school enrollment rates, and more construction of housing and at the same time a shorter life expectancy, a higher gross mortality, lower labor productivity, and inferior housing standards.

Perhaps the most thorny issue in comparing the performance of socialist and capitalist economies is the question of the comparative standard. Against which countries should the progress of the Soviet Union, Poland,

same as in Mexico and Venezuela. Zaslavsky (1987–8: 35) cites data according to which about half of bank deposits in the Soviet Union came from only 3 percent of the accounts. According to an interview in *Le Nouvel Observateur* (15–21 June 1989, p. 99), the per patient expenditure in the special hospitals for the nomenklatura was 111 rubles per day; in ordinary hospitals, 24 rubles. Note that Poland and the Soviet Union are the only two countries in the world where life expectancy has fallen in the past few years.

[43] See several tables in *Polacy 88: Dynamika konfliktu a szanse reform*.

[44] Military expenditures may help elucidate the puzzle, although the estimates are notoriously unreliable. According to the upper estimates, the Soviet Union spends 8 percent more of GNP than the United States. With a capital–output ratio of four, this is equivalent to a difference of 2 percent in growth rates.

or China be measured? Khrushchev set the United Kingdom as the target to surpass, but many comparisons match the Soviet Union against the United States, with which it competes militarily. Today, many Soviet and Western observers are beginning to see the Soviet Union as a third-world country. Yet Eastern Europe is in Europe; reference to the developed, capitalist West is made inescapable by the everyday demonstration of Western standards of living in the media and by the personal observation of people who travel. And this comparison is devastating and painful. Why cannot East Germany be like West Germany? I think this is the question to which the answer is "the economic system."

Finally, one must take into account frustrated expectations. Stalinism was developmentalist to the hilt. When I was growing up in Poland, every wall was plastered with thick red graphs that mounted up and up into what Aleksandr Zinoviev called the radiant future. Socialism would conquer nature; it would build everything – dams, steel mills, skyscrapers – bigger than under capitalism; it would usher societies into the realm of order and reason. But nature fought back. The worst ecological disaster in Europe today is the area where Czechoslovakia, East Germany, and Poland meet. "Bigger" turned out to apply also to mistakes: After the massive irrigation of Ukraine, the yield per hectare dropped as the soil became poisoned with salt.[45] And the irrationality was so pervasive that people were forced to spend most of their everyday lives coping with it.

There are thus good reasons for subjective perceptions to diverge from aggregate numbers. But what is of central importance is that neither capitalism nor socialism has succeeded in abolishing poverty. Moreover, both systems have failed to generate self-sustaining growth.

The postwar experiences of the socialist East and of several countries in the capitalist South constitute two different attempts to overcome underdevelopment and to establish economic independence. The Eastern European model has been one of state ownership of productive resources, allocating by centralized command, and an autarkic development strategy led by producer goods industries. The capitalist pattern, often identified as "associated dependent capitalist development," was one of private property, an active role for the state, and a fair dose of protectionism oriented toward import-substitution industrialization.

Both strategies were successful for a long time, and several countries

[45] On "gigantomania," see Zalyguine 1987.

established a significant industrial base. From 1960 to 1980, the gross domestic product of Latin American countries grew at an unweighted average of 5.2 percent, and in Eastern Europe the rate of growth exceeded 6 percent. Several countries experienced periods when industrial production grew at a rate in double digits.

But what is striking today is that this development simply collapsed in both the capitalist South and the socialist East in the late 1970s. Between 1980 and 1985, the average rate of growth of GDP in Latin America was 0.0 percent. During these years, the three Eastern European countries that furnish data to the IMF – Hungary, Poland, and Yugoslavia – had an average growth rate of 1.0 percent. Per capita consumption fell in many countries.[46] Neither model generated self-sustaining growth.[47] Indeed, the economic crises facing Argentina, Brazil, and Mexico and Hungary, Poland, and Yugoslavia are without precedent in the history of these nations.

Hence, reality is not enlightening. In the real world people do starve while the productive potential is underutilized or underdeveloped.

## What can be reformed?

Capitalism is irrational; socialism is unfeasible; in the real world people starve – the conclusions we have reached are not encouraging. But perhaps basic human needs can be universally satisfied even if the economic systems in which we live remain inferior to nineteenth-century utopias; even if they perpetuate some irrationality and some injustice. Can either socialism or capitalism be reformed partially, yet sufficiently to feed everyone?

[46] Between 1977 and 1983, per capita GDP declined 16 percent in Uruguay, 12 percent in Argentina, 11 percent in Chile, and 9 percent in Brazil (CEPAL data, cited in Weffort 1989). In Poland, per capita income fell by 8 percent between 1978 and 1985. In the Soviet Union, total housing construction was the same in 1985 as in the 1960s, and per capita agricultural production has not increased since 1978. The gross death rate increased from 6.7 per thousand in the 1960s to 10.6 per thousand in 1985, life expectancy fell from 70 to 68 years, and infant mortality increased (Agabengyan 1988). Between 1973 and 1984, total factor productivity has been falling at an average annual compounded rate of 1.58 in Argentina, 1.97 in Brazil, 0.92 in Chile, 0.64 in Mexico, and 1.40 in the Soviet Union (Maddison 1989: 91).

[47] Why this happened at more or less the same time in the capitalist South and the socialist East, I do not know. One possible explanation is debt, but that does not seem to be enough. As Comisso (1989) notes, citing a series of economic blunders, "even if Finance Capital provided the rope, someone else had to supply the hangman." Moreover, I have seen no studies that correlate debt and growth. Comisso places the burden on barriers to competition, due in the socialist countries to central allocation and in the capitalist countries to the monopolistic position of state firms. Yet the simultaneity of this collapse points to a common underlying cause.

*Reforming socialism*

Reform was an endemic phenomenon under socialism. Since economies based on central planning contain no automatic self-correcting mechanisms, a reform must be launched every time they generate flagrantly undesirable effects. Hence, reforms – of territorial administration, of economic management, of planning, of incentive systems – were always a regular rite in the socialist countries.[48] Yet today there is a widespread feeling that partial reforms cannot be effective; the very organization of the economic system is at fault.

The goals of reforms were largely the same everywhere: to rationalize the investment process and to equilibrate the consumer markets. Yet while the goals were shared, the methods diverged sharply. Some reforms were designed to "perfect" the existing central command system; others introduced markets. The East German reforms of 1963–70 represented the first orientation; the post-1968 reforms in Hungary went in the latter direction.

Can socialism be reformed? Consider the latest effort in the Soviet Union to preserve the basic features of the socialist system: the reforms of the late 1980s, designed to introduce firms' financial autonomy and responsibility, but not markets. In a programmatic statement, the architect of these reforms, Leonid Abalkin (1988: 44, 47), rejected all economic mechanisms that "are alien to social property, that is, all that provoke crises, anarchy of production, unemployment and the division of society into classes." He went on to argue that in the socialist system of production, price mechanisms function differently than under capitalism and "become instruments of the mechanism of planned economic management." Two economists spelling out the project in detail spoke in terms of "integrating price policy into the planning process" and distributed the responsibility for administering prices among the central planning office, intermediate levels of the bureaucracy, and associations of suppliers and consumers (Petrakov and Yassine 1988: 64).

Altogether, these reforms would enhance the role of economic incentives, step up administrative controls over investment, and reorient sectoral priorities – a mixture that has failed to achieve great results in the past.[49]

---

[48] The most complete exposition of this argument is Staniszkis's (1984), but the same reasoning can be found in Wiatr 1989 and Abalkin 1988.

[49] An excellent analysis of such reforms and the reasons they are doomed to fail is offered by Asselain (1984). See also Nove 1983: ch. 4 and Kornai 1986.

This failure has two well-known sufficient causes: (1) Profitability is useless as a criterion for allocating resources when profit is just the difference between the prices of inputs decided on by bureaucrats sitting in one room and the prices of outputs decided on in another room; (2) the pressures for recentralizing resource allocation come from below, since managers have no way of obtaining the required inputs other than through commands from above.[50] Hence, reforms that do not include market mechanisms fail to rationalize resource allocation and become subverted spontaneously even without the resistance of bureaucrats. In turn, the idea of introducing partial markets, of using market prices as an instrument of planning, is logically incoherent. As Nove points out with regard to the Lange model, one cannot have a market in final demand goods without a mechanism to make the producer goods sector respond to this market. This mechanism could be either a market in producer goods or a central planning office in which planners' only task is to guess what a market will do.[51]

Hence, I do not believe that the socialist system of allocating resources by command can be reformed.

*Market socialism*

My entire analysis has thus far been couched in terms of mechanisms of allocation of resources and distribution of income. This is because I am skeptical that we know if (1) forms of property have consequences for firm performance and (2) the observed distribution of forms of property, in particular the paucity of employee-owned cooperatives, is due to their performance. In spite of the popularity of the idea of market socialism, we still do not have a theory of the firm to justify this preference.[52]

First, some questions of definition. If market socialism is a system that

[50] As a Polish manager is supposed to have remarked, "We know we're independent, but who is going to tell us what to produce?" (Roger Thurow, "Poland Finds Economic 'Reforms' Don't Necessarily Produce Results," *Wall Street Journal,* 27 February 1986).

[51] I am not arguing that the planner cannot have priorities that diverge from the allocation of producer goods that would be required to equilibrate the consumer market. If socialist citizens voted through a democratic mechanism for an allocation of consumer goods different from the one they demanded through their actions in the market, the planner would be justified in seeking to realize this objective. But unless the consumer market allocation is itself modified by indirect state intervention, the economy as a whole will not balance when consumer goods are allocated by the market and producer goods are distributed by the planner.

[52] For a recent attempt to construct an endogenous theory of the firm, see Hansmann 1988.

legislates against only a few forms of property and allocates most resources using markets, then it is identical with capitalism. All capitalist countries reserve to the state the property of some enterprises, not only prisons and tax-collecting agencies, but often natural monopolies (industries that have increasing returns or externalities in consumption), and at times even salt mining, the production of matches, or the sale of alcohol. In fact, all capitalist economies are "mixed": The public sector ranges from 6 percent in Sweden to more than 50 percent in Austria. And outside the sectors not reserved for the state, cooperatives are not illegal under capitalism; it just happens – for reasons still poorly understood – that when people can form any kind of firm they want, the vast majority of firms end up combining private ownership of capital with hired labor.[53]

Hence, if market socialism is to be a distinct system, it must legally discriminate in favor of worker-owned cooperatives, as in Nove's blueprint of feasible socialism. In many capitalist countries, centralized state corporations distribute the mail, public enterprises produce cars, small-scale private firms run restaurants, and individual plumbers repair leaks. The difference between capitalism and market socialism is that under capitalism there are also large-scale private firms that distribute mail and produce cars; Nove (1983: 200; also Putterman 1986: 328) would ban these and reserve the field for cooperatives.

But who would decide what should be cooperative and what could be capitalist? Elster points out that the decentralized choices of producers can and in general will yield a different outcome than a vote. In the presence of

---

[53] One challenge to the feasibility of market socialism is the argument by Leijonhufvud (1986) that, because machines are more specialized than skills, firms that pool capital and hire labor are more efficient than firms that pool labor power and hire machines. "Workers cannot pool their labor power as the capitalists pool their physical capital," he maintains (p. 219), "in order to hire machines at a rental that would leave the joint rent going to workers of the labor-managed firm. Labor will not be owned and specialized machinery is not for hire. The producer cooperative is a possible compromise form but, on the whole, successful enterprises started as worker partnerships are going to end up owning capital and hiring labor – which is to say, end up as capitalist firms." In this situation, unionization of capitalist firms is the workers' best solution.

Yet Leijonhufvud's argument is not sufficient to explain why rich people assume ownership of firms. Most explanations of why capital hires labor rely on moral hazard: People with money become owners because if they merely loaned capital to direct producers, the latter would behave in excessively risky ways. The literature on this topic is too extensive to be discussed here; the best summary I know of is Cui 1990.

I am indebted to Zhiyuan Cui for his comments and for his inexhaustible supply of information.

externalities, people might vote to live in an economy with 70 percent cooperatives, but they might freely form only 30 percent.[54] As I see it, this situation presents an important dilemma: The result of democratic choice may be suboptimal, while free decentralized decisions have in the past resulted in capitalism.

These doubts aside, two arguments are frequently advanced for the superiority of cooperatives over capitalist firms: efficiency, notably higher labor productivity, and better distribution. Since the first of these claims has been reviewed recently by Elster (1989; also Elster and Moene 1989 and Putterman 1986), I offer only some marginal comments.

First, Elster is right to emphasize the importance of externalities: Cooperatives may perform differently depending on their environment. This is true not only under capitalism but also under socialism. Cooperatives have been spectacularly and obnoxiously profitable in Poland and the Soviet Union because the central allocation system was so inefficient that entrepreneurial and even "pure," Austrian profits fell like manna from heaven to anyone who was permitted to pursue them.[55] And if the performance of cooperatives depends on the presence of centralized state firms, public enterprises, and private companies, the optimal economic system may be a mixed one.[56]

Second, although according to Elster and Moene (1989: 27) empirical studies repeatedly show that labor productivity is higher in the few cooperatives that exist under capitalism, they note that "theoretical discussions usually conclude that the impact is negative." In my view, the results of theoretical analyses depend on (1) the model of labor process they ascribe to the capitalist firms and (2) the assumptions they are willing to make about mutual supervision. If one assumes, as Bowles and Gintis do in their recent papers, that under capitalism workers exert effort because they are individually supervised by the firm (and because job loss is costly) and if

---

[54] His fears are confirmed by a recent Polish survey: Whereas 72.2 percent of respondents support privatization of state enterprises, 52.3 prefer to work for state firms (*Życie Warszawy*, 25 June 1990, p. 4).

[55] Bauer (1989) points out, however, that private entrepreneurs operating in a system of administrative allocation are intimidated from behaving in a way oriented to full-fledged profits because the prices they can charge and the incomes they can earn are likely to evoke a political reaction. And they are right to be intimidated: Władysław Baka (1986: 130), a former Polish minister of the economy and the architect of the "second stage" of economic reform, warned that "fortunes resulting from using inefficiencies of systemic [i.e., state] solutions will not be tolerated."

[56] This assertion does not imply its converse. Some mixed systems may be terrible.

one assumes that mutual supervision would be the equilibrium strategy in a worker-owned firm, then it follows that labor cooperatives would be more productive; workers would work at least as hard, but the firm would save the costs of supervision.[57] This has been the traditional socialist micro-argument for socialization of the means of production. But both of these assumptions have been gravely undermined by Burawoy (1979), according to whom (1) workers in fact do supervise each other under capitalism and (2) the organization of production seems to be more a matter of firm size than of ownership. Burawoy seems to think that in fact the capitalist firm subcontracts jobs to groups of workers by negotiating the parameters of their collective performance and that these groups decide to what extent these parameters should be fulfilled and performance supervised.[58] And his USA–Hungary comparisons seem to show that firm size is the decisive factor in the organization of production.

Arguments about worker cooperatives concern, in addition to labor productivity, their effect on employment, investment, proclivity to adopt technological innovation, and risk postures. The effect on employment is most controversial. Earlier models arrived at the result that cooperatives will underemploy (maximizing average rather than total profit – Ward 1957), but this is no longer a shared conclusion. Moene's (1989: 87, 93) recent article is particularly enlightening, since he correctly compares the cooperative not with a "pure" capitalist firm but with one that has strong unions. His conclusions are that (1) "the capitalist firm tends to have fixed wages and variable employment, whereas the coop tends to have fixed employment and variable income" and (2) "underinvestment seems to be one of the main problems of capitalist firms with a unionised labour pool." In general, it seems that the conclusions one reaches with regard to any of these topics are highly sensitive to institutional issues: the rules that govern membership and financing of the cooperative.

Given all the uncertainties concerning cooperatives, Elster (1989: 110) concludes that on grounds of efficiency "there is no reason to experiment with this form of ownership. There are, after all, many reforms that *might*

---

[57] I am not sure whether "productive" is the same as "efficient" in this context. Judgments about efficiency have to take into account the fact that workers derive disutility from effort, including the effort to supervise. Bowles and Gintis assume, in effect, that mutual supervision is costless to workers.

[58] Zhiyuan Cui has pointed out to me that Holmstrom's (1982) model would provide microfoundations for Burawoy's claim. In this model, the reward schedule is such that each member of the team internalizes the full cost of shirking. Hence, shirking is deterred.

have good properties in the large even if they work badly in the small – but society cannot go ahead and try them out on the basis of a mere possibility." But then he pulls a rabbit out of the hat and announces that he would go ahead, since "the basic argument for cooperatives is one of economic justice."

Justice is a topic I have deliberately avoided, since I think it may be easier to agree that it is good to feed everyone than to agree why. Some people may want to eradicate poverty on the grounds of Kantian ("I might have been them") justice; others, simply out of compassion. But what, then, about the traditional socialist claim that capitalism is not only irrational but also unjust and that, conversely, only social ownership embodies the right of everyone to the full fruits of his or her labor?

Note first that distributional considerations have in the past provided and in many countries continue to furnish an important impulse toward socialism of some sort. One way to see the distributional cost of capitalism to wage earners, suggested a long time ago by Paul Samuelson, is to look at the proportion of net income consumed by owners of capital. The net output in any capitalist economy can be partitioned into the consumption of wage earners and the investment and consumption of capitalists. The last item is forever lost to wage earners; it is the price they pay for the private ownership of productive wealth. And this price varies enormously among capitalist countries: In 1985, for every dollar of value added in manufacturing, the consumption of capitalists ranged from about ten cents in Austria and Norway to under forty cents in the United Kingdom and the United States to about sixty cents in Brazil and seventy cents in Argentina.[59] Hence, in purely distributional terms Austrian and Norwegian wage earners have little to gain from nationalization or socialization.[60] Since nationalization has some inevitable costs, they are best off relying on their market power and electoral influence. British and U.S. workers have more to gain by squeezing profits or owning productive wealth directly: They

[59] Data, from the World Bank, are only for the manufacturing sector. The numbers are approximate; they are derived by subtracting from 100 percent the labor share and a part of investment, where this part is an educated guess ranging from 50 percent in Norway and Austria to zero in Argentina and Brazil.

[60] Note that income from property and self-employment does not constitute a major part of household incomes for the top quintile in the developed capitalist countries. This share is 17.3 percent in the USA (and the top quintile gets 35.9 percent of all incomes), 16.3 percent in Canada (33.2 percent of all incomes), 7.5 percent in the United Kingdom (31.9 percent), 4.8 percent in Sweden (27.1 percent), and 22.4 percent – mostly from self-employment – in Norway (30.3 percent). Data are from Rainwater, Torrey, and Smeeding 1989.

end up striking more. In turn, the distributional effect of nationalization in Argentina and Brazil would be enormous. If income differentials between the top and the bottom quintile were limited to a factor of five in socialist Brazil, the income of the poorest 20 percent would increase tenfold. Hence, in Argentina and Brazil nationalization is attractive to wage earners for purely distributional reasons.

Yet the paradox is that those working-class movements that may have the political muscle to bring about some form of socialism by legislation have no incentive to do so, while those movements that have much to gain by transferring productive wealth to the public realm have no power to do it. Hence, socialism as a program for public ownership of productive wealth is the political project of only those movements that cannot bring it about.

In the end, market socialism does appear attractive on distributional grounds. Even if we cannot exactly anticipate its effects on employment, investment, and labor productivity, a combination of cooperatives with markets would be superior to capitalism in equalizing income distribution. If we think of market socialism as a system in which there is a labor-cum-capital market – that is, if being a shareholder in a co-op constitutes simultaneously a right and the obligation to work in it, and these rights–obligations can be traded – then in equilibrium the rate of return to total endowments will be uniform throughout the economy. The distribution of income associated with this equilibrium will be more egalitarian than under capitalism, since employees receive the entire net income of the firm.[61]

In turn, the claim that market socialism would be a system of industrial democracy, in the sense that the process of production would be democratic, seems unfounded. If worker-owned firms compete and if one way of organizing production maximizes profits, then they will be forced to choose this organization. In turn, if more than one organization of production maximizes profits, then capitalists would be indifferent between them, and if workers prefer one, capitalists would adopt it. Hence, workers' co-ops would have nothing to change.

Moreover, since under market socialism the utilization of resources would depend on rates of return, this system would suffer from the social

---

[61] Yet efficiency considerations may argue against this kind of system. As Comisso (1989) notes, "diversified ownership of assets is critical for efficient allocation of capital and rational monitoring of management alike." She also points out that tying rights to the residual income to employment precludes investing abroad.

inaccessibility of technically feasible allocations of welfare – the irrationality we identified as characteristic of capitalism. Even if the instruments of production are owned cooperatively, the final distribution of income among cooperatives will depend on their initial endowments, and attempts to redistribute incomes would result in decreased output.[62]

Hence, market socialism would still be at odds with democracy. The principle that everyone has equal economic rights is not sufficient for democracy either in production or in the economy as a whole. Market socialism is not a full implementation of democracy in the economic realm.[63]

## Social democracy

Can capitalism be reformed? The answer is obviously positive: Some capitalist countries have succeeded in providing basic material security for everyone, though even in these countries capitalism can be criticized on several grounds.[64] But eradication of poverty is a sufficient criterion of success in a world in which billions of people suffer from material deprivation. When about thirty million people in the United States and about forty million in the Soviet Union live under conditions defined as absolute poverty – not to speak of China, India, or Brazil – material conditions in Sweden, Norway, and France are enviable.

Capitalist economies are extremely heterogeneous. They differ dramatically in levels of development, distribution of income, and the role of the state in ensuring material welfare. Per capita income is twenty times higher in the most developed capitalist countries than in the poorest ones.[65] A person born in Bangladesh or Zaire can expect to live thirty years less than someone in Western Europe. A worker employed in manufacturing takes home less than 20 percent of value added in most South American countries but almost 60 percent in the Netherlands and Austria. A person in the top 20 percent of households in Brazil or Peru has an income more than

---

[62] Moreover, O'Neill (1989: 209–10) points out that "problems of cooperation are not answered by defenders of market socialism. In particular, the problems of coordination that arise in market economies are not solved by transforming privately owned enterprises into workers' cooperatives. Cooperation *within* enterprises does not entail and, in the context of a market economy, would not result in cooperation *between* enterprises."

[63] Exponents of the contrary view include Dahl (1985) and Bowles and Gintis (1986).

[64] See the Epilogue in Przeworski 1985 for such a critique.

[65] According to GNP calculated at purchasing-power parities. It is seventy-five times higher according to conventional GNP figures as provided by the World Bank.

thirty times higher than someone in the bottom 20 percent, whereas in several Western European countries and Japan this disparity is reduced to less than five times. Finally, central governments allocate less than 2 percent of their expenditures to housing, social security, and welfare in Indonesia and Ecuador but more than one-half in Spain, Switzerland, Sweden, and West Germany.[66] Thus, for many people capitalism represents utter poverty, while for some others it generates affluence.

Looking for countries that have eradicated poverty – countries that are rich, that have an egalitarian distribution of earned incomes, and that have a developed welfare system – one finds a few robust patterns and lots of unknowns. (1) The very few countries where no one is poor are all capitalist.[67] (2) Statistical analyses of developed capitalist countries show repeatedly that better economic performance, less income inequality, and more extensive welfare services are to be found in those developed capitalist countries that combine strong unions with social democratic control of the government (see Bruno and Sachs 1985; Lange and Garrett 1985; Hicks 1988). (3) No unified body of theory can explain economic development.[68] (4) The impact of democracy in the political realm on economic development remains unclear. (5) The argument that the development of some capitalist countries was made possible only because they exploited other countries seems empirically false.

Clearly, the fact that capitalism has been reformed in Sweden does not imply that it can be reformed in Peru, even if Scandinavian affluence is not

[66] All this information is from the 1987 World Bank *Development Report* (diskette version). Except for distribution of household income, all data are for 1985.

[67] Among the countries for which data are available, the rate of absolute poverty before taxes and transfers (using the U.S. definition converted to local currencies at exchange rates giving parity in purchasing power) is 5.6 percent in Sweden, 5.8 percent in Switzerland, 7.4 percent in Canada, 8.3 percent in West Germany, 11.8 percent in the United Kingdom, 12.7 percent in the United States, and 13.2 percent in Australia (Rainwater et al. 1989). I should qualify this statement because of the paucity of data on poverty in the socialist countries. Matthews (1986) provides evidence that poverty is not rare in Hungary, Poland, or the Soviet Union, but data on East Germany are hard to find.

[68] As I understand it, a particularly thorny problem is to develop a theory that will make reasonable assumptions about technology and technical progress and will at the same time account for the persistent differences among countries. When at least one factor is mobile, constant coefficients technology leads to the conclusion that one country should be rich and all others poor; concave technologies lead to the conclusion that gaps among countries should vanish; increasing returns to particular endowments are inconsistent with evidence. Hence, Lucas (1988), for example, ends up placing his faith in the increasing returns that are due to externalities in human capital: Either particular individuals become more productive when they work in the presence of better-educated partners, or particular processes are more effective when they are adopted in the presence of other effective processes.

a result of exploiting South American poverty. But in some countries capitalism has been reformed: Everyone is fed. How is that possible?

The fundamental premise of social democracy is that nationalization of the means of production is not necessary to overcome the irrationality of capitalism, that is, to avoid the welfare losses caused by the rights inherent in private ownership of the means of production. This premise contradicts both the classic marxist analysis reconstructed above and the (identical) views of neoliberals.[69] According to these views, every attempt at redistributing income causes "deadweight losses," that is, withdrawal of resources from productive use. Taxes on earned incomes cause a reduction in labor supply; taxes on profits cause a decline in savings and investment. In turn, transfers make leisure cheaper and aggravate the effect of taxes by causing poor people to work less. Yet, as plausible as this argument appears, it is not very well supported by empirical analyses. At least within the observed range of tax rates, the labor supply of adult males and rates of saving and investment do not seem to be very sensitive to taxes.[70] One reason is that relatively few people can decide the number of hours they work; most must work full time or not at all. But most important for us, different forms of taxes and transfers have different consequences for the decisions of owners to utilize their endowments. At least on paper, taxes on potential earnings and on consumption from profits are neutral with regard to labor supply and investment respectively.[71] And even if completely neutral taxes are in fact impossible, different combinations of taxes and transfers do cause different magnitudes of deadweight loss (Becker 1976). Countries with strong unions and prolonged social democratic tenure in office exhibit better trade-offs between unemployment and inflation as well as between labor share and investment.

Hence, governments that want to eradicate poverty while minimizing losses of efficiency are not helpless in capitalist economies: The social

---

[69] A more extensive version of what follows can be found in Przeworski 1990: ch. 1.

[70] In a recent review of the evidence, Saunders and Klau (1985) failed to find clear evidence that taxes affect the tax base. They note that "the evidence to date has produced estimates of labour supply responses to taxation which are neither strong nor robust" (p. 166); that the effect of taxes on the demand for labor does not show in a cross-section of the OECD countries (p. 174); that "the view that countries with comparatively high tax burdens tend to be those with weak saving propensities cannot be supported on the basis of the data" (p. 177); and, finally, that the effect of taxes on investment cannot be assessed in aggregate terms (p. 185).

[71] For the argument that governments have instruments to control income distribution without reducing investment, see Przeworski and Wallerstein 1988.

democratic model is theoretically viable. Governments can encourage technological innovation; they can counteract economic fluctuations; and they can steer investment; they can facilitate labor mobility; they can deliver welfare services and maintain incomes. The degree of irrationality in capitalism is not a given. Governments elected with a mandate to assure everyone of material security do have instruments with which to pursue their mission.

## Could we feed everyone?

We have thus arrived at the following conclusions. The socialist critique of the irrationality of capitalism is valid, but the socialist alternative is unfeasible. In turn, either social democracy – a system in which no forms of private property are banned and in which the state plays an active role in regulating markets and in redistributing incomes – or market socialism – a system in which large firms are owned by the employees or by the public and the state plays the same role with regard to markets – both offer reasonable second-bests. Both can ensure that markets operate efficiently, and both can generate a humane distribution of welfare.

I see no grounds on which to choose between social democracy and market socialism. Ownership understood as the right to claim residual income and to make decisions about allocation of resources is not what matters for efficiency. If the state appropriately organizes and regulates markets, these should ensure that managers of firms – private, cooperative, or public – maximize profits. In turn, if the state chooses appropriate instruments of taxation and efficient ways of delivering social services and ensuring incomes, it can assure everyone of a welfare minimum.

It is true that retaining markets would preserve some features that socialists find deleterious. They would still be irrational in the sense that universal subsistence could be assured only at the cost of underutilizing productive potential. Moreover, they would still entail a large dose of inequality; indeed, the condition for efficiency is that owners of more productive factors receive a higher return. And since even markets with state intervention are a second-best, the current disenchantment with central planning may not stop us from searching for a better alternative: a system that would make the economy conform to the collective preference expressed by citizens through a democratic process without causing inefficiency.

Could we, then, feed everyone? This is a twofold question. First, what are the hypothetical conditions under which this would be possible? Second, can these conditions be realized? If the search for an answer took us through capitalism and socialism in their utopian, feasible, and historically realized embodiments, it was to eliminate those answers that do not provide sufficient conditions or those that seem unfeasible. What remains is to investigate whether we could feed everyone under systems that rely on markets, in spite of their irrationality.

A necessary condition for feeding everyone is "strong abundance," that is, a level of development of productive capacity sufficient to ensure universal subsistence even when the redistribution of incomes required to make satisfaction of needs universal may cause losses in output.[72] I assume a world market economy in which most decisions to utilize endowments are private and oriented by rates of return, which implies that their owners – private, cooperative, or public – have the right to withdraw resources from production when their return is reduced either by higher wage costs or by taxation. Hence, the productive capacity relevant for our purposes is not defined by the level of output that would be produced without any redistribution of income. This output may be sufficient to satisfy everyone's basic needs, but it would not be produced if these needs were to be satisfied: This is precisely the irrationality of capitalism. Higher productive capacity may be needed to produce enough for universal subsistence.

Is strong abundance already here? The answer depends on (1) the cost of satisfying everyone's basic needs, (2) the present technological and organizational capacity to produce, and (3) the extent to which this capacity would be underutilized if the rates of return were reduced because of income redistribution. I do not know the answer; too many technical issues are involved. But I suspect that we are not too far away.

Hence, even if market economies do perpetuate irrationality and injustice, under strong abundance a government entrusted with the popular mandate of eradicating poverty and having chosen those policies that minimize deadweight losses could see to it that everyone's basic needs are

---

[72] This answer approaches the views of van der Veen and van Parijs (1986). In fact, what follows relies on my earlier comments on their statement (Przeworski 1986a), though there I thought that the abundance required was weak rather than strong. In fact, what is needed is more than the level of development that would permit satisfaction of basic needs if all endowments were fully utilized; that would be weak abundance.

satisfied. All that is needed is a state that will organize efficient markets, tax those who can afford it, and use the revenue to ensure the material well-being of everyone. Yet somehow states almost nowhere succeed in this simple task.

# 4. The political dynamics of economic reform

## Introduction

The goal of recent economic reforms, undertaken in several countries around the globe, is to organize an economy that rationally allocates resources and in which the state is financially solvent.

These are market-oriented reforms. Rationalizing the allocation of resources requires organizing new markets, deregulating prices, attenuating monopolies, and lowering protection. Making the state solvent entails reducing public expenditures, increasing revenues, and at times selling public assets.

Such reforms necessarily cause a temporary fall in aggregate consumption. They are socially costly and politically risky. Perhaps in the long run reforms do accomplish all one former Polish minister of the economy announced they would: motivate, generate market clearing, and satisfy social justice (Baka 1986: 46). Yet meanwhile they hurt large social groups and evoke opposition from important political forces. And if that happens, democracy may be undermined or reforms abandoned, or both.

Even if governments that launch such reforms often hate to admit it, a temporary economic deterioration is inevitable. Inflation must flare up when prices are deregulated. Unemployment of capital and labor must increase when competition is intensified. Allocative efficiency must temporarily decline when the entire economic structure is being transformed. Structural transformations of economic systems are costly.

Can such transformations be accomplished under democratic conditions?[1] The question about the relationship of democracy and reforms

---

[1] By posing the question in this manner, I do not want to imply that they would in fact be accomplished under a dictatorship. Remmer (1986) provides persuasive evidence that the rate of success of the IMF's Standby Agreements, albeit not very high, was slightly higher for democratic than for authoritarian regimes in Latin America between 1954 and 1984. Haggard (1986) found that among the thirty cases of Extended Fund Facility programs he examined,

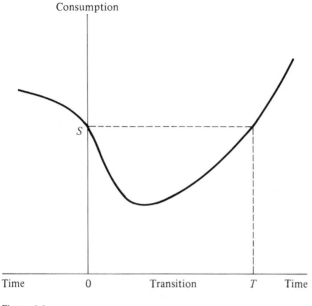

Figure 4.1

concerns transitional effects. The reason is the following: Even if the post-reform system would be more efficient – more, even if the new steady state would be Pareto-superior to the status quo, that is, no one would be worse off in the new system and someone would be better off – a transient deterioration of material conditions may be sufficient to undermine either democracy or the reform process.

Examine Figure 4.1, in which the vertical axis measures the welfare a person expects to experience and the horizontal axis measures time in equal units to the left and right of the current situation $S$. Hence, the downslope around $S$ indicates changes in welfare in the immediate future, and the peaks represent the levels of welfare associated with stable economic systems. Suppose the right-hand hill is higher than the left, but the status quo lies on the left slope. Then a move to the right causes a temporary deterio-

IMF disbursements were interrupted or canceled for noncompliance in all the democratic countries except for the special case of India, but the rate of success among the "weak" authoritarian regimes he considered was not different. In turn, Stallings and Kaufman (1989) found in their analysis of nine Latin American countries that whereas "established democracies" did about as well as authoritarian regimes with regard to stabilization, only the latter progressed with regard to both stabilization and structural reform.

ration, which lasts during the period of transition. This "valley of transition" must be traversed before we climb the higher hills.[2]

Structural economic transformations are being undertaken in many countries, South and East, under nascent democratic institutions. Four outcomes may occur under such conditions: (1) Reforms may advance under democratic conditions, (2) reforms may be forced through by a dictatorship, (3) democracy may survive by abandoning reforms, and (4) both reforms and democracy may be undermined. Market-oriented economic reforms were pursued by authoritarian governments in Chile and in Mexico, while in the Soviet Union some economists laid down a program for transition to a market economy "from totalitarianism via authoritarianism" (Migranyan 1988). In turn, under democratic conditions, where the discontent can find political expression at the polls, even the most promising reform strategies may be abandoned. Either politicians are concerned about electoral support and reverse policies that will cause them to lose elections, or they lose to competitors more attuned to the political consequences of structural transformation. And in some cases, egalitarian ideologies with strong populist and nationalistic overtones can be mobilized against both democracy and reforms.

Can structural economic transformation be sustained under democratic conditions, or must either reforms or democracy be sacrificed? This is a threefold question: (1) What are the economic costs of such transformation? (2) Under what political conditions are such costs most likely to be tolerated? (3) What is the effect of transformation on democratic institutions? These questions are, respectively, the subject of the next three sections.

The analysis that follows places transitions from command to market economies in the light of Latin American experiences. This analysis is no more than speculation, informed on the one hand by economic theory and on the other by the meager historical experience we have thus far. Neither source is very useful: We have no theory of structural transformation, and the empirical evidence is scanty. Market-oriented reforms are a plunge into

[2] In fact, reforms are being undertaken in many countries as a response to a prolonged economic crisis. Per capita income declined during the 1980s in most Latin American countries as well as in a number of Eastern European nations. Hence, the left side of the status quo may be downward-sloping; staying with the present system can mean that consumption will continue to deteriorate with no hope that the future will be different. Yet to avoid the continuing deterioration it is still necessary to suffer through a period of transition.

the unknown, a risky historical experiment born out of desperation and driven by hope, not by justifiable benefits.

## Transitional costs of reforms

The purpose of this section is to speculate about the economic costs of reforms in Eastern Europe by relying on the Latin American experience. First, the conditions inherited by newly democratic governments on both continents are compared. The subsequent two sections focus, respectively, on the aggregate and distributional costs of reforms.

### Conditions and strategies

Students of command economies tend to see the difficulties involved in economic reforms in Eastern Europe as more profound than those facing the less developed capitalist countries, specifically those in Latin America. The typical view is spelled out by Bruszt (1989: 716): "Changes in Eastern Europe are often compared with the processes of democratization that have taken place in South America and Southern Europe. In spite of the obvious similarities, one factor basically distinguishes Eastern European changes . . . , namely, that in these countries the transition to political democracy is accompanied by the radical transformations of the economic system. The issues of economic and political transition cannot be separated from each other. Increasingly, mounting tensions in the economy are posing a direct threat to the process of political transition."

I take issue with such assertions, since I see the economic transformations in Latin America as radical; to some extent different, but radical. In Latin America, transitions to democracy have been accompanied by attempts to transform the economic system radically, and the tensions in the economy do pose a threat to democracy. It is not an accident that a headline in a Polish newspaper read "Menem like Balcerowicz."[3]

A glance at the macroeconomic indicators at the time of democratic transition suffices us to conclude that Latin American countries did not enjoy an easier situation than Eastern European countries. Adding Bolivia

---

[3] *Gazeta,* Warsaw, 13 December 1989, p. 6. Carlos Menem is the president of Argentina elected in 1989. Leszek Balcerowicz was economic tsar of the Mazowiecki government in Poland.

and Peru, on the one hand, and Romania and Yugoslavia, on the other, would not change this picture. Except in Chile, Latin American democratic governments came into office in the midst of an acute economic crisis; except perhaps in Czechoslovakia, so did Eastern European ones. But, at least as portrayed by the macro indicators, the situation was worse in Latin America. (Table 4.1.)

One can argue, however, that these indicators do not manifest the true state of the respective economies. Perhaps Eastern European economies are in fact in worse shape, but their crisis is yet to unfold. Or they are in worse shape because they have much farther to go before they will grow again: Although their crisis is not as acute as in Latin America, their present economic structure is harder to transform. Whereas in Latin America the crisis of growth is a conjunctural phenomenon due to the changing international division of labor, in Eastern Europe it is a structural phenomenon due to the economic system. Hence, economic reforms in Latin America are a matter of, at most, "structural adjustment," while in Eastern Europe they call for a transition from system to system, from socialism to capitalism.

Yet let us look beneath the labels, at what we can see.[4] Both Latin American and Eastern European countries have had (1) states vulnerable to pressures from large firms, (2) a high degree of monopoly and protectionism, (3) overgrown bureaucracies, (4) weak revenue-collecting systems, and (5) rudimentary and fragmentary systems for income maintenance and welfare delivery. Some important features, however, did systematically differ between these groups of countries: (1) Centralized allocation of physical resources and administrative price setting were more prevalent in Eastern Europe than in capitalist countries, and (2) income distribution is incomparably more unequal in Latin America than in Eastern Europe.

In my view, states have been weak as organizations in Eastern Europe as well as in most Latin American countries: They were unable to resist

---

[4] Eastern Europeans can always find nightmares to buttress their view. But consider the following passage: "Everyone has horror stories about countries where subsidized gasoline is cheaper than drinking water, or where subsidized bread is so cheap that it is fed to pigs, or where telephone calls cost a cent or so because someone forgot (or lacked the courage) to raise prices to keep pace with inflation or where subsidized 'agricultural credit' is designed to buy the support of powerful landowners, who promptly recycle the funds to buy government paper" (Williamson 1990: 11). Only the last example reveals that these are stories about Latin America.

Table 4.1. *Economic conditions at the time of democratization*

| Economic indicators | Uruguay 1984 | Chile 1989 | Brazil 1983 | Argentina 1983 | Poland 1989 | Hungary 1989 | Czechoslovakia 1989 |
|---|---|---|---|---|---|---|---|
| GNP/CAP[a] | 2,710 | 2,370 | 1,590 | 1,650 | 1,520 | 2,210 | — |
| ΔGDP (%) | -3.9 | 10.5 | -1.3 | 2.6 | 0.5 | 0.8 | 3.0 |
| Δ3 GDP (%) | -24.8 | 26.4 | -9.1 | -13.3 | 11.1 | 4.8 | 8.0 |
| INFLATION (%) | 66.1 | 21.1 | 179.2 | 433.7 | 180 | 17 | 0.2 |
| DEBT/CAP ($)[b] | 1,128 | 1,539 | 750 | 1,556 | 1,112 | 1,656 | — |
| DEBT/EXP (%) | 520 | — | — | 485 | 540 | 293 | 87 |
| SERV/EXP (%) | 65 | 27.2 | 28.8 | 24.5 | 76 | 32 | 16 |
| GOV EXP/GNP (%) | 18.8 | 33.4 | 23.2 | 26.8 | 40.4 | 58.3 | — |
| PUB DEF/GNP (%) | -5.6 | 0 | -4.3 | -1.4 | -1.8 | -3.6 | — |
| CUR ACT BAL/GNP | -2.7 | -1.3 | -3.3 | -3.8 | -0.2 | -1.4 | -0.0 |
| INT RES[c] | — | 5.2 | — | — | 1.5 | 2.3 | — |
| LABOR SHARE (%) | 21.0 | 15.4 | 19 | 19.2 | 23.4 | 34.9 | — |
| Δw/PERIOD (%) | -50/10 | -28/5 | — | -23/10 | -10/7 | — | — |
| UNMPLMNT[d] (%) | 14.3 | 11.0 | 6.7 | 4.0 | 0.0 | — | — |
| INF MORT (%) | 28.8 | 20.0 | 69.4 | 34.4 | 17.5 | 17.5 | — |
| SEC SCH ENR (%) | 70.0 | 74.0 | 35.0 | 65.0 | 80.0 | 70.0 | — |

*Note:* Most data are from the *World Tables* (World Bank, 1989). Δ3 GDP is the cumulative change in per capita GDP during the three preceding years; Δw/PERIOD is the fall in the average wage from its most recent peak, where PERIOD stands for the number of years since the peak.
[a]1980 U.S. $ (World Bank Atlas method).   [b]Current dollars.
[c]Gross international reserves in months of import coverage.
[d]Urban areas for Latin America; all but agriculture for Poland.

pressures from large firms for subsidies and protection and incapable of collecting revenue from these firms (or their private owners) and of evoking compliance with rules and regulations. The image of the "totalitarian" state whose orders evoke the compliance of economic agents is at best an ideological relic of the Stalinist period. Although details differ, there is an overwhelming consensus that central command systems were in fact not plan, but bargain, economies, bargained between central governments and their particular branches and firms as well as directly among firms seeking to avoid government control. And for various reasons, economic and political, governments were vulnerable to pressures from large firms in both designing and implementing policies. To this extent, the situation in Hungary or Poland was not different from that in Argentina or Brazil, where governments also conformed to the demands of large firms, public and private, in the design and implementation of economic policies. As a result, governments South and East tended to subsidize and protect large, often monopolistic, firms.[5]

The degree of monopoly is probably much greater in Eastern Europe than in Latin America; industrial plants tend to be enormous in Eastern Europe, and retail distribution networks are monopolized by the state or by pseudo-cooperatives.[6] The degree of protection is difficult to assess, but I suspect that it is not much different. Nominal tariff rates were very high in Latin America when democratic governments first came into office, but import restrictions were mainly due to licensing: Those imports that were licensed were subject to a low effective rate (see Cardoso and Dantas 1990 for a study of Brazil). In this respect, the situation is not different from Eastern Europe.

Large public bureaucracies combined with weak revenue-collecting sys-

[5] In a recent article, Balcerowicz (1989: 46) observed: "That the enterprises are the main beneficiaries of fiscal distribution distinguishes the centrally planned from the market economies." Little did he know that in the United States, subsidies to firms, including tax expenditures, amount to more than social welfare spending by the federal government. Subsidies in Poland were running at about 30 percent of central government expenditures, but a large part of these subsidies went to consumer prices. I do not know how much went to firms. Latin American countries subsidized public firms, provided grants and tax breaks for exports, and supported agricultural prices.

[6] Kornai (1986: 1699) reports that in Hungary in 1975 the three largest producers supplied more than two-thirds of the output for 508 out of 637 industrial products. Sales networks were highly monopolized, too: All the food in Warsaw was distributed by two firms. In turn, I am told that if U.S. antimonopoly legislation were applied to Brazil, the thirty largest conglomerates would be affected.

tems generate public deficits. In several Latin American countries, the state is so bankrupt that the only way it can survive from day to day is by borrowing money from would-be taxpayers. Under such conditions, the state cannot collect taxes other than at borders, if at all; in some years, Bolivia collected 1 percent of GNP in taxes, and Peru 2 percent.[7] Except for Chile, all democratic governments in Latin America inherited not only an enormous external and internal debt but also a structure of revenues and expenditures that generates large and increasing deficits. The situation in Eastern Europe is not as drastic, although Poland experienced a 4 percent deficit in 1988. It may become worse before an effective tax system is introduced.

Finally, a comment is needed on the state of social services. It may seem that here the situation of Eastern Europe is far superior, and to some extent it is. But it is important to realize that even if the level of welfare services might have been relatively high in Eastern Europe during the 1960s, the command economies did not have a social welfare system. Welfare services were distributed in the same way as everything else: The planner allocated steel, furniture, meat, doctors' visits, school places, and retirement pensions. This system disintegrated along with the rest of central planning. Eastern European societies are still far from having large sectors of the population completely outside the network of social services, but they will have to rebuild this network from scratch.

The central difference between Eastern Europe and Latin America was the manner of allocating resources and, to a lesser extent, the frequency of administered pricing. Note that this is not just a matter of the size of the public sector: 55.2 percent in Poland in 1987 is probably not much larger than in Brazil or Mexico.[8] Price regulation was probably also much more prevalent in Eastern Europe, except in Hungary, where the post-1968 reforms did free most prices from administrative control. Indeed, price deregulation turned out to be the stumbling block for reforms under the

[7] In Argentina in 1985, the government derived 3.1 percent of its revenues from taxing incomes, as opposed to 13.3 percent from customs and tariffs (World Bank); taxpayer rolls, including actual and nominal persons, are said to contain 30,000 names; and comparison of a list of the hundred largest firms and the hundred largest taxpayers showed no name in common (Lopez 1990).

[8] Poland, however, had a smaller public sector than other Eastern European countries, because most land was privately owned. In industry, state firms produced about 40 percent of output in Latin America, 80 to 90 percent in Eastern Europe. Around 1980, there were 530 public firms in Brazil, 1,155 in Mexico (Schneider 1990), and about 8,000 in Poland.

communist systems.[9] However, price regulation – of food and foodstuffs, utilities, and varieties of other goods, in particular gasoline – was also ubiquitous in Latin America.[10]

Another important difference is income inequality. As shown in Table 4.2, the gap between Eastern Europe and the Far East on the one hand, and Latin America and Turkey on the other, is indeed enormous.

This is, then, the underlying structure of Latin American and Eastern European economies at the time of transition to democracy. Do Eastern European countries have farther to go before they reach economies that are competitive and in which the state is solvent and everyone enjoys a modicum of material security? Are the transformations that await them any more radical than those that face Latin America? If this brief survey is accurate, the answer to such questions is certainly not apparent; the road may not be the same, but it is long on both continents.

There is still another way to address the issue: by looking at what is to be done. Let us, then, examine the reforms that have been made or are being undertaken.

One way to think about reforms is in the traditional terms of international financial institutions,[11] distinguishing stabilization, structural adjustment, and privatization. Stabilization consists of short-term measures designed to slow down inflation, reduce the balance-of-payments deficit, and cut the government deficit. Structural adjustment is the set of measures designed to make the economy competitive. It is the most heterogeneous category, comprising everything from trade liberalization to price deregulation to tax reform. Privatization is self-explanatory. In these terms, Latin American countries, except for Chile, shared with Poland the urgent need to stabilize the economy at the time of transition, whereas other Eastern European countries did not suffer from inflation. In turn, Eastern Europe

[9] In spite of a two-stage reform, the share (in percent of total sales) of prices of producer goods fixed by the government increased in Poland from 20 in 1982 to 29 in 1987; the share of such administered prices for consumer goods increased from 35 to 45; and prices that were not directly fixed were subject to increased regulation (Balcerowicz 1989: 45).

[10] In 1985, out of nine basic necessities, the Argentine, Brazilian, Colombian, Peruvian, and Venezuelan governments controlled the prices of all nine; the Mexican government, of five; and the Chilean government, of none. Of five basic industrial goods, Argentines, Brazilians, Colombians, Mexicans, and Peruvians controlled all five, Venezuelans three, and Chileans none. A ceiling on interest rates existed in all these countries except Venezuela (based on Balassa et al. 1986: Table 4.3).

[11] I say "traditional" because recently the World Bank has become much more concerned about income distribution and, hence, taxation and poverty. See the 1989 *Development Report*.

Table 4.2. *Income distribution in selected countries*

| Country | Ratio of incomes of top to bottom quintile of households | | | Labor share in net value added in manufacturing | | |
|---|---|---|---|---|---|---|
| | Date | Source | Ratio | Date | Source | Ratio |
| Argentina | 1970 | WB | 11.4 | 1985 | WB | 19 |
| Brazil | 1983 | WB | 26.1 | 1985 | WB | 19 |
| Mexico | 1977 | WB | 19.9 | 1985 | WB | 25 |
| Peru | 1972 | WB | 32.1 | 1985 | WB | 15 |
| Hungary | 1987 | WB | 3.0 | 1985 | WB | 32 |
| Poland | 1987 | WB | 3.6 | 1984 | WB | 24 |
| Soviet Union | 1972 | B | 4.4[a] | 1988 | A | 37[b] |
| Yugoslavia | 1978 | WB | 5.9 | 1985 | WB | 29 |
| South Korea | 1976 | WB | 7.9 | 1985 | WB | 27 |
| Japan | 1979 | WB | 4.3 | 1985 | WB | 35 |
| Turkey | 1973 | WB | 16.1 | 1985 | WB | 23 |
| Portugal | 1973 | WB | 9.4 | 1985 | WB | 44 |
| Spain | 1980 | WB | 5.8 | 1985 | WB | 41 |
| Belgium | 1978 | WB | 4.6 | 1985 | WB | 50 |
| France | 1975 | WB | 7.7 | | | |
| Italy | 1977 | WB | 7.1 | 1984 | WB | 38 |
| Sweden | 1981 | WB | 5.6 | 1985 | WB | 35 |
| West Germany | 1978 | WB | 5.0 | 1985 | WB | 47 |
| United States | 1980 | WB | 7.5 | 1985 | WB | 40 |

[a]Urban households, post-tax.
[b]Labor share in gross value added.
*Sources*: WB, *World Bank Development Report* (1987); B, Bergson 1984; A, According to Nicolai Schmelyev, cited in *New York Times,* 17 October 1989.

has more to privatize, if it finds buyers. And whatever public sector is left on both continents will have to be reorganized.

Another way of looking at reforms is provided by Williamson (1990), who examined the progress of several Latin American countries with regard to nine categories of measures, oriented toward (1) fiscal discipline, (2) changing priorities in public spending, (3) tax reform, (4) financial liberalization, (5) a competitive exchange rate, (6) trade liberalization, (7) foreign direct investment, (8) privatization, and (9) deregulation. New democratic governments in Latin America faced all these reforms, and many have pursued them. Eastern Europeans also face these reforms. But are there some other steps Eastern Europeans must undertake that make their task more radical?

The reforms already under implementation, announced, or expected in several Eastern European countries include mixtures of the following steps:

1. Rationalizing the investment process by (a) making firms financially autonomous and responsible and (b) getting the right prices for capital goods, which in practice means lowering protection.
2. Equilibrating consumer goods markets by (a) deregulating most prices and (b) eliminating or reducing price subsidies.
3. Building mechanisms for eliminating inefficient firms and processes by (a) allowing bankruptcy and unemployment, (b) organizing financial markets, (c) organizing labor markets and manpower programs, and (d) adopting antimonopoly measures, including measures against state monopolies.
4. Reducing budget deficits by (a) reducing expenditures or (b) increasing tax revenues and (c) selling state enterprises.
5. Restructuring the social welfare and income-maintenance network, including unemployment insurance.

Comparing this list with the Latin American measures enumerated by Williamson leads to four questions: (1) Will the inflation resulting from price deregulation in command economies be a transitional phenomenon *sui generis*, or will it assume the inertial character characteristic of Latin America? (2) Will unemployment turn out to be a transitional phenomenon, remedied once financial and labor markets are organized and capital and labor are reallocated? (3) Will private entrepreneurship replace the state after a brief period of learning? (4) Will the distributional effects of reforms turn out to be transitional, or will they lead to a permanent increase in inequality? These questions are discussed in turn in the following sections.

## Aggregate effects

In examining reforms, we can distinguish two categories of effects. Some consequences are permanent, characteristic of the steady state of the already transformed system. Others are transitional, inherent in the process of transformation. Some effects, in particular those concerning efficiency, are aggregate; other consequences are distributional. Combining these distinctions yields four types of effects: (1) Permanent aggregate outcomes are presumably positive. Reforms are undertaken because the current economic structure is inefficient or otherwise undesirable, and its flaws can be remedied by transforming the economic system. (2) Some permanent consequences are distributional. Those groups whose interests are protected in the old system may find themselves absolutely or relatively less well off in the post-reform economy. (3) The process of reforms causes temporary inflation, unemployment, and allocative inefficiencies. Hence, it generates transitional aggregate costs. Finally, (4) the process of reforms may generate transitional distributional effects: volatile changes in relative incomes.

Aggregate transitional costs may include inflation, unemployment of capital and labor, and temporary misallocations of resources. I analyze these costs in the context of the "bitter pill" strategy, in which everything is done at once. This strategy is based on the admission that transition costs will be significant. Their central assumption is that the more profound are the reforms, the shorter will be the transitional effects. In this conception, people are willing to undergo an unpleasant cure if it does not last long.

*Inflation.* Inflation is the most complex issue. The central question is whether it is possible to experience transitional inflation and not generate inertia.

Examine first the inflation that must occur with deregulating prices: a one-shot transition from administered to market prices. I use Polish data as an illustration, but the logic is generic to all situations of price deregulation.

Imagine an economy in which prices are administratively set and in which demand at these prices exceeds supply. This is the status quo.[12] Take Poland, where on December 31, 1989, for each 1,000 Zł in the hands of the population there were about 333 Zł worth of goods and services available in the stores. In such a system, money is not sufficient to access goods and services, which are distributed by queues or unofficial barter. Note that standing in line is a major welfare cost: A kilogram of oranges costs 222 Zł and one hour in line; a kilogram of meat, 111 Zł and two hours.[13]

Suppose now that on January 1 all prices are deregulated;[14] there are perfect competition, no saving, and no change in the money supply; nomi-

---

[12] It is a separate question why in a system of administered prices and centralized control over wages such a disequilibrium ever occurs. I leave this question aside.

[13] An interesting question is why stores are not empty under such conditions. They were almost, but not quite. I suspect there are several reasons: (1) complete uselessness of some products – no one wanted them at zero price; (2) budget constraints – given the income distribution, people kept money in case goods they wanted became available ("appeared," in popular terms); (3) transaction costs of waiting in line; (4) saving due to risk aversion.

[14] And some – say, utilities – are administratively adjusted to reflect true opportunity costs.

nal incomes remain constant; and output is the same. After a brief tâtonnement, all prices adjust to reflect preferences and scarcities, and the market clears. Oranges now cost 333 Złl/kg, meat 667 Zł/kg; there is no excess demand. Next month the supply of goods and of money is the same, the market clears again, and prices remain constant at their new levels. The deregulation operation is completed.

Prices increased threefold; what before cost 333 Zł now costs 1,000 Zł. There was thus 300 percent inflation in one month, but this was only a transitional effect. Once the operation was accomplished, prices remained constant. Moreover, in aggregate terms the welfare of the population has increased. The 666 Zł of excess money supply was useless; before the reform, everyone had three lottery tickets for one prize, and now everyone has one prize for certain. But transaction costs were reduced by the hours people had to spend in lines, and the time had amounted to several hours per day per household. Moreover, the new prices are rational; the ratio of the price of oranges to meat now reflects tastes and relative scarcities.[15] But for future reference, note a distributional effect: People with lower earning power who value time less, in particular the retired, may actually have suffered a reduction in consumption, while people with more money and less time increased their consumption.

Moreover, note the role of price subsidies. In the old system, several prices were subsidized; the state paid higher prices to producers than the prices it charged the consumers.[16] Suppose these subsidies are completely eliminated. Then nominal incomes fall, and so does demand; after the initial excess incomes have been spent, prices decline.

Hence, inflation turned out to be only transitional: It occurred once and stopped. It is misleading, therefore, at this stage to draw an analogy with the inflation that reigns in Latin America by calling this phenomenon demand inflation. This label judges that the phenomenon has constant causes, and this is precisely what needs to be determined.

What might undermine the success of this transitional operation? Price reform will be successful if it does not generate inertia; if it does not create mechanisms that will continue to push prices upwards. Four mechanisms

[15] It will be fascinating to compare the market prices that emerge from the deregulation with the administered prices that reigned before. I wonder how irrational the relative prices in fact were.

[16] In Poland in 1989, subsidies amounted to 31 percent of the state budget, about 15 percent of GNP. In the Soviet Union, the subsidies for meat alone are equivalent to one month's wage bill.

can take effect: (1) wage pressure, (2) monopolies, (3) government deficits, and (4) the effects of competition on supply.

The issue of wage pressure is perhaps the most complex; whether it ensues depends on a number of political conditions. I leave the discussion of this mechanism to the next section.

Monopolies are an obvious threat. They are one of the two central mechanisms propelling inflation in Latin America, where the degree of protection and the degree of concentration are both very high; and we have seen that Eastern European economies are even more monopoly-ridden. Hence, price reforms must be accompanied by radical antimonopoly measures.[17] Yet note that in Latin America antimonopoly measures have been timid and singularly unsuccessful. Nationalistic ideologies work against expanding foreign competition, which is particularly paradoxical given that the great mass of monopolies are multinationals anyway. Often the feeble attempts to pursue industrial policies have perpetuated the monopolistic structure of the economies. The danger in combating monopolies by lowering protection is that it will cause massive unemployment, while fighting them through legislation turns out to be ineffective, since they seem to perpetuate themselves even without explicit collusion. Hence, the monopolistic structure of the economy inherited from the prereform system is likely to continue to drive prices up.

Government deficits are in my view an even greater threat. Again, they play a crucial role in propelling inflation in Latin America. The Argentine case is extreme, but as such it serves as a memento. In Argentina, the state has hovered for several years now on the verge of bankruptcy. It survives financially only by continually refinancing its debt, and the only way it can find lenders is by paying higher and higher interest rates. It announces every few months spectacular measures designed to stop this spiral, but it is incapable of acting on the underlying causes. The main reason the state is bankrupt is that it is incapable of collecting revenues; instead of taxing, it borrows from those whom it could tax. In turn, as Lopez (1990) reports, lending to the state is the most lucrative economic activity in Argentina.

Can this situation be avoided by countries not yet caught in this vicious

[17] These are not simple to introduce. It turned out that in Poland the pressure groups that most vigorously defended their interests were peak associations of retail trade "cooperatives." The parliament passed a law making it illegal for such cooperatives to associate, but they quickly turned into private firms and continue to function as before. On the other hand, competition does eat away at monopoly rents: Producers sell direct to consumers, very often on the streets in front of the stores.

cycle? In my view, the answer is to a large extent unknowable. The budgetary predictions that governments can make at the moment of adopting the bitter-pill strategy can be no more than guesses. Governments can predict neither their revenues nor the expenditures to which they are legally committed. Revenues – from taxation, nontax charges, and their own activities – depend on the level of demand and the efficacy of tax collection, and at least the former is to a large degree unpredictable when structural reforms are launched. Expenditures – mainly those for income maintenance – depend on the effect of reforms on income levels and their distribution, again unpredictable at the moment when inflation rockets up to several hundred percent and firms close under the pressure of competition. Consider one example. The Polish government committed itself to paying unemployment compensation at the level of 70 percent of previous wages. But the estimates of what unemployment would be after a few months of reform varied between 300,000 and 4,000,000 people, a factor of 13. In fact, no one knew how much there would be. And this also means that no one knew the amount of revenue the government could collect. Hence, it is likely that the government will find that to fulfill its statutory obligations it must run deficits that exceed the planned targets and that as a result it must raise interest rates and print money.[18]

The role of foreign aid thus seems crucial. Stabilization funds counteract the inertial effects of deficits. The open question is whether the amounts are sufficient. If deficits set in and stabilization funds are insufficient, the only way to prevent inertial inflation is to reduce expenditures. Whether this is politically feasible is discussed below.

Suppose, then, that prices are deregulated and protection is lowered to induce competition. Then many firms and activities will go under. Both supply and demand will temporarily decline. The effect on price dynamics cannot be determined in general terms; it depends on the structure and the international competitiveness of the particular economy. If supply declines faster than demand, an inertial mechanism will appear.

In summary, the crucial question concerning a one-shot price deregulation is whether inertial mechanisms can be avoided. These inertial mechanisms can consist of wage pressures, monopoly pricing, government defi-

---

[18] Indeed, the Mazowiecki government in Poland, which had religiously professed its commitment to a balanced budget, when confronted with political pressure decided six months after its program had been launched to increase social expenditures at the cost of tolerating a deficit.

cits, and lags in supply. The Latin American experience leads to pessimistic conclusions. Antimonopoly measures turn out to be politically difficult – governments are vulnerable to pressure from large firms – and socially costly – they may require reduction of protection and cause unemployment. Government deficits are difficult to avoid, since reduction of spending is often politically unfeasible. In general, as Hirschman noted a long time ago, inflation is a political phenomenon. Whether a stable level of moderate inflation can be maintained depends largely on the willingness of political forces to wait out the transitional costs.

If inertial mechanisms do take effect governments can revert to anti-inflationary "shocks": freezing prices, wages, or profits. The experience of such treatments has been mixed: Neither the Plan Austral nor its offspring, the Plano Cruzado, nor the successive *pacotes* have worked longer than a few months, and pent-up pressures exploded with a vengeance each time. Such treatments are conceived as buying time for structural reforms, but in Argentina and Brazil they have not in fact been accompanied by such reforms. In Mexico and Bolivia, and for specific reasons in Israel, anti-inflationary shocks have been effective. In the context of the bitter-pill strategy, they may be necessary but politically very costly: Since the strategy is to pass as quickly as possible from a system of controlled to market prices, a freeze signals a suspension of reforms. Moreover, freezing prices and wages at whatever happen to be their current relative levels induces allocative inefficiency and reintroduces the mechanisms of political bargaining. Hence, from the economic point of view, freezes are no more than a palliative. Politically, they may respond to popular demand for slowing down the reforms, but they also weaken the determination to suffer through the period of adjustment.

Inflation is thus likely to follow a trajectory pernicious from the political point of view. The initial burst does not diminish, and it may increase, welfare. Yet if inertia sets in, inflation will linger. And if the government responds with a freeze, political confidence in reforms may be undermined.

*Unemployment of capital and labor.* The purpose of reforms is to transform the economic structure from one that is administratively regulated, monopolistic, and protected to one that reflects domestic preferences and both domestic and international opportunity costs. If these two structures differ – and they do, for otherwise no reforms would be needed – a transition to market mechanisms must cause some activities to be undertaken at a modified scale, some capital stock that is not fully depreciated to be physically abandoned, and some labor services to be withdrawn from their current employment. Unless these adjustments occur instantaneously, temporary unemployment of capital and labor must ensue, and the level of output will decline.

Why would transitional unemployment occur? First, in economies that are protected and monopolistic, the only way to rationalize the allocation of producer goods is to let the world market determine relative prices. Using world prices as a proxy for fixing internal prices is not enough; these prices may reflect opportunity costs elsewhere, but if opportunities are never exploited, resource allocation remains irrational. Steel may be cheaper than aluminum on the world market, but it makes no sense to price it lower in a country that never buys steel or sells aluminum. Hence, a true capital goods market must be built, and this means that tariff barriers must be lowered and other protectionist devices abolished. And since some activities and some firms involved in them are inefficient by international standards, activities will be abandoned, and firms will go under.

Second, the effect of internal competition and the effect of a sudden change of relative prices will be the same. Some activities are undertaken in administered economies only because they are mandated or subsidized and firms do not internalize their full costs. Elimination of subsidies will drive them out.

Note that some plants will simply close down and scrap their capital stock: It will have a zero price given the opportunity costs. Some other plants will be streamlined and reorganized to engage in new activities.

Agriculture is a case that merits separate attention. The bitter-pill strategy, when taken to its Polish extreme, risks destroying this sector. For various reasons, the rate of return to agricultural activities tends everywhere in the world to be lower than to industry and services. Agriculture is minutely regulated and heavily subsidized in all the developed capitalist countries. Hence, eliminating subsidies to agricultural outputs while introducing competitive markets in agricultural inputs creates a major danger to the entire sector. Moreover, this danger is compounded by food aid from abroad. Such aid may be needed to defend the urban population during the period of transition, and it is useful to counteract inertial inflation, but it imposes on the domestic agricultural sector competition it may not survive.

Third, unemployment of capital and labor may result from wage pressure. This is not, however, a specifically transitional effect. Moreover, the question of whether unemployment is due to wage pressure is a matter of continuing controversy even under stable developed capitalism.

Finally, one source of transitional labor unemployment is specific to command economies. It is well known that these economies overemploy. Since supplies arrive at firms in a highly arrhythmic fashion and the firms are concerned to fulfill the plan, they tend to hoard labor. If they cease to do so, they will reduce employment.

Lowering protection, introducing competition, giving in to wage pressure, and eliminating labor hoarding will cause some capital stock to be abandoned, some economic activities to be undertaken at a lower rate, and some workers to be laid off. The magnitude of these effects depends on the structure of the particular economy and the international economic conditions in which the reforms are undertaken. For all practical purposes, these magnitudes are probably unpredictable. Estimates that per capita GNP would fall by 20 percent in Hungary and Poland in 1990 were nothing but guesses.[19] The only way to proceed is to plunge in and see what happens.

The central question is again whether unemployment will be transitional, but now the issue is not one of inertia but of new sources of capital and of new activities replacing the old ones. Administered economies, particularly in Eastern Europe, had a seriously underdeveloped service sector and a virtual absence of petty entrepreneurship. State monopoly extended to car mechanics, and state regulation stifled street vendors. Hence, a large reservoir of initiative and employment is available, and it may be liberated to replace the activities abandoned. Yet this is not enough.

Suppose that financial markets exist, so that firms that go bankrupt are purchased by someone else and the capital stock that has more than scrap value is reemployed. Suppose that labor markets operate with little friction and manpower programs quickly retrain the laid-off workers. Finally, suppose that the whip of unemployment increases labor productivity and the democratization of credit stimulates petty entrepreneurship. Under such conditions, the economic structure adjusts quickly, and unemployment rapidly declines.

Clearly, the role of markets is crucial in determining whether the adjustment will occur. Without financial markets, unprofitable firms can only be

---

[19] In fact, output (at least the output that is officially recorded) fell by 35 percent in Poland after six months of the Balcerowicz plan.

closed down, and their capital stock can only be scrapped. Without credit markets, formation of new firms will be rare. Without labor markets and manpower programs, structural unemployment will be enormous. Yet even this is not the whole story, since the effects of structural reforms cannot be divorced from changes in the forms of property. Two questions must be asked: (1) What forms of property are likely to emerge? (2) What will their effect on employment, investment, and labor productivity be? Let me caution immediately that the answer to neither question is apparent, for reasons discussed in the preceding chapter. Even if everyone suspects that forms of property do have effects on the performance of firms, we are far from having an endogenous theory of the firm, a theory that would explain why particularly types of firms emerge in terms of their relative performance.

The only property transformation associated with reform in several different countries is the privatization of state enterprises, including some public utilities. Under the impetus of international financial institutions, privatization has been an almost universal ingredient in recent reforms. I do not think that the selling of public firms can be justified by the criterion of efficiency; efficiency could be improved by introducing competition among state firms without privatizing. The motive for privatization is to fill the state treasury, and so it is an appealing step for any deficit-ridden government.[20]

But what does it mean, to privatize? Suppose the state sells all or most of its productive assets; what property structure can be expected to emerge? Note first that many forms of property may appear. Once decisions about resource allocation are decentralized and material rewards are linked to performance, the question of property becomes threefold: Who decides, who produces, and who benefits? Answers to these questions no longer distinguish just two, or even three, forms of property: state, cooperative, and private. Let me list some possibilities:[21]

1. The state firm that pays wages according to some centrally determined pay scale and has no right to invest out of its own revenue or

[20] Several authors make this point in Vernon 1988.

[21] A theoretically motivated classification of ownership forms by Hansmann (1988) distinguishes firms as (1) investor-owned, (2) consumer-owned, (3) worker-owned, and (4) without owners (not-for-profit). He demonstrates that in the United States the incidence of these forms differs substantially across sectors. He explicitly ignores state ownership.

to borrow on capital markets. This is the traditional socialist firm – in China today and in Poland before 1982.

2. The state firm that makes autonomous decisions. This firm is owned by the state, which is financially responsible for it (such a firm can be closed down but cannot go bankrupt). It may or may not pay taxes.

3. The public firm that makes autonomous decisions and is owned by the state but is financially autonomous, that is, can go bankrupt and pays taxes in the same way as private firms.[22]

4. The "cross-owned" corporation. This is a Hungarian proposal according to which public corporations would be owned by one another.

5. The "public bodies" corporation. Again, a Hungarian proposal according to which all organizations and associations thus far on the state budget would instead become owners of for-profit enterprises.

6. The "social" corporation. This firm is controlled by boards of directors that include representatives of employees, of the government, and of the public. It must disburse all residual income.

7. The cooperative in which all employees and only employees are members. Members cannot be expelled or suspended.

8. The cooperative that employs nonmembers who receive wages but do not share in surpluses.

9. The cooperative in which all employees are members but where some shareholders do not work for the firm.[23]

10. The investor-owned publicly held firm.

11. The investor-owned privately held firm.

. . . Mixtures.

Now, one striking feature of the reforms is that, while they are driven by highly idealized blueprints of competitive markets, the property structure is emerging spontaneously, not guided by any design. In fact, governments have been trying to sell public enterprises to whoever would buy them.

Indeed, the process has thus far involved a fair amount of corruption. In

---

[22] Note that in each of the state firms the management can be appointed by the state, or the state may delegate this property right to the employees.

[23] On the difficulties of defining a cooperative, see Elster and Moene 1989.

the last months of its tenure, the Chilean dictatorship sold some firms to members of the military and to civilian politicians on terms that raise suspicion. In Poland, a full-fledged process of "appropriation" of the nomenklatura has unfolded as factory managers and other members of the bureaucracy developed ways of putting their hands on state property. As Tarkowski (1989) put it, they converted from being apparatchiks into being entrepreneurchiks.

Whatever property structure emerges as the result of privatization, it will be largely by default. Wholesale plans for selling state property are simply unrealistic. The savings of households and of domestic private firms are minuscule in relation to any reasonable estimate of the value of the public sector. In Poland, private savings amounted to about one-third of GNP, or about 8 percent of the capital stock, by the end of 1989, and the numbers cannot be very different elsewhere. Foreign buyers look attractive from the economic point of view, but nationalistic reactions set in quickly. "You're selling the country out to foreigners" is an accusation no government can withstand. Hence, a large sector of the economy may remain in state hands because there are no buyers.

The alternative to selling is some kind of free, subsidized, or credit-financed distribution to employees, to managers, or to the public. One Hungarian blueprint, for example, was to transfer the ownership of state firms to all bodies now subsidized by the state budget: local governments, universities, voluntary associations, and so forth. In Czechoslovakia, a popular proposal was to distribute to all citizens shares in mutual funds that would hold the stock of privatized companies. Another alternative, for which there was a fair amount of support in Poland, was to sell some of the shares to employees on credit. In any case, it seems likely that a large employee-owned sector will emerge, particularly in industry.

The spontaneous nature of property transformations is well illustrated by the peregrinations of the Lenin Shipyard in Gdansk, the cradle of Solidar-ność. The last communist government found that the firm was unprofitable and decided simply to close it down. In defense of their interests, workers began looking for a private buyer and found a candidate in a Polish-American millionaire. But the group of German experts she employed to assess the value of the shipyard found that it was worth almost nothing, and the transaction did not materialize. At this stage, workers exerted pressure on the new, postcommunist, government to turn the shipyard into an employee-owned firm and to extend credit for the transfer of ownership. This is where matters stand as this text is being written.

According to current plans, if the shipyard does end up in the hands of employees, employment will be reduced by 60 percent, some sections of the plant will be abandoned, and new customers will be sought. Would the same happen if the state had remained the owner? Would it if the firm had been sold to an American millionaire? The system that is likely to emerge as a result of privatization will still combine a large state sector, perhaps a sizable employee-owned sector, and a mixture of large and small private firms. Whether this mixture will behave differently from the mixed economies that we know is anyone's guess; we still do not know enough about the effects of ownership on firm performances.

Since the property structure remains to be determined, and since we know little about the effects of different mixtures of property forms on firm performance, all predictions concerning the dynamic of investment, employment, and technological innovation remain tenuous. Even if we assume that the new property structures will behave in the same way as the mixed economies that we do know from experience, many imponderables remain concerning the feasibility of creating markets. Financial markets are not easy to establish when there are no savings; labor markets will not operate when there is no housing market. Credit markets everywhere discriminate against venture entrepreneurs, since they have no collateral.

Yet, if the bitter pill is in fact implemented, the trajectory of output and employment is likely to correspond to the politically more tolerable pattern of quick decline and gradual recovery. If the lowering of protection and price deregulation are brutal to begin with, their effects should be immediate. Afterward, unless the government induces a recession to combat inflation, a recovery, even if a very slow one, should set in.

*Allocative inefficiencies.* Even if in the long run reforms would end up improving allocative efficiency, they induce transitional misallocations. As Comisso (1988) argued concerning the Hungarian experience, "the problem lay not simply in a poorly planned or improperly implemented reform, but in the shape of the industrial structure that had evolved prior to the reform." She pointed out that in the presence of monopolies, absence of financial markets, and an unclear property structure the onset of reforms may increase the misallocation of resources.

One reason is that reforms increase uncertainty: Things are in flux, and no one knows what will happen. Under such conditions, firms will increase their preference for liquidity (see Vickers 1987), and investment will decline.[24] Another reason is that several markets, in particular futures markets, are missing.

My only comment concerns the ideological credo that guides the present reforms. Note that the very term "reform" has in the last few years become synonymous with a transition from an administered to a market economy. Twenty years ago this term conjured up distribution of land to peasants in Latin America or tinkering with the planning system in Eastern Europe. Today it is tantamount to the reign of markets.

Markets are the only efficient mechanism we know of for allocating resources. But the assumption that if individuals internalize the costs and benefits of their decision everyone will respond to price stimuli is nothing but an article of faith. Powerful cultural barriers must be broken and well-entrenched habits must be eroded if people are to behave like market actors. To cite just one piece of evidence, it takes a 20 to 30 percent difference in expected rates of return plus some other conditions to persuade peasants to change crops (Shapiro and Taylor 1989: 12). Modernization, the process by which individuals became acculturated to market relations, took decades or longer in Western Europe. Moreover, whereas, as Lenin once remarked, any cook can be taught to administer a socialist economy, the market economy is a world of accountants, stockbrokers, investment planners, and financial wizards. It takes time for cooks to become MBAS.

One structural bottleneck of the Polish planned economy is the food processing industry. Every June the supply of strawberries is almost infinite; a few weeks later the berries that have not been eaten or processed by households rot. Their price in June is very low; demand for frozen or canned fruit is high in the winter. Will individual entrepreneurs respond to this opportunity, guided by a rational price system? Perhaps they will if they can transport the strawberries from farm to factory, if they can store the product, if they can communicate with potential buyers. Now they

---

[24] A cousin of mine used to breed chickens in Poland. When prices were deregulated, the feed became excessively costly and interest rates went up. His main consideration in deciding what to do next concerned reducing uncertainty; as he said to me, "The prices of inputs I know today, but who knows what the prices of outputs will be when I am ready to sell?" He decided to go in for cucumbers because their growing cycle is the shortest.

cannot: There are few roads, few trucks, no telephones that work. Will these be made available as a result of the profit-maximizing behavior of individuals? This is what the monetarist credo leads us to believe. But massive reallocation of resources has not occurred spontaneously anywhere; it was the state that made it happen.

In several capitalist countries in which private entrepreneurship was feeble – Brazil, France, Mexico, South Korea – the state not only led the accumulation of capital but in time created a local bourgeoisie. Eastern European countries have no local bourgeoisie, and the prevailing mood is so radically antistatist that the state cannot play the same role in the near future. Capitalists are expected to mushroom in the market.

Moreover, one difference in favor of Latin American countries is their longer exposure to market relations and the existence of some dynamic modern capitalist firms that can serve as models. In Eastern Europe, this experience is limited and knowledge of markets is scant. In the 1970s Poles tried to sell consumer durables in the West without offering any after-sale services, and they predictably failed. Today, my informal conversations indicate, they are ready to do the same; they still believe that if a product is competitive it will sell itself.

This is not an argument against market-oriented reforms. But one should expect that transitional allocative inefficiencies will result from intangible factors: missing markets, lack of knowledge about the way markets operate, and learning involved in property transformations, and the absence of local capitalists.

### Distributional effects

The transition to another system would be agreed to by unanimous vote if everyone expected to be better off under the new system or had a strong normative commitment. If individuals care only about their welfare, two conditions suffice: (1) The new system is more productive, and (2) the distribution of welfare under the new system preserves the relative differences of the old one.[25] If people have conceptions of justice that lead

---

[25] Note that Marx thought that revolutions are Pareto-superior moves because they occur when the relations of production fetter the development of productive forces to such an extent that the postrevolutionary system liberates enormous productive potential. Schumpeter thought the transition to socialism would be Pareto-superior because it would occur at a time when there would be no capitalists to speak of, only employees of capital, and these managers would be equally needed under socialism.

them to have preferences over mechanisms of distribution independent of their outcomes, they might unanimously vote for a system that is more productive and that satisfies some norms of equity, fairness, or justice violated under the current system.[26] Yet even if revolutions unfurl universalistic slogans, they alter distributions of income and welfare. If any group expects to be worse off in absolute terms under the new system, it is likely to oppose the transition. And it is not apparent that normative commitments always operate to support structural transformation.

But our question is whether distributional effects undermine the reform process even if the steady state of the post-reform system were to be Pareto-superior to the old one and even if there were no envy. There are good reasons to expect that transitional distributional effects will be pronounced and that changes in absolute consumption levels will be volatile and perhaps even life-threatening. Some of these changes are easily predictable; others may be unforeseen.

Some distributional effects are easy to predict, as are the social bases of opposition. Many higher-level bureaucrats held their positions because of the nomenklatura system – political control over the most important administrative positions. If they have no professional skills that can be gainfully employed in the market economy and if they did not use their public positions to amass private fortunes, they find themselves out on the street. Of course, unskilled workers are the ones most likely to suffer from the onset of unemployment. In turn, public sector employees lose jobs as a result of reductions in public spending and the streamlining of the government bureaucracy. Note that in Latin America public sector unions are in the forefront of resistance to market-oriented reforms. Hence, the antireform coalition is likely to comprise bureaucrats without professional training or private incomes, unskilled workers, and public employees, and this is indeed what is shown by analyses of Eastern Europe (Bruszt 1988; Kolarska-Bobinska 1988; Zaslavskaya 1988).[27]

Yet who swallows the pill depends on the relations of political forces. Elimination of subsidies will inevitably hurt large firms, and layoffs will inevitably hurt unskilled workers and public employees; this much cannot

[26] For example, Habermas (1975) has argued, and recent Polish survey data confirm, that people may be more tolerant of inequalities engendered by markets than by administrative decisions when these are seen as arbitrary.

[27] Note that Chinese workers opposed both what they called corruption (bureaucracy-generated wealth) and profiteering (market-generated wealth).

be avoided. But reduction of public deficits can be achieved in two ways: by restricting expenditures or by raising revenues via taxation. The crucial question is whether the particular state is capable, politically and administratively, of collecting tax revenue from those who can afford it and delivering welfare services or maintaining the incomes of those who are hurt by the market. Reforms need not have pronounced regressive effects if the state can collect taxes, efficiently deliver welfare services, and maintain incomes.[28]

The system for welfare delivery and income maintenance has to be built from scratch. The welfare system in market economies is designed to protect people against misfortunes they suffer in the market. Market incomes are assessed, revenues are taxed or otherwise retained, welfare services are delivered, and some minimal incomes are maintained. Hence, a completely new system must be built in Eastern Europe; a bureaucracy that used to command the economy must be transformed overnight into one that collects and transfers incomes. A huge tanker must be turned around in one sweep.

Under these conditions, large categories of people may fall overboard; reforms may turn out to be life-threatening for those who have no income from employment or property and who are not yet assisted by the state. Such people cannot wait for reforms to work themselves out. True, they may have little political power, particularly since they are likely to comprise the aged, peasants who are geographically isolated, and people with the least education. But they constitute a potential ally for other sectors that suffer from the distributive effects of reforms.

*Conclusion*

Whatever their long-term consequences, in the short run reforms are likely to cause inflation, unemployment, and resource misallocation as well as to generate volatile changes in relative incomes. These are not politically popular consequences anywhere. And under such conditions, democracy in the political realm works against economic reforms. In Comisso's (1988) words, a hierarchy may reemerge because the market failed to deliver efficient results.

[28]A careful study by Cortés and Rubalcava (1990) shows that, while average income did fall, inequality did not increase in Mexico in the aftermath of the 1982 adjustment program, contrary to widespread belief.

# Political dynamics of reforms: a model

Both political reactions to reform and their eventual success or failure depend not only on their economic effects but also on political conditions. In November 1987 a program of reforms failed to win majority support in a referendum organized by the communist government in Poland. Yet economic reforms by the postcommunist government enjoyed overwhelming support. The program was almost the same; it was the government that changed. Hence, the question is not only how deep and wide is the valley of transition but also which political forces are most apt to traverse it. This is the question examined here.

Three somewhat stylized facts organize this analysis. First, it seems that reforms are almost invariably launched by surprise. Second, they often generate widespread initial support that erodes as social costs set in. Last, reforms tend to follow a stop-and-go pattern.

## The choice of strategies

To consider how reform strategies are chosen, compare first the three paths of consumption portrayed in Figure 4.2. Under the radical strategy, path $R$, consumption declines rapidly and profoundly and recovers early. The radical strategy is a "bitter pill," adopted with the belief that anything that tastes that bad must be good for you.[29] Under the gradual strategy, path $G$, consumption falls slowly, does not diminish as much as under the radical strategy, and returns to the initial level later.[30] Once the initial level has

---

[29]   The best example of radical reform before the Polish Balcerowicz plan of 1989 was the Bolivian package of 1985. According to one of its designers (Cariaga 1990: 43ff.), it included imposition of an indirect tax on fuel; devaluation of the currency; an increase in the rates charged by state-owned enterprises to the level of their international counterparts; wideranging tax reform; elimination of all subsidies, including those on food and foodstuffs, as well as those in the guise of low rates and fares charged by the state-owned companies; elimination of all illegal bonuses paid in cash and kind; a freeze on the salaries of all public-sector employees; tight fiscal discipline; reduction of tariffs to a single uniform rate with no exceptions whatsoever; and, one year later, the closing down of mining operations.

[30]   One example of gradual reform was Władysław Baka's program in Poland. His plan was to introduce markets or other decentralized mechanisms with regard to investment goods but not to touch the final goods markets. Only after investment was rationalized and output increased was the consumer market to be deregulated. Since supply would increase while nominal incomes were still being controlled, the eventual deregulation of consumer prices would not cause inflation. The obvious problem with this strategy is that, even if it is eventually effective, it requires time. Moreover, this strategy is vulnerable to reversals; witness the repeated instances in which Eastern European economies were recentralized after initial attempts to introduce financial autonomy for firms.

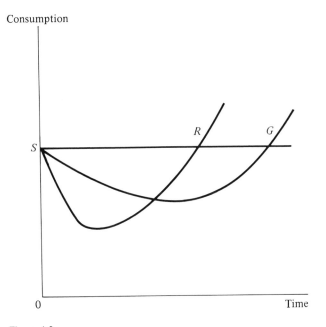

Figure 4.2

been reached again, marking the end of the transition, the economy grows at the same rate under the two strategies. These paths are deliberately constructed so that the social cost is higher under the radical strategy, where social cost is defined as the cumulative decline in consumption during the period of transition.[31] If neither reform strategy is adopted, consumption remains at the status quo level, $S$.[32]

The choice among these alternatives depends on the attitudes of three actors: technocrats, politicians in office, and the population. I assume that people want to eat, technocrats want to succeed, and politicians want to

[31] If the gradual strategy is so slow that its cumulative social cost is higher than that of the radical strategy, then the gradual strategy will never be chosen, and the entire problem reduces to a choice between a radical strategy and the status quo.

[32] Here is a numerical example. Take the initial level of consumption as 100, so that $R(0) = G(0) = S(0) = 100$. Under the radical strategy, consumption follows the following path: 70, 50, 60, 70, 80, 90, 100 (end of transition), 110, 120, . . . , +10 during each new period. Under the gradual strategy, the path is 95, 90, 85, 80, 75, 70, 80, 90, 100 (end of transition), . . . , +10 during each new period. Under the status quo, $S(t) = 100$ for all $t$. Total consumption during the first ten periods is $C(R) = 850$, $C(G) = 865$, $C(S) = 1,000$. Social costs are $-180$ for the radical strategy, $-145$ for the gradual strategy and, by definition, 0 for the status quo.

enjoy support.[33] Let us examine their preferences concerning reforms, beginning with the population. Would people ever agree voluntarily to suffer transitional costs; would they ever vote for a party that proposes to lower their consumption? And would they ever opt for a strategy that engenders higher costs than its more gradual alternatives?

There are several reasons why under some conditions people may support a radical program. Standard assumptions suffice to identify such conditions. Suppose that individuals maximize the present value of their future consumption, discounting the future on the grounds of risk.[34] Voters examine the consumption stream they face under each strategy: status quo, gradual, and radical. If they are confident of the success of the particular strategy, they value the consumption they will receive after many periods almost as much as their present consumption. If they have little confidence in the strategy, they attach small value to distant outcomes and concentrate on the most proximate ones. They opt for the strategy they value most given the projected consumption stream and their confidence in the future under this strategy.[35]

Given these assumptions, people will vote for the party that proposes to traverse the valley if they believe that their future after reforms will be sufficiently superior to the status quo to compensate for temporary deterioration. And if voters are highly confident about the future, they choose the radical strategy, although it entails a higher social cost than the gradual one. If the decisive voter is confident that reforms will succeed, the ranking of strategies will be $R > G > S$.[36] If this voter is somewhat less certain about the future, the ranking will be $G > R > S$. As confidence declines further, the preference ordering passes through $G > S > R$ to $S > G > R$: If voters have no confidence in reforms, they opt for the status quo.

[33] Obviously, technocrats and politicians also want to eat. But they are quite certain to eat enough even if reforms engender profound social costs. I say this to avoid a paradox inherent in Downs-like support-maximizing models, in which voters care about policy outcomes and politicians do not.

[34] This is not to exclude pure time preferences. I ignore them because they have no effect on comparative results unless we have a theory about the way they are formed.

[35] There are several other reasons why people may prefer a short period of excruciating pain to a long stretch of a gnawing one. The assumption on which I rely here is maximizing the present value of future consumption, the classic (von Neumann–Morgenstern) grounds. Alternative assumptions are discussed below.

[36] The notation $X(t) > Y(t)$ stands for "$X$ is preferred to $Y$ at time $t$." We are now at the initial period, $t = 0$. Under our illustrative paths – and one can think of many others – voters opt for the radical strategy over the gradual one and over the status quo as long as the rate of discount is less than 12 percent per period; they prefer $G > R > S$ as long as the rate of discount is less than 12 percent but no more than 16 percent; they reject reforms if they discount the future at a rate faster than at 18 percent per period.

Hence, radical reforms, though they engender high social costs, are not necessarily always imposed on the population by technocrats and politicians. If people trust the government, voters may opt for the "horse therapy," to use the Polish description of the Balcerowicz plan. Indeed, evidence from a number of countries, including Poland (Balcerowicz plan), Brazil (Plano Collor), Argentina (under Menem), and even Peru (under Fujimori), indicates that reform packages enjoy support when they are launched even if they cause a decline in the standard of living.[37]

Yet suppose that voters opt for either reform program over the status quo but prefer gradual to radical reform. Will the gradual program be chosen?

For the economic team, to use the current terminology, success is defined in terms of realizing its blueprint for transforming the economy, of achieving the goals of stability, solvency, and efficiency. They want results, and they are not particularly concerned about social costs. Hence, they prefer radical reforms to gradual ones and to the status quo. If they are at all concerned about political reactions, they still want to proceed as far as possible before these reactions set in. In the words of an OECD statement, *Transition from the Command to a Market Economy* (1990: 9), "While a gradualist approach may cause lesser social tensions, a long period of moderate reforms entails the danger that both reformers and the population will 'become tired of reforms,' as they do not seem to bring visible changes. Also during a long period of reforms various anti-reform and other lobbies may mobilize their forces and may gradually strangle the reform process." Or, as Nelson (1984: 108) observed, "Advocates of 'shock treatment' are convinced that public tolerance for sacrifice is brief and that the courage of politicians is likewise limited. If the adjustment process is too gradual, opposition will gather and the process will be derailed."

---

[37] In Poland, an overwhelming proportion of the population ($\pm 90$ percent) supported the Mazowiecki government in spite of the drastic deterioration in living conditions during the first months of the new economic program. Moreover, 60 to 70 percent of respondents stated their readiness to suffer the costs of reform (*Gazeta Wyborcza*, various issues). In Brazil, 68 percent expressed confidence in President Collor when his plan was announced (*Latin American Weekly Report*, WR–90–37, 27 September 1990, p. 11). In Peru, President Fujimori suffered an immediate decline of support when he betrayed his supporters by embracing the bitter-pill strategy, but the minister of the economy who directed the adjustment program enjoyed the confidence of 58 percent of respondents (ibid., WR–90–36, 20 September 1990, p. 2). Spanish survey data indicate that workers were willing to sacrifice wage demands expressly in order to consolidate democracy. Moreover, while workers were not willing to moderate wage demands in exchange for a direct economic quid pro quo in the form of employment or investment, they were ready to do so in exchange for democracy in the political realm.

Elected politicians are in a more ambivalent situation. They sense that reforms are inevitable, but they expect popular opposition. Politicians have only a limited understanding of reform programs; these are pretty technical matters.[38] They experience pressure from international lenders, they fear that their country will be left out of the new international division of labor, and they are concerned about growing poverty. Hence, they have a sense that something drastic must be done. Yet politicians are concerned about social peace and popular support. What they decide, therefore, depends on the one hand on their confidence in the economic team and on the other on their theories about popular reactions. My conjecture is that they think as follows. They know that some measures are certain to provoke fierce resistance, and those they try to avoid.[39] Otherwise, they care most that the economy should be on the upward curve when the next election comes; they believe that once things turn around, voters will be optimistic and will forget past deprivations. Hence, politicians opt for radical strategies whenever they trust the assurances of technocrats that the economy will turn around before the next date on the institutional calendar.

If politicians are persuaded before elections that reforms are necessary, they will be tempted to manipulate the agenda, offering initially a choice between one reform program and the status quo or to keep their economic plans vague until they get into office. But even if the victorious candidates campaigned against reforms, criticizing them for their social cost, they may still surprise everyone once they are in office by adopting a radical strategy. While all kinds of considerations may be insufficient to propel them onto the path of reforms, one is irresistible. If the government is bankrupt – if it runs a deficit and cannot borrow money – all politicians, regardless of their ideological orientations, electoral programs, and social bases, will be willing to do what it takes to restore creditworthiness.

In Bolivia in 1985, Victor Paz Estenssoro was seen as the populist candidate against Hugo Banzer. The election took place on 15 July; no candidate won a majority, and the Congress elected Paz on 6 August. Two weeks later, in a speech entitled "Bolivia Is Dying," he announced the

---

[38] Nelson (1984: 104) reports on the basis of her study of five countries that "only a very small number of economic officials have the training to grasp complex and abstract economic relationships and the implications of alternative macro-economic policies. Furthermore, aspects of conventional stabilization and adjustment programs are counter-intuitive." See also Conaghan 1983.

[39] The evidence concerning IMF programs (Haggard 1986; Remmer 1986) shows that reduction of government spending – in practice, of public employment – is the target least frequently fulfilled.

most radical package of market-oriented reforms in the history of Latin America. In Argentina, Carlos Menem was vague about his economic policy throughout the 1989 presidential campaign, while leading everyone to expect he would behave like a Peronist. In fact, he wholeheartedly embraced a traditional anti-Peronist economic policy, including wholesale denationalization. In Brazil, all members of Congress, including the majority leader, Fernando Henrique Cardoso, were informed about the Plano Cruzado only when the president's decree reached the media (Sola 1990: 21). In Poland, the Mazowiecki government came into office in August 1989 as an aftermath of the Magdalenka agreements of April and the elections of June. The first glimpse of the economic program was given to the public on 29 September, and the program was formally presented by Balcerowicz during a press conference on 5 October. It differed drastically from the April agreements (for the text of those, see *Porozumienia Okraglego Stolu,* 1989). Indeed, the Solidarity leader in the Sejm, Bronislaw Gieremek, complained, "It is unacceptable that members of Parliament should find out from newspapers what the economic program of the government is" (Domaranczyk 1990: 193). In Hungary, the party that advocated radical reforms, SZDSZ, lost the election against the MDF, which presented a traditional centralizing posture. It now seems that the MDF will pursue market-oriented reforms.

Hence, reform programs tend to be adopted regardless of whether or not they are supported in elections. Candidates' stance in a campaign is a poor predictor of what they will do in office.

*The dynamic of popular support*

Even when people do support the radical treatment at the outset, the limited data we have indicate that this support erodes, often drastically, as social costs are experienced.[40] Opposition is expressed in public opinion surveys, elections, strikes, and, at times, riots.

---

[40] In Poland, 50.2 percent of respondents supported the Balcerowicz plan when it was adopted at the end of December 1989, and 14.2 percent were against it. By June 1990, 32 percent were for, 25 percent against (*Gazeta Wyborcza,* various issues). In Brazil, confidence in Collor fell from 68 percent in May, when his plan was announced, to 60 percent in September (*Latin American Weekly Report,* WR–90–37, 27 September 1990, p. 11), while positive views of his plan remained almost stable at around the 40 percent level, against 27 percent negative views (*Folha de S. Paulo,* 15 September 1990). The fall in support for Alan García in Peru, Raúl Alfonsín in Argentina, and the Plano Cruzado in Brazil was much more dramatic.

Why would people support a particular reform package at the onset and then turn against it? If one assumes that people initially supported the reform program on von Neumann–Morgenstern grounds, that is, they chose the program that maximized expected utility, the erosion of support can be explained only in terms of declining confidence in the success of reforms.

Confidence does play a crucial role in shaping popular reactions. People's evaluation of their future streams of consumption depends on how certain they feel that their consumption will in fact increase as a result of present sacrifices. They are willing to suffer in the short run if they believe in the long run. This confidence is to a large extent endogenous. The reason is that people do not know how costly and how long the transition will be. Structural transformations of the economy are a plunge into opaque waters: The people do not know where the bottom is and how long they will have to hold their breath. All they know is what they were told would happen and what is happening: whether they are still plunging or already emerging, whether things have turned around.

Confidence is a stock: It can be depleted and it can be accumulated. It can be eroded in two ways: by erroneous forecasts and by vacillations.

If politicians promise immediate improvements but consumption in fact declines, the competence of the government is put in question, and perhaps even its good faith. And note that technocrats have good reason to believe optimistic forecasts: They have to persuade politicians that the transition will not be too long or too costly. In turn, politicians find it difficult to campaign by promising that incomes will decline if they are elected; depression is anathema in most countries. The result is that politicians tend to make unrealistic promises about the immediate effects of reforms, and people soon learn that the government was either incompetent or dishonest.[41] To the best of my knowledge, no Latin American government, except for the one in Bolivia in 1985, prepared its population for a decline in incomes when it announced a reform package. Even in Poland, where the government was forthcoming about the prospective difficulties, the depression turned out to be much sharper than predicted. And when people learn not to trust the government, their confidence in the future declines and with it their support for reforms.

---

[41] Calvo (1989: 228) observed that to be effective, policy announcements have to be simple, but that simple policies are not credible with regard to many problems. "Some announcements," he concluded, "are not credible simply because they *are* incredible."

Vacillations are perhaps even more pernicious. If a government goes back on a particular reform package and then launches new programs, people, knowing that reforms have failed in the past, are less likely to believe they will succeed now. In Brazil, where people experienced the failure of three major and several minor reform programs, 75 percent of respondents thought that inflation would increase or remain the same when the fourth package, the Plano Collor, was launched (*Folha de S. Paulo,* 15 September 1990). This learning process affects the behavior of individuals as economic agents and as political actors. Firms and consumers learn to act on the expectation that reforms will fail; political forces learn not to publicize their support for reforms. Yet politicians have no choice but to vacillate. As we shall see, if they are concerned about the progress of reforms, their best bet is to adopt a radical strategy with full knowledge that they will have to moderate it under popular pressure: The optimal strategy is inconsistent. True, repression of the general strike in Bolivia in 1985 did persuade the population that the government was resolute, and parties supporting continued reform did win 65.4 percent of the vote in the next elections, in May 1989 (Cariaga 1990). But such resolve is risky, and not only for politicians; it is risky for democracy. Politicians concerned about popular support must abandon their initial resolve if they meet too much opposition.

If confidence is eroded, radical programs cannot be undertaken again under democratic conditions. Governments must first rebuild confidence. Under such conditions, which typically involve accelerating inflation, only gradual – more precisely, partial – reform can be undertaken. This is why heterodox stabilization programs, although they are often accompanied by announcements that structural reforms will follow, constitute attempts to accumulate confidence without subjecting people to the costs inherent in opening up the economy, reducing public employment, or increasing taxation. If stabilization packages are successful, they open the door to proceeding farther; if they fail, willingness to suffer transitional costs declines even more.

Declining confidence explains the erosion of support for reforms if people are assumed to maximize the expected utility of future consumption. But several alternative interpretations of their initial preference for a radical strategy lead to the conclusion that this support will erode even if confidence remains the same, just because actual costs are being experienced.

One interpretation is that people opted for a radical strategy seeking to commit themselves. Suppose that the status quo is terrible; people are fed up with the present system, whether because of hyperinflation or because of shortages. Yet people know that once their consumption falls below the status quo, they will be tempted to return to it. Then the radical strategy will be preferred because it creates irreversibility; it offers a clear break with the past. (Elster [1984] analyzed this kind of rationality.) But once the costs of reform set in, people do want to go back.

The second is that people may have distinct attitudes toward risk and intertemporal substitution of consumption (Kreps and Porteus 1978, 1979a and b). Suppose that people know that their consumption will follow the path $C, C, C, \ldots, C', C', C', \ldots$, where $C'$ is a lottery with the same expected value as the certain value of $C$, but they do not know at what time the switch from $C$ to $C'$ will occur.[42] It has been shown (Weil 1990: 32) that "lotteries in which uncertainty resolves early are less risky than late resolution lotteries with the same distribution of prizes." Hence, risk-averse individuals will prefer early resolution. They will prefer to see as early as possible what will happen to them as the result of reforms, and they will opt for radical reforms. But suppose that once the uncertainty is resolved, at least some people find that their condition has deteriorated sharply. They will prefer to return to the certain level $C$ they experienced before.

Finally, a third reason has been suggested by Loewenstein (1987), who cited experimental evidence to the effect that some people do not like waiting for a certain unpleasant event to occur. He argued that people value consumption separately from anticipation. When the event itself is "fleeting and vivid," anticipation dominates in evaluating consumption paths: Some people prefer to get it over with. Again, people opt for radical reforms because they do not like to wait knowing that they will have to experience hardships at some time or other; but once they experience the hardships, they do not like them.

These assumptions lead to the conclusion that people may prefer $R$ to $G$, but once $R$ is launched and costs are experienced, they change preferences,

----

[42] Imagine, for example, that you suffer from a constant level of pain. You know that at some time you will have to undergo an operation as a result of which you will either recover completely or will have to be confined to bed for a year: events that have the same expected value as the current pain.

opting for *G* or even *S*. Hence, the dynamic described below follows regardless of assumptions about popular support.

## The dynamic of reforms

Even if the initial strategy was adopted with a wide consensus, it is unlikely that the path of reform will be smooth, and it remains uncertain that the valley will be traversed. What can be shown is that radical programs are likely to advance farther than gradual ones even if voters prefer gradual strategies over radical ones. By "advance farther" I mean that more reforms are accomplished; that is, their announced goals are reached, and governments continue to pursue reform.[43]

Suppose that, depending on what the government decided, either gradual or radical reform has been launched. At fixed periods – say, each quarter – public opinion is read in some way (including noting strikes and riots) to see whether people want to continue on the current path or change to a different program.

Examine the situation at the end of the first period, $t = 1$. The path *GS* (to be read as "gradual to status quo ante") in Figure 4.3 represents abandoning gradual reforms in favor of a return to the status quo ante,[44] the

---

[43] I follow the approach of Nelson and her collaborators (1990: 336), who sought to explain "the degree to which policy decisions were carried out rather than economic outcomes of the measures taken." The reason I hesitate to use the term "success" is that the causal relation between reforms and the performance of the economy is not unambiguous. Williamson (1990: 406) shows that among ten Latin American countries that have pursued full or partial reform, four were growing in 1988–9, and six were stagnant or declining; among eleven countries that did not pursue reforms or had only recently undertaken them, one was growing, and ten were stagnant or declining. There is some correlation, but it is not overwhelming. Remmer (1986: 7) reports with regard to IMF Standby Programs that there is "only a moderate correlation between the implementation of IMF prescriptions and the achievement of desired economic results." Dornbusch (1990: 312) worries that successful stabilization programs in Mexico and Bolivia have failed to restore growth. One can think of at least three reasons why reforms may not unambiguously improve economic performance. First, there are exogenous events, for example the fall in the prices of Bolivian exports in 1986. Second, some reforms have as their stated objectives outcomes that involve a temporary deterioration of the economy. For example, the weeding out of inefficient firms by eliminating subsidies creates unemployment. Third, some reform measures may be badly designed and may have unintended consequences; see the Plano Cruzado in Brazil.

[44] Several reform programs aimed at decentralizing socialist economies were reversed when managers did not know what to do, and chaos ensued. Nelson (1990) lists the programs of Belaunde (Peru, January 1983 to March 1984), Kaunda (Zambia, December 1982 to May 1987), Sarney (Brazil, February 1986 to January 1987), and García (Peru, mid 1985 to mid 1987) as cases where reform collapsed.

Consumption

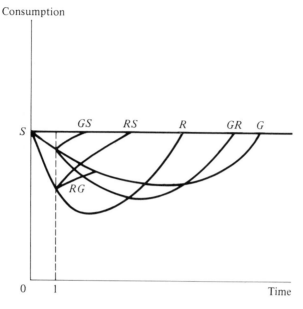

Figure 4.3

path *GR* represents an acceleration of reforms (switch from *G* to *R*),[45] the path *RS* stands for abandoning radical reforms for a return to the status quo ante, and the path *RG* portrays the effects of slowing down the reforms (shift from *R* to *G*).[46] The important assumption is that the return to the status quo ante is gradual; its pace depends on how far the old system has already been transformed. The following can be then shown to be true:[47]

(1) If at $t = 0$ people voted for *G* or *R* over *S* on grounds of maximizing expected utility, and if the rate of time preference remains the same, the return to the status quo ante will not be chosen at $t = 1$. But if confidence in the future has been undermined by whatever happened during the first

[45]Wałęsa launched his presidential campaign in Poland in May 1990 with the slogan "acceleration of reforms," specifically, privatization.

[46] Examples are innumerable. A typical situation is one in which the announced package consists of stabilization and some structural reforms, particularly a reduction in public employment, but only the stabilization part is implemented. In Poland, bankrupt firms were supposed to be closed down on 1 July 1990, but the government did not have the nerve to act on this part of its program.

[47] These results are based on reasoning about Figure 4.3 and numerical examples that satisfy the assumptions. These examples work with reasonable time paths of consumption and a wide range of time preferences. But I have not constructed a full-fledged model.

period, or if people changed preferences as they experienced costs, voters may prefer to abandon reforms rather than to continue. But since the radical strategy generated a profound transformation of the economy during the first period, the cost of turning back is greater than under the gradual program. Hence, it is possible that at $t = 1$ voters would vote for *GS* over continuing with *G* but for continuing with *R* over *RS*. Bridges have been burned; they would have to be reconstructed for steps to be retraced.[48]

(2) If voters preferred *G* to *R* at $t = 0$ but *R* was adopted, people will want to slow down the reforms at $t = 1$: $RG(1) > R(1)$. But even if $S(0) > G(0) > R(0)$, they may still prefer $RG(1)$ to $RS(1)$. Hence, if politicians respond to public opinion, reforms will be slowed at $t = 1$ but need not be abandoned. Moreover, even if $GS(1) > G(1)$ and $RG(1) > R(1)$, it does not necessarily follow that $GS(2) > G(2)$: At $t = 2$, the post-transition future is nearer, and the prospect of increased consumption may overwhelm the remaining transition costs. Reforms will again be slowed at $t = 2$, but they will not be abandoned. And so on.

(3) If reforms are not reversed at some time, they will not be reversed later. At some moment they pass through a point of no return. The sooner consumption bottoms out under the radical strategy, or, equivalently, the sooner the consumption level under the radical strategy exceeds (still declining) consumption under the gradual program, the earlier this point of no return occurs.

Conclusions are thus the following:

(1) If voters have a high degree of confidence that they will benefit in the future from the transitional sacrifice, and if this confidence remains unshaken during the transition, they will vote for the radical strategy to begin with and ratify this choice at each time. If confidence declines, or if the initial preference was not motivated by expected values, reforms will be slowed or temporarily reversed.

(2) If voters have only moderate confidence in the future, they will prefer gradual reforms to radical ones. If a gradual strategy is chosen under these conditions, it may be abandoned if confidence declines, whereas if a radical program is launched, it may be only slowed.

(3) If voters prefer gradual reforms, but radical reforms are proposed and launched, these may be reversed at the first voting opportunity. If they are

---

[48] An interesting case of burned bridges is the Collor plan. By freezing almost all assets, the government made certain that it would not be able to finance deficits by borrowing on the local market.

not reversed at this time, they will not be later. In turn, voters will prefer to slow down the reforms as long as consumption declines rapidly under the radical program.

These findings add up to a startling result. The strategy most likely to succeed is not the one that minimizes social costs. Radical programs are more likely to advance reforms farther under democratic conditions even if voters would have preferred to start with a more gradual strategy. Hence, if politicians are concerned about the progress of reforms, they have an incentive to impose a radical strategy even against popular preferences and even when they know that this strategy will have to be moderated under popular pressure. Their optimal strategy is inconsistent.

*The effect of income distribution*

Note, however, that so far we have treated all voters as if they were identical. Suppose that reforms are fair; that is, the transitional costs are identical for all individuals under each reform strategy: The time paths of consumption are determined only by the initial position. Such time paths are portrayed for three individuals in Figure 4.4a. If these voters have the same time preferences, then the vote at each time will be unanimous. But voter preferences are obviously not identical, for individuals may have different time preferences and may face different time paths of consumption under each reform strategy. And if reforms are to continue under democratic conditions, they must be supported from time to time by majority vote.

One way to analyze the dynamic of support for reforms would be to assume that the consumption paths facing all voters are identical, save for the initial level, but that individuals differ in their time preferences. Suppose that voter $W$ (wealthy) has no confidence in any reforms and prefers $S > G > R$; voter $M$ has some confidence, and his preferences are $G > R > S$; while voter $P$ (poor) is fed up with waiting and prefers $R > G > S$. Then, at $t = 0$ either $G$ or $R$ beats $S$ in pairwise majority voting, and $G$ beats $R$. If parties control the agenda in such a way as to offer only a choice of $R$ and $S$, $R$ beats $S$, and radical reforms are launched, with the subsequent dynamic analyzed above.

But reforms have not only aggregate but also profound distributional consequences; they affect the welfare of different categories differently. Suppose that voters have the same time preferences but that the consump-

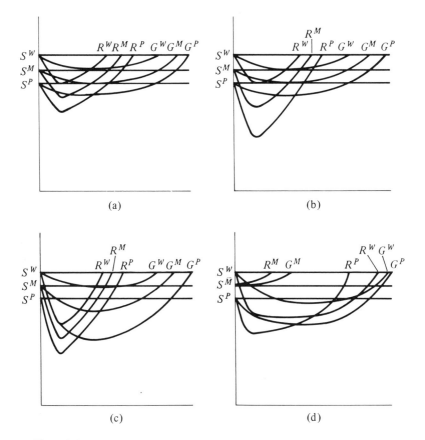

Figure 4.4

tion paths they face under each strategy differ. Examine the case, presented in Figure 4.4b, where radical reforms increase inequality, and the gradual strategy is fair. Then $W$ prefers the radical program over the gradual one; $P$ would be badly hurt by radical reforms and prefers gradual ones; and the outcome of majority rule depends on voter $M$, who is the median voter. Inversely, if radical reforms are fair, while gradual reforms increase inequality, as in Figure 4.4c, $W$ would vote for gradual reforms, and $P$ would vote for radical ones, while $M$ would again be decisive.

Hence, the distributional consequences of reforms matter for their political dynamics independently of their aggregate costs. Unfortunately, to venture beyond this truism would be an empty speculation. Structural reforms of economic systems alter class relations. Depending on their position in the old system, some people have good reason to expect that they will be worse off as far into the future as they can imagine; others, that they will benefit immediately from the reforms; still others, that their consumption will follow one of the patterns described above. Hence, while it makes sense to think that the futures people face under different reform programs depend on their position in the structure of the old system, the group with median income in the old economy need not have the median preference about reform strategies. Indeed, I have cited evidence to the effect that, at least in Eastern Europe, people with the highest and lowest incomes are likely to be hurt by radical reforms more than people with middle incomes in the old system. Let me merely offer two hunches:

(1) If groups with the highest incomes get hurt as a result of reforms, and sectors with middle incomes do well, as in Figure 4.4d, the decisive vote belongs to the poorest people. In this case, analysis of the preferences of the median voter, which is what we implicitly conducted in Figure 4.3, concerns those sectors of the population that are poor under the status quo ante. Since remaining in the old system means that their poverty will be perpetuated, they support a reform program. If the difference in their consumption paths under radical and gradual reforms is not too great, and if they have confidence in the government, they will initially support radical reforms; otherwise they support gradual ones, with the dynamic analyzed above.

(2) The entire analysis thus far has assumed that people consider the future. But reforms may be life-threatening to some sectors of the population. If consumption falls below some minimal level, they cannot wait for different strategies to work themselves out. Hence, political reactions may be subject to thresholds: Groups that fall under the level of absolute poverty because of reforms have to oppose them even if their future is radiant if they survive the reforms.

Are reforms politically easier or more difficult in countries that have a more egalitarian distribution of income? Let us analyze the political impact of reforms by comparing stylized cases, patterned after Brazil and the Soviet Union, of countries with the same pre-reform per capita consumption but very different income distributions, and by assuming that people who freshly fall under the threshold of poverty immediately turn against reforms, since they cannot wait. In Brazil, income is distributed highly

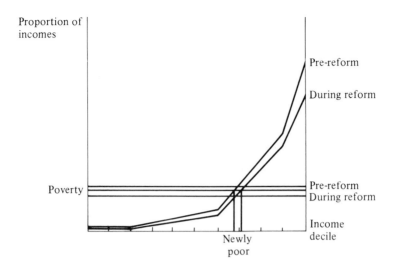

Figure 4.5

unequally. The popular way of capturing the pattern of consumption is the word "BelIndia": a Belgium for the upper class surrounded by an India for the rest of the population. In the Soviet Union, income equality is low by comparative standards, but most of the population hovers just above the poverty level; it has been estimated that the average diet constitutes just 105 percent of the minimum calorie requirement (Matthews 1986).

Suppose, first, that market-oriented reforms only lower aggregate consumption; distribution remains the same. Both curves in Figure 4.5 then shift downward. The number of poor households increases somewhat in Brazil. But in the stylized Soviet Union, everyone falls below the threshold of poverty! On our assumptions, opposition to reforms is universal.

Distributional effects that increase inequality do attenuate this contrast somewhat: More people fall under the poverty threshold in Brazil, fewer in the Soviet Union. But the proportion of the population that finds itself living in absolute poverty as a result of reforms is still higher in the originally more egalitarian country.

Moreover, redistributive measures are much easier in the country with a more unequal distribution. In Brazil, taxing the highest quintile of income recipients at an additional 30 percent rate would collect 20 percent of GNP and quadruple the standard of living of the bottom two quintiles of households.[49] In the Soviet Union, taxing higher incomes would increase the newly poor proportion of the population.

Hence, if reforms have the same aggregate cost in the two countries, the proportion of the population that would fall under the poverty threshold as a transitional result of reforms would be higher in the originally more egalitarian country. This analysis is highly stylized, but it shows that, at least under these *ceteris paribus* assumptions, reform may be politically more palatable in Latin America than in Eastern Europe.

Tolerance of inequality is important in shaping attitudes toward reforms. The one value that socialist systems have successfully inculcated is equality, and this value may undermine pro-market reforms under conditions of democracy. Yet the legacy of egalitarianism is a complicated issue, as is shown by Kolarska-Bobinska (1989) in her analysis of Polish survey data. She argues that Polish society was intolerant of inequalities, but only because these inequalities were seen as unjust. In fact, the author shows, tolerance of inequalities and of unemployment has greatly increased since 1980. In 1980, 70.6 percent of respondents accepted "without reservations" the principle of limiting the highest incomes. In 1981, this proportion fell to 50.7 percent, and in 1984 to 29.6 percent; and by 1988 it had reached 27.5 percent. Attitudes to equality are instrumental: Blue-collar workers, groups with low incomes and little education, and those in non-managerial positions are most intolerant of income differentials. Intergroup differences became profound; in 1981, 68.8 percent of specialists with higher education accepted this principle ("with or without reservations"), against 71.6 percent of skilled workers, while by 1988 only 37.0 percent of specialists supported limits on the highest incomes, against 63.0 percent of skilled and 70.0 percent of unskilled workers. Moreover, it is far from evident that Eastern European societies have more egalitarian values than Latin American ones. In a recent survey, 78 percent of Brazilians agreed with the statement "Everything society produces should be divided among everyone in the most equal way possible,"[50] and 60 percent disagreed that "If the country were rich, it does not matter that there would be many social inequalities."[51]

---

[49] Assuming no deadweight losses. Indeed, about 2 percent of national income would be sufficient to move everyone above the poverty line. See Cardoso and Dantas 1990: 148.

[50] Maravall (1981: 33) asked Spanish workers the identical question in 1977; 62 percent responded positively.

[51] *Folha de S. Paulo*, 24 September 1989, p. B-8. I am grateful to José Álvaro Moisés for bringing this survey to my attention.

*Conclusion*

Given their political dynamic, how far can one expect reform to advance? We have seen that the path of reform will not be smooth. The most likely path is one of radical programs that are eventually slowed or partly reversed, initiated again in a more gradual form with less popular confidence, and again slowed or reversed, until a new government comes in and promises a clean break, and the cycle starts again. Indeed, the Latin American experience shows that political forces that oppose radical reforms while in opposition pursue them once in office, and vice versa. Thus, we should expect reforms neither to "succeed" nor to "fail," but to proceed in spurts: advancing, stumbling, retreating, and advancing again.[52] The record of reforms in Latin America – as distinct from the record of economic performance – shows that reforms have advanced during the 1980s in spite of all the blunders, collapses, and vacillation (for the record, see Williamson 1990).

What is the effect of past failures on new attempts? Bogdanowicz-Bindert (1983: 65–70) concluded that past failures improve the chances of success. Díaz-Alejandro (1981: 120), however, thought that "the longer the history of failed stabilization plans, the smaller the chances of success . . . of any new plan." Contrary to Nelson (1990: 360), these assertions are not necessarily contradictory; they may concern different actors. On the one hand, elites learn from past mistakes to design better programs. On the other hand, individuals – as economic agents and political actors – learn from past failures to expect that new reforms will also fail. If this is true, then we should expect that more comprehensive and consistent programs will be offered each time to a more skeptical population. But if economic agents do not believe policy announcements, the policies themselves will be less effective: As Calvo (1989: 217) has shown, "policies

---

[52] This hypothesis implies an important methodological point: cross-sectional evaluation of the success of reforms can be very misleading. Just note the controversies over Chile. In 1980, views were sharply divided; the economy was growing, inflation was low but unemployment was high, wages had declined disastrously, and social expenditures were painfully reduced. By 1982–3, the country was an unmitigated disaster; the economy was in the throes of its worst recession since the 1930s. By 1986, the economy was growing slowly, but the standard of living of the bottom 40 percent of the population was lower than in 1973, per capita income was barely higher than in 1971, there was a public deficit, private investment was negative, and so on. In 1989, the economy grew at a fast rate and there was a widespread consensus, which included the democratic politicians who inherited the legacy of authoritarian reforms, that it was exceptionally healthy.

that would be optimal under full credibility turn out to be inoptimal under incomplete credibility." Hence, volatility should increase with each new attempt: Elites become more self-assured in their blueprints and more willing to adopt them independent of public opinion, and individuals become more predisposed to wait until they fail or to resist them.

Can democratic institutions be consolidated under such conditions? Haggard (1986: 164) argued that "democratic stalemate thus produces a zigzag or stop–go effort to adjust but need not lead to political destabilization, repression, or authoritarian installation." My view is different: In spite of these zigzags, reforms can advance quite far under democratic conditions, but they are politically destabilizing.

## Political consequences of economic reforms

If reforms are to proceed under democratic conditions, distributional conflicts must be institutionalized; all groups must channel their demands through democratic institutions and abjure other tactics. Regardless of how pressing their needs may be, the politically relevant groups must be willing to subject their interests to the verdict of democratic institutions. They must be willing to accept defeat and to wait, confident that these institutions will continue to offer opportunities the next time around. They must adopt the institutional calendar as the temporal horizon of their actions, thinking in terms of forthcoming elections, contract negotiations, or at least fiscal years.[53] They must assume the stance put forth by John McGurk, chairman of the British Labour party, in 1919: "We are either constitutionalists or we are not constitutionalists. If we are constitutionalists, if we believe in the efficacy of the political weapon (and we do, or why do we have a Labour Party?) then it is both unwise and undemocratic because we fail to get a majority at the polls to turn around and demand that we should substitute industrial action" (Miliband 1975: 69).

Reforms can progress under two polar conditions of the organization of political forces: The latter have to be very strong and support the reform program, or they have to be very weak and unable to oppose it effectively. Reforms are least likely to advance when political forces – in particular, opposition parties and unions – are strong enough to be able to sabotage them and not large enough to internalize the entire cost of arresting them.

---

[53]This notion of institutional time is due to Norbert Lechner.

As Haggard and Kaufman (1989: 269) put it, "The greatest difficulty comes in intermediate cases where labor is capable of defensive mobilization, but uncertain about its long-term place in the political system."[54] To put it bluntly, reform-oriented governments face a choice of either cooperating with opposition parties and unions, as did the Spanish Socialist government, or destroying them, as did the Bolivian government of Paz Estenssoro with regard to unions.

The role of unions is crucial for two reasons. On the one hand, they organize the people whose demands are the potential source of wage pressure. If workers and salaries employees have market power, they can exercise this power to push for wage increases. And during reforms, wage pressure is a source of inertial inflation; it slows down the recovery and results in increasing differentials among different sectors and occupations. Wage restraint is a necessary condition for the success of reforms. On the other hand, union federations can control the behavior of their constituents. Whether by using coercive powers delegated by the state or by relying on their persuasive powers, the leadership of a union can persuade the rank and file to wait for reforms to bear fruit. Unions have what is best described by the Spanish term *poder convocatorio:* the power to discipline the behaviors of their constituents in the collective interest.

To function as partners, unions must constitute encompassing, centralized organizations and must trust in the good faith of the government. Such organizations must be encompassing: They must associate large parts of their potential constituencies. And they must be centralized: They must be able to control the behavior of their constituents. Finally, they must have confidence in the government: They must trust that the government will not be unfair in distributing the costs and the benefits of reforms and that it will be competent in conducting reforms.

This assertion is supported not only by extensive evidence from the developed countries, where encompassing, centralized unions are willing to restrain their wage demands when social democratic parties are in office, but also by the experience of some newly democratic countries. In post-1976 Spain, a Socialist government has advanced a program of indus-

[54] The best example of unions that are neither strong enough nor large enough comes, again, from Argentina. As I am writing this text, the Argentine Union Federation (CGT) has called for price controls on all basic consumer goods, imposition of exchange controls, an end to the government's plans for privatization, abandonment of the plans to streamline public administration, and massive wage increases (*Latin American Weekly Report*, WR–90–11, 22 March 1990).

trial modernization under conditions of very high unemployment – until recently with the consent of the unions. In Poland, Solidarność offered a striking moratorium to facilitate the reforms initiated by the postcommunist government. In Brazil, a movement of "results-oriented unionism" was willing to do the same, and it is significant that its general secretary is the first union leader to become a minister of labor.[55]

Political parties represent more heterogeneous interests, and their impact is potentially wider. They play the central role in presenting alternatives and molding attitudes with regard to particular governments as well as with regard to the very project of structural transformation. Yet parties, at least modern noncommunist parties, do not have the same power to discipline their constituents as do unions. They may refuse to process demands they find untimely or inappropriate, but they face competition from other parties and the threat that popular mobilization will assume extraparliamentary forms.

In sum, to advance reforms, governments must either seek the broadest possible support from unions, opposition parties, and other encompassing and centralized organizations, or they must work to weaken these organizations and try to make their opposition ineffective. Obviously, the latter strategy raises the question of democracy. Is a government that resorts to a state of siege to counter opposition to reforms democratic? Moreover, if a government adopts the strategy of forcing reforms against popular opposition, the posture of the armed forces becomes relevant. This posture largely defines whether nondemocratic alternatives are perceived as feasible, either by those who are tempted to force reforms against democratically organized opposition or by the groups that are determined to defend their interests in any way possible against a democratically organized pro-reform majority. When the armed forces are independent of civilian control and are present as a political actor, various groups in the civil society engage in what Huntington (1968) termed praetorian politics: strategies such as "If you do not moderate your demands, we will ask the military to intervene" or "If you do not concede to our demands, we will create a disorder which will provoke the military to intervene." The competitive political process in the presence of an autonomous military creates the permanent possibility of military intervention.

[55] Antonio Rogerio Magri broke ranks with Brazilian unionism when, as president of the Electrical Workers, he made statements such as "All we workers want is that firms invest, so that the economy will expand. There is no better guarantee of employment than economic expansion" (*Journal da Tarde*, São Paulo, 27 July 1987, p. 12).

Responding to this bipolar choice, the new democratic governments can pursue two contrasting political strategies to control economic conflicts, placing different emphases on economic logic and on participation. Reform-oriented governments can insulate themselves from popular demands and impose economic policies from above. Or, trying to mobilize support for reform programs, they can seek to orchestrate consensus by engaging in widespread concertation with parties, unions, and other organizations. Hence, governments face the choice of either involving a broad range of political forces in the shaping of reforms, thus compromising their economic soundness, or of trying to undermine all opposition to the program. Confronted with this dilemma and the resistance that the social costs of reforms inherently engender, governments tend to vacillate between the technocratic political style inherent in market-oriented reforms and the participatory style required to maintain consensus.

Market-oriented economic reforms are an application of a technical economic blueprint based on theories developed inside the walls of North American universities and often forced on governments by the international lending agencies. They are based on a model of economic efficiency that is highly technical. They involve choices that are not easy to explain to the general public and decisions that do not always make sense to popular opinion. Moreover, they call for some measures that are most successful if they are introduced by surprise.[56]

From the political point of view, reforms are thus a strategy of control from above. The particular measures implement technicians' ideas; they are adopted without consultation and sometimes announced by surprise. A reform policy is not one that emerges from broad participation, from a consensus among all the affected interests, from compromises. As we have seen, parties that want to complete structural transformation have an incentive to manipulate the agenda in such a way as to push the electorate to accept radical reforms. And the success of the bitter-pill strategy depends on its initial brutality, on proceeding as quickly as possible with the most radical measures, on ignoring all the special interests and all immediate demands. Any government that is resolute must proceed in spite of the clamor of voices that call for softening or slowing down the reform pro-

---

[56] If everyone knows that the price of a particular commodity will be deregulated, there will be a rush on it before the measure is adopted; if everyone knows that wages and prices will be frozen on a particular day, they will be pushed as high as possible before the freeze takes place; if everyone knows savings will be frozen, money will be withdrawn from the banks.

gram. Since reformers know what is good and since they are eager to go ahead as fast as possible, political conflicts seem just a waste of time. Hence, market-oriented reforms are introduced by decree or are rammed through legislatures. Thus, worried that the Sejm might be unable to process eleven important pieces of economic legislation in seven days to beat the deadline imposed by the IMF, Wałęsa proposed that the government be given power to rule by decree. Desperate about the collapse of his original plan, President Menem of Argentina considered not convoking the scheduled session of the Congreso and governing by decree. According to Conaghan, Malloy, and Abugattas (1990: 20–1), decree powers were used extensively in getting reform packages adopted in Bolivia, Ecuador, and Peru. Of the 675 laws promulgated in Peru between 1980 and 1984, 463 were executive decrees. This potential is inherent in the very conception of reforms.[57]

At the same time, reforms require political support from individuals at the polls, from unions and professional associations in the workplaces, and at times from opposition parties in the legislature. And since they engender transitional costs, reforms inevitably provoke resistance. Voices are raised to the effect that social costs are excessive and the program should be moderated. Others point out that their situation is in some way special and that they should be accorded special treatment. In this situation, governments are tempted to seek consensus, to explain and justify their program, to listen and to compromise. They seek to involve opposing parties, unions, and employers' associations in economic policy making, hoping that this will reduce conflicts and induce economic actors to behave in ways consistent with continuation of at least the basic lines of the reform program.

The social pacts that are sought in bargaining typically consist of the granting of wage restraint by the unions in return for some welfare programs together with economic policies that control inflation and encourage investment and employment.[58] Both in post-1958 Venezuela and in Spain,

---

[57] One North American adviser to the Polish government recently remarked at a conference, "It is now up to the Poles whether the program will succeed. From the economic point of view, the program is sound. It can be undermined only by people who will succumb to populist appeals." I hear echoes of Brecht: "Would it not then be simpler for the government to dissolve the People and elect another?"

[58] The economic logic and the political preconditions of such pacts are discussed by Lechner (1985) and Przeworski (1987b). Reviews of experience from various countries include Cordova 1985, Pappalardo 1985, and dos Santos 1987.

the first of such pacts established the rudiments of the industrial relations system, while subsequent accords attempted, with varying degree of success, to regulate specific wage and employment targets.[59] Yet there are several reasons why such pacts seem unlikely to succeed in most new democracies.

(1) Social pacts are always exclusive; Schmitter (1984: 365) correctly incorporates this feature into their very definition. Unionized workers represent only one of the popular sectors in Latin America (Grossi and dos Santos 1983: 143). "Can the union movement based in the sphere of production," Lechner (1985: 30) asks rhetorically, "represent a popular movement founded in the context of reproduction?"

(2) Unions will participate in such pacts only if they are strong: encompassing, centralized, and politically influential. Otherwise they have no reason to expect that they will benefit in future from the present underutilization of their power. Yet, while employers may be favorably disposed to make immediate concessions, they fear strong unions and fight against extending to unions rights that might be used against them in the future. Governments, too, have an ambivalent attitude toward unions; they want their cooperation in controlling wages, but they do not want them so strong that they can dictate economic policy.

(3) Even if unions in the private sector may be willing to participate in a pact, public sector unions have no incentive to do so. In the profit sector, unions trade wage restraint for employment and investment, but neither employment nor investment in public services depends on their employees' wage rates. Hence, public sector unions face neither the stick of unemployment nor the carrot of investment. Moreover, reforms normally involve measures to reduce public spending, a threat to the public sector unions.

These obstacles are so overwhelming that most of the time attempts to conclude social pacts collapse. And even when such pacts are ceremoniously signed, they are rarely observed.

Since a temporary deterioration of material conditions is inherent in any reform process, neither decrees nor concertation generate immediate economic improvement. Governments learn that decrees evoke opposition and

---

[59] A useful descriptive comparison of the Venezuelan and the Spanish experience with social pacts is given by Córdova (1985). On Spain, see García 1984, Gonzalez 1985, and Perez-Díaz 1986. Venezuela, I think, is a case apart because of the rent income derived from oil. Karl (1987) and McCoy (1987) offer contrasting analyses of social pacts in Venezuela, but in my view the first exaggerates and the second underrates the role of oil.

pacts do not result in what they wanted to achieve by decree. They discover, in the words of a former Argentine vice-minister of the economy, that "requirements of participation conflict with those of competence."[60] And as pressures mount, governments begin to vacillate between *decretismo* and *pactismo* in search of a peaceful resolution of conflicts. Since the idea of resolving conflicts by agreement is alluring, they turn to making bargains when opposition against reforms mounts; they turn back to the technocratic style when the compromises involved in pacts imperil reforms. They promise consultation and shock the eventual partners with decrees;[61] they pass decrees and hope for consensus. As a result, governments appear to lack a clear conception of reforms and the resolve to pursue them. The state begins to be perceived as the principal source of economic instability.[62] Then comes the time for sorcerers with yet another magic formula. Once confidence in reforms is eroded, each new government tries to make a clean break with the past by doing something that people have not yet learned to distrust. Reforms are addictive; a stronger dosage is needed each time to soothe the accumulated desperation. Market-oriented reforms may be based on sound economics. But they breed voodoo politics.

The effect of this style is to undermine representative institutions. When candidates hide their economic programs during election campaigns or when governments adopt policies diametrically opposed to their electoral promises, they systematically educate the population that elections have no real role in shaping policies. When governments announce vital policies by decree or ram them through legislatures without debate, they teach parties, unions, and other representative organizations that they have no role to play in policy making. When they revert to bargaining only to orchestrate support for policies already chosen, they breed distrust and bitterness.

Democracy is thus weakened. The political process is reduced to elections, executive decrees, and sporadic outbursts of protest. The government rules by decree, in an authoritarian fashion but often without much

---

[60] Juan Carlos Torre, speaking at the seminar Transição política: Necessidades e limites da negociação at the University of São Paulo in June 1987. See Guilhon Albuquerque and Durham 1987.

[61] The Pacote Bresser was announced on the eve of a meeting that was designed to investigate the feasibility of a social pact at the personal instigation of President Sarney.

[62] For complaints about the inconstancy of government policies, see the presentations by both representatives of employers' associations and union leaders during the São Paulo seminar on social pacts (Guilhon Albuquerque and Durham 1987).

repression. All the power in the state is concentrated in the executive, which is nevertheless ineffectual in managing the economy. People get a regular chance to vote, but not to choose. Participation declines. Political parties, unions, and other representative organizations face a choice between passive consent and extraparliamentary outbursts.

These consequences are perhaps not inevitable. Indeed, the reason why the whole pattern of stop–go reforms sets in is that democracy is incomplete to begin with. In a country with constitutional provisions that force the executive to seek formal approval for policies before they are launched, with effective representative institutions and widespread political participation, governments could not set out on the path of reform independent of the support they could muster. Reforms would have to emerge from widespread consultation channeled through the representative institutions and ratified by elections. The Spanish Socialist government did proceed in this fashion and succeeded in conducting the country through a painful program of industrial reconversion with widespread support (Maravall 1990).[63] But this seems an exceptional case among new democracies.

Once democracy is weakened, pursuit of reforms may become politically destabilizing. At some point, the alternative may become either to abandon reforms or to discard the representative institutions altogether. Authoritarian temptations are inevitable. The clamor of discordant voices, the delay caused by having to follow procedures, and the seeming irrationality of conflicts inescapably cause impatience and intolerance among the proponents of reforms. For them, reforms are obviously needed and transparently rational: Doubts, oppositions, insistence on procedures appear to be symptoms of irrationality. Technocracy hurls itself against democracy and breeds the inclination to proceed against popular resistance: to suppress *glasnost* in order to continue with *perestroika*. And, on the other side, as suffering persists, confidence erodes, and the government seems less and less competent, temptations are born to defend one's interests at any cost, even at the cost of democracy.

---

[63] Note that when the Italian Communist party decided in 1976 to support the austerity policy of the government, it processed one million workers through evening school for a course in economics that explained the need for austerity.

# Conclusions

"If it had not been for 'the system,' we would have been like the West" – this is the premise of the Eastern European syllogism. But there are many countries that never experienced communist rule, yet remain part of the South; half of the world's population lives in countries that are capitalist, poor, and ruled by intermittent outbursts of organized violence. As a Brazilian business leader remarked, "Our businessmen think that communism has failed. They forget that our capitalism is also a monstrous failure."[1] Poverty, inequality, inefficiency, repression, and foreign domination are the daily experience of billions of people for whom the West remains the North.

What warrant do we have, therefore, to complete the syllogism, to believe that now, once "the system" is gone, Eastern Europe will find a path to "democracy, markets, and Europe," to the West? This is the question that motivated this book.

Conclusions are not the place to be cautious or nuanced. Let me, therefore, first summarize the results established above and then go out on a limb and speculate about the future of Eastern Europe.

To be consolidated, democratic institutions must at the same time protect all major interests and generate economic results. Yet the institutions that have emerged from recent transitions to democracy seem to be to a large extent haphazard, adopted under the understandable pressure to terminate fundamental conflicts as quickly as possible. Hence, the new democracies are likely to experience continual conflict over basic institutions. The political forces that suffer defeat as a result of the interplay of these institutions will repeatedly question the institutional framework. And wherever

---

[1] Roberto Nicolau Jehu, vice-president of the Department of the Economy of the São Paulo Employers Association (FIESP) interviewed in *Veja*, 25 October 1989, p. 5.

the armed forces have remained free of civilian control, the "military question" is a permanent source of instability for the democratic institutions.

Moreover, not all anti-authoritarian movements are pro-democratic. Some groups join under the slogan of democracy only as a step toward devouring their authoritarian opponents and their allies in the struggle against the old authoritarian regime. Once democratic institutions are established, they use them to establish their own monopoly on representing "the national interest," to repress opposing views, and to eradicate all conflict.

The durability of the new democracies will depend, however, not only on their institutional structure and the ideology of the major political forces, but to a large extent on their economic performance. Profound economic reforms must be undertaken if there is to be any hope that the deterioration in living conditions experienced by many nascent democratic countries will ever cease.

Yet structural transformations of economic systems are a plunge into the unknown; they are driven by desperation and hope, not by reliable blueprints. For political reasons, the reform strategy most likely to be undertaken is not the one that minimizes social costs. It is the bitter-pill strategy that combines a turn toward markets with transformations of property. And even if such reform programs enjoy initial support among individuals and organized political forces, this support is likely to erode as time passes and the suffering continues. Inflation is likely to flare up again and again under inertial pressures. Unemployment, even if temporary, is difficult to tolerate. Increasing inequality stokes conflicts with suspicions that the support of some groups for reform is simply self-serving. And in the face of political reactions, governments are likely to vacillate between the technocratic political style inherent in market-oriented reforms and the participatory style required to maintain consensus. They abandon or postpone some reforms, only to try them again later. And each new time they encounter a smaller stock of initial confidence. Ultimately, the vacillations of financially bankrupt governments become politically destabilizing.

Authoritarian temptations are thus inevitable. The clamor of discordant voices, the delay caused by having to follow procedures, the seeming irrationality of conflicts inescapably cause impatience and intolerance among the proponents of reforms. And, on the other hand, the continuing material deprivation, the technocratic style of policy making, and the ineffectiveness of the representative institutions undermine the popular support for democracy.

What does this analysis suggest about the future of Eastern Europe? I see two implications: Political developments in Eastern Europe will not be different than in those countries where the transition to democracy occurred earlier, and economic transformations will stop far short of the blueprints.

The main reason to hope that Eastern Europe will escape the politics, the economics, and the culture of poor capitalism, that it will soon join the West, is geography. This is the central premise of the Eastern European syllogism: "There is only one Europe" – the single European civilization, of which Eastern European countries have been traditional members, only temporarily separated by the curtain lowered by Soviet domination. All that is needed now is for Bulgaria, Poland, and Slovenia to find their rightful place in the European family of nations.

Geography is indeed the single reason to hope that Eastern European countries will follow the path to democracy and prosperity. There is no place in Europe today for nondemocratic politics; democratic institutions are a sine qua non for any country that seeks to become a member of this community. Yet whether the location will also attract flows of investment is already an open question. Thus far, it has not. And otherwise I see no reason why the future of Czechoslovakia, Hungary, or Romania should be different from that of Argentina, Brazil, or Chile.

Eastern Europeans tend to regard Latin America with an air of superiority. They see across the ocean a land of military coups, landed oligarchies, populist movements, jungles, and beaches: exotic, perhaps attractive, but uncivilized. And they place themselves at the origins of the highest, the European, culture. They forget their own military coups, their own landed oligarchies, their own populist movements, their own nationalism and xenophobia. Yet I know many a Polish village where Gabriel García Márquez would feel right at home; I hear the allure of the tango to the Polish ear; I have sensed on my shoulders the weight of hundreds of thousands of people propelling me to kneel before a sacred image of the Virgin Mary, the Queen of Czestochowa and the Tiranita of Santiago del Estero. And can you imagine a Western European parliament that, facing an agenda of several pieces of fundamental economic legislation, would plunge into a debate about whether a cross should be placed on the crown of the emblematic eagle?

Forget geography for a moment and put Poland in the place of Argentina, Hungary in the place of Uruguay. You will see states weak as organizations; political parties and other associations that are ineffectual in representing and mobilizing; economies that are monopolistic, overprotected, and overregulated; agricultures that cannot feed their own people; public bureaucracies that are overgrown; welfare services that are fragmentary and rudimentary. And will you not conclude that such conditions breed governments vulnerable to pressure from large firms, populist movements of doubtful commitment to democratic institutions, armed forces that sit menacingly on the sidelines, church hierarchies torn between authoritarianism and social justice, nationalist sentiments vulnerable to xenophobia?

None of the above implies that the future of Eastern Europe is given or that prospects for Latin America are doomed. For one thing, the roads to prosperity and democracy are not closed: Spain, Portugal, and Greece did succeed in escaping poverty and authoritarianism, and perhaps South Korea and even Taiwan and Thailand are on their way. Such accomplishments may be exceedingly rare, but they are possible. For another, the prospects of particular countries on either continent are not the same: Chile has borne the brunt of economic transformation under authoritarian rule, while Brazil still faces a deteriorating economy; Czechoslovakia has almost no foreign debt, while Hungary has a crippling one; Uruguay seems to have solved the military problem, while Argentina continues to live under the fear of the putsch; Hungary already has a party system and legitimate institutions, while Romania still has neither. Geography, with whatever it implies, is just not enough to shape economic and political futures.

The bare facts are that Eastern European countries are embracing capitalism and that they are poor. These are conditions Eastern Europeans share with masses of people all over the world who also dream of prosperity and democracy. Hence, all one can expect is that they too will confront the all too normal problems of the economics, the politics, and the culture of poor capitalism. The East has become the South.

# References

Abalkin, Leonid. 1988. "Politico-Economic Bases of the Radical Reform of the Economic Mechanism." In *Sovietskaia ekonomitcheskaia reforma: Poiski i reshenia*, pp. 38–54. Moscow: Nauka.

Abreu, Dilip. 1988. "On the Theory of Infinitely Repeated Games with Discounting." *Econometrica* 56: 383–96.

Agabengyan, Abel G. 1988. "Economic Reforms." In *Perestroika, 1989*, pp. 73–109. Abel G. Agabengyan, ed. New York: Scribner.

Andrade, Régis de Castro. 1980. "Política social e normalização institucional no Brasil." In *América latina: Novas estrategias de dominação*, pp. 87–114. Luis Maira, ed. Petropolis: Editora Vozes.

Arrow, Kenneth J. 1951. *Social Choice and Individual Values*. New York: Wiley.
1964. "The Role of Securities in the Optimal Allocation of Risk Bearing." *Review of Economic Studies* 9: 91–6.
1971. "Political and Economic Evaluation of Social Effects and Externalities." In *Frontiers of Quantitative Economics*. M. D. Intrilligator, ed. Amsterdam: North-Holland.

Ash, Timothy Garton. 1990. *The Uses of Adversity: Essays on the Fate of Central Europe*. New York: Random House.

Asselain, Jean-Charles. 1984. *Planning and Profits in a Socialist Economy*. Oxford: Blackwell Publisher.

Auerbach, Paul, Meghnad Desai, and Ali Shamsavari. 1988. "The Transition from Actually Existing Capitalism." *New Left Review* 170: 61–80.

Aumann, Robert. 1987. "Correlated Equilibrium as an Expression of Bayesian Rationality." *Econometrica* 55: 1–18.

Aumann, Robert J., and Mordecai Kurz. 1977. "Power and Taxes." *Econometrica* 45: 1137–61.

Axelrod, Robert. 1984. *The Evolution of Cooperation*. New York: Basic.
1986. "An Evolutionary Approach to Norms." *American Political Science Review* 80: 1095–113.

Baka, Władysław. 1986. *Czas reformy*. Warsaw: Ksiazka i Wiedza.

Balassa, Bela, Gerardo M. Bueno, Pedro-Pablo Kuczynski, and Mario Henrique Simonsen. 1986. *Hacia una renovación del crecimiento económico en América latina*. Mexico City: El Colegio de México.

Balcerowicz, Leszek. 1989. "Polish Economic Reform, 1981–1988." In *Eco-*

*nomic Reforms in the European Centrally Planned Economies,* pp. 42–52. Economic Commission for Europe, Economic Studies, no. 1. New York: United Nations.

Bauer, Thomas. 1989. "The Unclearing Market." In *Alternatives to Capitalism,* pp. 71–83. Jon Elster and Karl Ove Moene, eds. Cambridge: Cambridge University Press.

Beck, Nathaniel. 1978. "Social Choice and Economic Growth." *Public Choice* 33: 33–48.

Becker, Gary S. 1976. "Comment [on Peltzman]." *Journal of Law and Economics* 19: 245–8.

Bence, Gyorgy. 1990. "Political Justice in Post-Communist Societies: The Case of Hungary." Manuscript, Eptvos Lorand University of Budapest.

Benhabib, Jeff, and Roy Radner. 1988. "Joint Exploitation of a Productive Asset: A Game-Theoretic Approach." Manuscript, New York University and A.T.&T.

Bergson, Abram. 1984. "Income Inequality under Soviet Socialism." *Journal of Economic Literature* 22: 1052–100.

Bideleux, Robert. 1985. *Communism and Development.* London: Methuen.

Bobbio, Norberto. 1989. *Democracy and Dictatorship.* Minneapolis: University of Minnesota Press.

Bogdanowicz-Bindert, Christine A. 1983. "Portugal, Turkey, and Peru: Three Successful Stabilization Programs under the Auspices of the IMF." *World Development* 11: 65–70.

Bowles, Samuel. 1985. "The Production Process in a Competitive Economy." *American Economic Review* 75: 16–37.

Bowles, Samuel, and Herbert Gintis. 1986. *Democracy and Capitalism: Property, Community, and the Contradictions of Modern Social Thought.* New York: Basic.

Braybrooke, David. 1976. "The Insoluble Problem of the Social Conflict." *Dialogue* 15: 3–37.

Brennan, Geoffrey, and Loren E. Lomasky. 1989. "Introduction." In *Politics and Process,* pp. 1–11. Geoffrey Brennan and Loren E. Lomasky, eds. Cambridge: Cambridge University Press.

Bresser Pereira, Luiz Carlos. 1978. *O colapso de uma alianca de classes.* São Paulo: Editora Brasiliense.

1984. *Development and Crisis in Brazil, 1930–1983.* Boulder, Colo.: Westview.

Bruno, Michael, and Jeffrey Sachs. 1985. *Economics of Worldwide Stagflation.* Cambridge, Mass.: Harvard University Press.

Bruszt, Laszlo. 1988. "'Without Us but for Us?' Political Orientation in Hungary in the Period of Late Paternalism." *Social Research* 55: 43–77.

1989. "The Dilemmas of Economic Transition in Hungary." *Südost Europa* 38:716–29.

Buchanan, Allen. 1985. *Ethics, Efficiency, and the Market.* Totowa, N.J.: Rowman and Allanhead.

Buchanan, James, and Gordon Tullock. 1962. *The Calculus of Consent.* Ann Arbor: University of Michigan Press.

Burawoy, Michael. 1979. *Manufacturing Consent: Changes in the Labor Process under Monopoly Capitalism.* Chicago: University of Chicago Press.

Butenko, Anatoli. 1988. *Sovremennyi socializm: Aktualnyie teoreticheskiyie problemi.* Moscow: Nauka.

Calvo, Guillermo A. 1989. "Incredible Reforms." In *Debt, Stabilization and Development: Essays in Memory of Carlos Díaz-Alejandro,* pp. 217–34. Guillermo Calvo, Ronald Findley, Pentti Kouri, and Jorge Braga de Macedo, eds. London: Blackwell Publisher.

Campbell, Donald E. 1987. *Resource Allocation Mechanisms.* Cambridge: Cambridge University Press.

Cardoso, Eliana, and Daniel Dantas. 1990. "Brazil." In *Latin American Adjustment: How Much Has Happened?* pp. 129–54. John Williamson, ed. Washington, D.C.: Institute for International Economics.

Cardoso, Fernando Henrique. 1972. *O modelo político brasileiro.* São Paulo: Difel.

1979. "Authoritarianism at the Crossroads: The Brazilian Case." Wilson Center, Washington, D.C., Latin American Program Working Paper, no. 93.

1983. "O papel dos empresarios no proceso de transição: O caso brasileiro." *Dados* 26: 9–27.

Cariaga, Juan L. 1990. "Bolivia." In *Latin American Adjustment: How Much Has Happened?* pp. 41–54. John Williamson, ed. Washington, D.C.: Institute for International Economics.

Carr, Raymond, and Juan Pablo Fusi Aizpurua. 1979. *Spain: Dictatorship to Democracy.* London: Allen and Unwin.

Carrillo, Santiago. 1974. *Demain l'Espagne.* Paris: Seuil.

Casper, Gerhard. 1989. "Changing Patterns of Constitutionalism: 18th to 20th Century." Manuscript, University of Chicago.

Castroriadis, Cornelius. 1979. *Le contenu du socialisme.* Paris: Editions du Seuil.

Cohen, G. A. 1978. *Karl Marx's Theory of History: A Defense.* Princeton, N.J.: Princeton University Press.

Cohen, Joshua. 1989. "The Economic Basis of Deliberative Democracy." *Social Philosophy and Policy* 2:25–51.

Coleman, Jules. 1989. "Rationality and the Justification of Democracy." In *Politics and Process,* pp. 194–221. Geoffrey Brennan and Loren E. Lomasky, eds. Cambridge: Cambridge University Press.

Collard, David. 1978. *Altruism and the Economy: A Study in Non-Selfish Economics.* Oxford: Oxford University Press.

Comisso, Ellen. 1988. "Market Failures and Market Socialism: Economic Problems of the Transition." *Eastern European Politics and Societies* 2: 433–65.

1989. "Crisis in Socialism or Crisis of Socialism? A Review Essay." *World Politics* (forthcoming).

Conaghan, Catherine M. 1983. "Industrialists and the Reformist Interregnum:

Dominant Class Political Behavior and Ideology in Ecuador, 1972–1979." Ph.D. dissertation, Yale University.

Conaghan, Catherine M., James M. Malloy, and Luis A. Abugattas. 1990. "Business and the 'Boys': The Politics of Neoliberalism in the Central Andes." *Latin American Research Review* 25: 3–29.

Córdova, Efrén. 1985. *Pactos sociais; Experiência internacional, tipologia e modelos.* Brasilia: Instituto Brasileiro de Relacoes do Trabalho.

Cortés, Fernando, and Rosa Maria Rubalcava. 1990. "Algunas consequencias sociales del ajuste: México post 82." Manuscript, El Colegio de México.

Coser, Lewis. 1959. *The Functions of Social Conflict.* New York: Free Press.

Covre, Maria de Lourdes M. 1986. *A cidadania que não temos.* São Paulo: Editora Brasiliense.

Cui, Zhiyuan. 1990. "Marx, Theories of the Firm and the Socialist Reform." M.A. thesis, University of Chicago.

Cumings, Bruce. 1989. "The Abortive Abertura: South Korea in the Light of Latin American Experience." *New Left Review* 173: 5–33.

Dahl, Robert A. 1971. *Polyarchy: Participation and Opposition.* New Haven, Conn.: Yale University Press.

1985. *A Preface to Economic Democracy.* Berkeley and Los Angeles: University of California Press.

1990. "Transitions to Democracy." Manuscript, Yale University.

Delich, Francisco. 1984. "Estado, sociedad y fuerzas armadas en la transición argentina." In *Transición a la democracia.* Augusto Varas, ed. Santiago: Associatión Chilena de Investigaciones para la Paz.

de Pablo, Juan Carlos. 1990. "Argentina." In *Latin American Adjustment: How Much Has Happened?* pp. 111–29. John Williamson, ed. Washington, D.C.: Institute for International Economics.

Díaz-Alejandro, Carlos. 1981. "Southern Cone Stabilization Plans." In *Economic Stabilization in Developing Countries.* William R. Cline and Sidney Weintraub, eds. Washington, D.C.: Brookings Institution.

Diniz, Eli. 1986. "The Political Transition in Brazil: A Reappraisal of the Dynamics of the Political Opening." *Studies in Comparative International Development* 21: 63–73.

Dmowski, Roman. 1989. *Myśli nowoczesnego polaka* (1903). 8th ed. Warsaw: Wydawnictwo Grunwald.

Dobb, Maurice. 1969. *Welfare Economics and the Economics of Socialism: Towards a Commonsense Critique.* Cambridge: Cambridge University Press.

Domaranczyk, Zbigniew. 1990. *100 dni Mazowieckiego.* Warsaw: Wydawnictwo Andrzej Bonarski.

Dornbusch, Rudiger. 1990. "Comment." In *Latin American Adjustment: How Much Has Happened?* pp. 312–27. John Williamson, ed. Washington, D.C.: Institute for International Economics.

dos Santos, Mario R. 1987. *Concertación política-social y democratización.* Buenos Aires: CLACSO.

Dunn, John. 1984. *The Politics of Socialism: An Essay in Political Theory*. Cambridge: Cambridge University Press.

Edgeworth, Francis Y. 1881. *Mathematical Physics*. London: C. Kegan Paul.

Elson, Diane. 1988. "Socialization of the Market." *New Left Review* 172: 3–44.

Elster, Jon. 1975. "Optimism and Pessimism in the Discussion of the Standard of Living during the Industrial Revolution in Britain." Paper presented at the 14th International Congress of Historical Sciences, San Francisco.

   1984. *Ulysses and the Sirens: Studies in Rationality and Irrationality*. Rev. ed. Cambridge: Cambridge University Press.

   1986. "Self-Realization in Work and Politics: The Marxian Conception of Good Life." *Social Philosophy and Policy* 3: 97–126.

   1989. *Solomonic Judgements*. Cambridge: Cambridge University Press.

Elster, Jon, and Karl Ove Moene. 1989. "Introduction." In *Alternatives to Capitalism*, pp. 1–38. Jon Elster and Karl Ove Moene, eds. Cambridge: Cambridge University Press.

Elster, Jon, and Rune Slagstad, eds. 1988. *Constitutionalism and Democracy*. Cambridge: Cambridge University Press.

Farrand, M., 1966. *The Records of the Federal Convention*. 4 vols. New Haven, Conn.: Yale University Press.

Fischer, Franklin M. 1989. "Adjustment Process and Stability." In *General Equilibrium*, pp. 36–43. John Eatwell, Murray Milgate, and Peter Newman, eds. New York: Norton.

Fontana, Andres. 1984. "Fuerzas armadas, partidos políticos y transición a la democracia en la Argentina." In *Transición a la democracia*. Augusto Varas, ed. Santiago: Associación Chilena de Investigaciones para la Paz.

   1987. "La política militar del gobierno constitucional argentino." In *Ensayos sobre la transición democrática en la Argentina*, pp. 375–418. José Nun and Juan Carlos Portantiero, eds. Buenos Aires: Puntosur Editores.

Fudenberg, Drew, and Eric Maskin. 1986. "The Folk Theorem in Repeated Games with Discounting or with Incomplete Information." *Econometrica* 54: 533–54.

García, Manuel Alonso. 1984. "En Torno a una política de relaciones laborales." In *España: Un presente para el futuro*, vol. 2: *Las instituciones*. Madrid: Instituto de Estudios Economicos.

Gauthier, David. 1986. *Morals by Agreement*. Oxford: Oxford University Press.

Geddes, Barbara. 1990. "Democratic Institutions as Bargains among Self-Interested Politicians." Paper presented at annual meeting of the American Political Science Association, San Francisco, September.

Golbery do Couto e Silva. 1981. *Conjuntura política nacional: O poder executivo e Geopolítica no Brasil*. Rio de Janeiro: Livraria Jose Olimpio.

González, Fernando Suárez. 1985. "El Marco institucional de la relaciones laborales." *Papeles de Economía Española* 22: 265–81.

Grossi, María, and Mario R. dos Santos. 1983. "La concertación social: Una perspectiva sobre instrumentos de regulación económico-social en procesos de democratización." *Crítica y Utopia* 9: 127–48.

Guilhon Albuquerque, José A., and Eunice Ribeiro Durham, eds. 1987. *Transição política: Necessidades e limites da Negociaciao.* São Paulo: Universidade de São Paulo.

Habermas, Jurgen. 1975. *Legitimation Crises.* Boston: Beacon.

Haggard, Stephan. 1986. "The Politics of Adjustment: Lessons from the IMF's Extended Fund Facility." In *The Politics of International Debt,* pp. 157–86. Miles Kahler, ed. Ithaca, N.Y.: Cornell University Press.

Haggard, Stephan and Robert Kaufman. 1989. "The Politics of Stabilization and Structural Adjustment." In *Developing Country Debt and the World Economy,* pp. 263–74. Jeffrey D. Sachs, ed. Chicago: University of Chicago Press.

Hahn, F. H. 1989. "Auctioneer." In *General Equilibrium,* pp. 62–8. John Eatwell, Murray Milgate, and Peter Newman, eds. New York: Norton.

Hankiss, Elemer. 1989. *East European Alternatives: Are There Any?* Budapest: Institute of Sociology, Hungarian Academy of Sciences.

Hansmann, Henry. 1988. "Ownership of the Firm." *Journal of Law, Economics, and Organization* 4: 267–304.

Hardin, Russell. 1987. "Why a Constitution?" Manuscript, University of Chicago.

Hardin, Russell, Stephen Holmes, and Adam Przeworski. 1988. "The Constitution of Democracy." Manuscript, University of Chicago.

Hayward, J. E. S. 1983. *Governing France: The One and Indivisible Republic.* 2d ed. London: Weidenfeld and Nicolson.

Herrero de Miñon, Miguel. 1979. "Les sources étrangères de la Constitution." *Pouvoirs* 8: 97–109.

Hicks, Alexander. 1988. "Social Democratic Corporatism and Economic Growth." *Journal of Politics* 50: 677–704.

Hirschman, Albert O. 1985. "Against Parsimony: Three Ways of Complicating Some Categories of Economic Discourse." *Economics and Philosophy* 1: 7–21.

———. 1986. "On Democracy in Latin America." *New York Review of Books,* 10 April.

Holmstrom, Bengt. 1982. "Moral Hazard and Incentives in Teams." *Bell Journal of Economics* 13: 324–40.

Huntington, Samuel P. 1968. *Political Order in Changing Societies.* New Haven, Conn.: Yale University Press.

Hurwicz, Leonid. 1973. "The Design of Resource Allocation Mechanisms." *American Economic Review* 63: 1–30.

Kalyvas, Stathis N. 1989. "The Politics of Nationalization and Privatization in Great Britain, 1973–1983." Manuscript, University of Chicago.

Karl, Terry Lynn. 1987. "Petroleum and Political Pacts: The Transition to Democracy in Venezuela." *Latin American Research Review* 22: 63–94.

Kavka, Gregory S. 1986. *Hobbesian Moral and Political Theory.* Princeton, N.J.: Princeton University Press.

Kirzner, Israel M. 1988. "Some Ethical Implications for Capitalism of the Socialist Calculation Debate." *Social Philosophy and Policy* 6: 165–83.

Kishlansky, Marc. 1986. *Parliamentary Selection.* Cambridge: Cambridge University Press.

Knight, Jack. 1990. "Institutions and Distribution." Manuscript, Washington University, St. Louis.

Kolarska-Bobinska, Lena. 1988. "Social Interests, Egalitarian Attitudes, and the Change of Economic Interests." *Social Research* 55: 111–39.

——— 1989. "Poczucie niesprawiedliwosci, konfliktu i preferowany lad w gospodarce." In *Polacy 88*, pp. 81–159. Warsaw: CPBP.

Kornai, Janos. 1986. "The Hungarian Reform Process: Visions, Hopes and Reality." *Journal of Economic Literature* 24: 1687–737.

Kreps, David M., and Evan L. Porteus. 1978. "Temporal Resolution of Uncertainty and Dynamic Choice Theory." *Econometrica* 46: 185–200.

——— 1979a. "Temporal von Neumann–Morgenstern and Induced Preferences." *Journal of Economic Theory* 20: 81–109.

——— 1979b. "Dynamic Choice Theory and Dynamic Programming." *Econometrica* 47: 91–100.

Kuroń, Jacek. 1990. *Wiara i Wina: Do i od komunizmu.* Warsaw: Niezależna Oficyna Wydawcza.

Lamounier, Bolivar. 1979. "Notes on the Study of Re-Democratization." Wilson Center, Washington, D.C., Latin American Program Working Paper, no. 58.

Lancaster, Kevin. 1973. "The Dynamic Inefficiency of Capitalism." *Journal of Political Economy* 81: 1098–109.

Lane, Frederic C. 1979. *Profits from Power: Readings in Protection Rent and Violence Controlling Enterprises.* Albany: State University of New York Press.

Lange, Peter, and Geoffrey Garrett. 1985. "The Politics of Growth: Strategic Interaction and Economic Performance in the Advanced Industrial Democracies, 1974–1980." *Journal of Politics* 47: 792–827.

*Latin American Weekly Report.* Published by Latin American Newsletters, London.

Lavoie, Daniel. 1985. *Rivalry and Central Planning: The Socialist Calculation Debate Revisited.* Cambridge: Cambridge University Press.

Lechner, Norbert. 1985. "Pacto social nos processos de democratização: A experiência latino-americana." *Novos Estudos* 13: 29–44.

——— 1986. "Responde la democracia a la busqueda de la certidumbre?" *Zona Abierta* 39–40: 69–94.

Leijonhufvud, Axel. 1986. "Capitalism and the Factory System." In *Economics as a Process.* Richard N. Langlois, ed. Cambridge: Cambridge University Press.

Lenin, V. I. 1959. *Against Revisionism.* Moscow: Progress Publishers.

Levhari, D., and L. J. Mirman. 1980. "The Great Fish-War: An Example Using the Cournot–Nash Solution." *Bell Journal of Economics* 11: 322–4.

Lewis, David. 1969. *Conventions: A Philosophical Study.* Cambridge, Mass.: Harvard University Press.

Linz, Juan. 1984. "Democracy: Presidential or Parliamentary. Does It Make a Difference?" Manuscript, Yale University.

——— 1990. "Transitions to Democracy." *Washington Quarterly,* Summer: 143–64.

Lipset, Seymour Martin. 1960. *Political Man.* Garden City, N.Y.: Doubleday.

Lipset, Seymour Martin, and Stein Rokkan. 1967. *Party Systems and Voter Alignments: Cross-national Perspectives*. New York: Free Press.

Littlechild, Stephen C. 1986. "Three Types of Market Processes." In *Economics as a Process*. Richard N. Langlois, ed. Cambridge: Cambridge University Press.

Loewenstein, George. 1987. "Anticipation and the Valuation of Delayed Consumption." *Economic Journal* 97: 666–94.

Lopez, Juan. 1990. "Political Determinants of Private Investment in Argentina: Field Work Impressions." Manuscript, University of Chicago.

López-Pintor, Rafael. 1980. "Transition toward Democracy in Spain: Opinion Mood and Elite Behavior." Wilson Center, Washington, D.C., Latin American Program Working Paper.

Lucas, Robert E., Jr. 1988. "On the Mechanics of Economic Development." *Journal of Monetary Economics* 22: 3–42.

Luxemburg, Rosa. 1970. *Reform or Revolution*. New York: Pathfinder.

McCoy, Jennifer. 1987. "State, Labor, and the Democratic Class Compromise in Venezuela." Paper presented at meeting of the Southeastern Conference on Latin American Studies, Mérida, Mexico.

McKelvey, Richard D. 1976. "Intransitivities in Multidimensional Voting Models and Some Implications for Agenda Control." *Journal of Economic Theory* 12: 472–82.

Maddison, Angus. 1989. *The World Economy in the 20th Century*. Paris: OECD.

Mandel, Ernest. 1986. "A Critique of Market Socialism." *New Left Review* 159: 5–38.

1988. "The Myth of Market Socialism." *New Left Review* 169: 108–21.

Manin, Bernard. 1987. "On Legitimacy and Political Deliberation." *Political Theory* 15: 338–68.

Maravall, José María. 1981. *La política de la transición, 1975–1980*. Madrid: Taurus.

1990. "Economic Reforms in New Democracies: The Southern European Experience." University of Chicago, ESST Working Papers, no. 2.

Marx, Karl. 1952. *The Class Struggle in France, 1848 to 1850*. Moscow: Progress Publishers.

1967. *Capital*. 3 vols. New York: International Publishers.

Matthews, Mervyn. 1986. *Poverty in the Soviet Union*. Cambridge: Cambridge University Press.

Mellor, John W., and Bruce F. Johnston. 1984. "The World Food Equation: Interrelations among Development, Employment and Food Consumption." *Journal of Economic Literature* 22: 531–74.

Migranyan, A. M. 1988. "Perehod ot totalitarno-avtoritarnii regimov k demokratsii." In *Politicheskie reformy v stranakh sotsializma*. E. A. Armbarstumov and J. M. Kliamkin, eds. Moscow: Akademia Nauk SSSR.

Miliband, Ralph. 1975. *Parliamentary Socialism: A Study in the Politics of Labour*. 2d ed. London: Merlin Press.

Moatti, Gerard. 1989. "Les jeunes deviennent capitalistes." *L'Expansion*, 18 May.

Moene, Karl Ove. 1989. "Strong Unions or Worker Control?" In *Alternatives to Capitalism*, pp. 83–98. Jon Elster and Karl Ove Moene, eds. Cambridge: Cambridge University Press.

Moisés, José Álvaro. 1986. "Sociedade civil, cultura política e democracia: Descaminhos da transição política." In *A cidadania que não temos*, pp. 119–51. Maria de Lourdes M. Covre, ed. São Paulo: Editora Brasiliense.

Montesquieu. 1905. *Extraits de l'Esprit des lois et des oeuvres diverses*. Camille Jullian, ed. Paris: Librairie Hachette.

Moore, Barrington, Jr. 1965. *Social Origins of Dictatorship and Democracy*. Boston: Beacon.

Moulin, Hervé. 1986. *Game Theory for the Social Sciences*. 2d ed. New York: New York University Press.

Murilo de Carvalho, José. 1987. "Militares e civis: Um debate alem da contituinte." Paper presented at the Eleventh Annual Meeting of ANPOCS, Aguas de São Pedro.

Nelson, Joan M. 1984. "The Politics of Stabilization." In *Adjustment Crisis in the Third World*. R. E. Feinberg and V. Kallab, eds. New Brunswick, N.J.: Transaction Books.

Nelson, Joan M., 1990. *Economic Crisis and Policy Choice: The Politics of Adjustment in the Third World*. Princeton, N.J.: Princeton University Press.

Newbery, David, and Joseph Stiglitz. 1981. *The Theory of Commodity Price Stabilization*. Oxford: Oxford University Press.

Nove, Alec. 1983. *The Economics of Feasible Socialism*. London: Allen and Unwin.

1987. "Markets and Socialism." *New Left Review* 161: 98–104.

O'Donnell, Guillermo. 1978a. "Reflections on the Patterns of Change in the Bureaucratic-Authoritarian State." *Latin American Research Review* 13: 3–38.

1978b. "State and Alliances in Argentina, 1956–1976." *Journal of Development Studies* 15: 3–33.

1979. "Notas para el estudio de procesos de democratización a partir del estado burocrático-autoritario." *Estudios CEDES* 5.

1989. "Argentina, de nuevo." Manuscript, CEBRAP, São Paulo.

O'Donnell, Guillermo, and Philippe C. Schmitter. 1986. *Transitions from Authoritarian Rule: Tentative Conclusions about Uncertain Democracies*. Baltimore: Johns Hopkins University Press.

Offe, Claus. 1985. *Disorganized Capitalism*. Cambridge, Mass.: MIT Press.

Olson, Mancur, Jr. 1965. *The Logic of Collective Action*. Cambridge, Mass.: Harvard University Press.

O'Neill, John. 1989. "Markets, Socialism, and Information: A Reformulation of a Marxian Objection to the Market." *Social Philosophy and Policy* 6: 200–211.

Organization for Economic Cooperation and Development. 1990. *Transition from the Command to Market Economy*. Summary of a meeting held at the Vienna Institute for Comparative Economic Studies. Paris: OECD.

Ostrowski, Krzysztof. 1989. "The Decline of Power and Its Effects on Democratization: The Case of the Polish United Workers Party." In *Eastern Europe and Democracy: The Case of Poland,* pp. 15–28. New York: Institute for East–West Security Studies.

Ostrowski, Krzysztof, and Adam Przeworski. 1965. "Trade Unions and Economic Planning in Poland." *Polish Roundtable* 1.

Pappalardo, Adriano. 1985. *Il governo del salario nelle democrazie industriali.* Milan: Franco Agneli.

Pareto, Vilfredo. 1927. *Manuel d'économie politique.* 2d ed. Paris: Giard.

Perez-Díaz, Victor. 1986. "Economic Policies and Social Pacts in Spain during the Transition." In *Political Stability and Neocorporatism.* Ilja Scholten, ed. Beverly Hills, Calif.: Sage.

Petrakov, Nikolai, and Evgeni Yassine. 1988. "Economic Methods of Planned Centralized Management." In *Sovietskaia ekonomitcheskaia reforma: Poiski i reshenia,* pp. 54–86. Moscow: Nauka.

Pigou, A. C. 1932. *The Economics of Welfare.* 4th ed. London: Macmillan.

Pizzorno, Allesandro. 1978. "Political Exchange and Collective Identity in Industrial Conflicts." In *The Resurgence of Class Conflicts in Western Europe since 1968.* Colin Crouch and Allesandro Pizzorno, eds. London: Macmillan.

*Porozumienia Okraglego Stolu.* 1989. Warsaw: NSSZ Solidarność.

Przeworski, Adam. 1982. "'The Man of Iron' and Men of Power in Poland." *PS* 15: 18–31.

1985. *Capitalism and Social Democracy.* Cambridge: Cambridge University Press.

1986a. "The Feasibility of Universal Grants under Democratic Capitalism." *Theory and Society* 15: 695–709.

1986b. "Marxism and Rational Choice." *Politics and Society* 14: 379–409.

1986c. "Some Problems in the Study of the Transition to Democracy." In *Transition from Authoritarian Rule,* vol. 1. Guillermo O'Donnell and Philippe C. Schmitter, eds. Baltimore: Johns Hopkins University Press.

1987a. "Democracy as a Contingent Outcome of Conflicts." In *Constitutionalism and Democracy.* Jon Elster and Rune Slagstad, eds. Cambridge: Cambridge University Press.

1987b. "Capitalismo, democracia, pactos." In *Transição política: Necessidades e limites da negociaciao.* José A. Guilhon Albuquerque and Eunice Ribeiro Durham, eds. São Paulo: Universidade de São Paulo.

1990. *The State and the Economy under Capitalism.* Chur: Harwood Academic Publishers.

Przeworski, Adam, and John D. Sprague. 1986. *Paper Stones: A History of Electoral Socialism.* Chicago: University of Chicago Press.

Przeworski, Adam, and Michael Wallerstein. 1982. "The Structure of Class Conflicts under Democratic Capitalism." *American Political Science Review* 76: 215–38.

1988. "Structural Dependence of the State on Capital." *American Political Science Review* 82: 11–31.

Putterman, Louis. 1986. "On Some Recent Explanations of Why Capital Hires Labor." In *The Economic Nature of the Firm*, pp. 312–28. Louis Putterman, ed. Cambridge: Cambridge University Press.

Rainwater, Lee, Barbara Torrey, and Timothy Smeeding. 1989. "Poverty and Low Incomes: International Evidence from Household Income Surveys." Manuscript.

Rasmusen, Eric. 1989. *Games and Information: An Introduction to Game Theory*. Oxford: Blackwell Publisher.

Remmer, Karen L. 1986. "The Politics of Economic Stabilization." *Comparative Politics* 19: 1–24.

Riker, William H. 1962. *The Theory of Political Coalitions*. New Haven, Conn.: Yale University Press.

1982. *Liberalism against Populism: A Confrontation between the Theory of Democracy and the Theory of Social Choice*. San Francisco: Freeman.

Roemer, John. 1989a. "Public Ownership and Private Property Externalities." In *Alternatives to Capitalism*, pp. 159–79. Jon Elster and Karl Ove Moene, eds. Cambridge: Cambridge University Press.

1989b. "Decentralization, Duplicity, and Minimal Equity." Manuscript, University of California at Davis.

Roland, Gerard. 1989. "Complexity, Bounded Rationality and Equilibrium: The Soviet-Type Case." Manuscript, Université Libre de Bruxelles.

Rolicki, Janusz. 1990. *Edward Gierek: Przerwana dekada*. Warsaw: Wydawnictwo FAKT.

Rousseau, Jean-Jacques, 1986. "Considerations on the Government of Poland." In *Rousseau: Political Writings, Selections*. Frederick Watkins, trans. and ed. Madison: University of Wisconsin Press.

Rubinstein, Ariel. 1988. "Comments on the Interpretation of Game Theory." Paper delivered as the Walras-Bowley Lecture at meeting of the North American Econometric Society, June.

Rustow, Dunkwart A. 1955. *The Politics of Compromise: A Study of Parties and Cabinet Governments in Sweden*. Princeton, N.J.: Princeton University Press.

1970. "Transitions to Democracy: Toward a Dynamic Model." *Comparative Politics* 2: 337–63.

Saguir, Julio. 1990. "On the Origins of the Argentine Constitution." Manuscript, Department of Political Science, University of Chicago.

Sartre, Jean-Paul. 1960. *Critique de la raison dialectique*. Paris: Gallimard.

Saunders, Peter, and Friedrich Klau. 1985. *The Role of the Public Sector: Causes and Consequences*. OECD Economic Studies 4. Paris: OECD.

Schmitt, Carl. 1988. *The Crisis of Parliamentary Democracy* (1923). 1st English ed. Cambridge, Mass.: MIT Press.

Schmitter, Philippe C. 1974. "Still the Century of Corporatism?" *Review of Politics* 36: 85–131.

1984. "Patti e transizioni: Messi non-democratici a fini democratici?" *Rivista Italiania di Scienza Politica* 14: 363–82.

Schneider, Ben Ross. 1990. "The Politics of Privatization in Brazil and Mexico:

Variations on a Statist Theme." Conference Paper, no. 23, Columbia University.

Schotter, Andrew. 1981. *The Economic Theory of Social Institutions.* Cambridge: Cambridge University Press.

1986. "The Evolution of Rules." In *Economics as a Process,* pp. 117–34. Richard N. Langlois, ed. Cambridge: Cambridge University Press.

Schumpeter, Joseph A. 1950. *Capitalism, Socialism and Democracy.* 3d ed. New York: Harper Bros.

Shapiro, Daniel. 1989. "Reviving the Socialist Calculation Debate: A Defense of Hayek against Lange." *Social Philosophy and Policy* 6: 139–60.

Shapiro, Helen, and Lance Taylor. 1989. "The State and Industrial Strategy." Manuscript, MIT.

Smith, William C. 1987. "The Political Transition in Brazil: From Authoritarian Liberalization and Elite Conciliation to Democratization." In *Comparing New Democracies,* pp. 179–340. Enrique A. Baylora, ed. Boulder, Colo.: Westview.

Sola, Lourdes. 1990. "The Politics of Hetherodox Schock in Brazil: Tecnicos, Politicians, Democracy." Manuscript, University of São Paulo.

Stallings, Barbara, and Robert Kaufman. 1989. "Debt and Democracy in the 1980s: The Latin American Experience." In *Debt and Democracy in Latin America,* pp. 201–23. Barbara Stallings and Robert Kaufman, eds. Boulder, Colo.: Westview.

Staniszkis, Jadwiga. 1984. *Poland's Self-Limiting Revolution.* Princeton, N.J.: Princeton University Press.

Stanton, Kimberly A. 1990. "The Chilean Constitution of 1925." Manuscript, Department of Political Science, University of Chicago.

Stepan, Alfred. 1978. *The State and Society: Peru in Comparative Perspective.* Princeton, N.J.: Princeton University Press.

Stigler, George. 1972. "Economic Competition and Political Competition." *Public Choice* 13: 91–106.

Sugden, Robert. 1986. *The Economics of Rights, Cooperation and Welfare.* New York: Blackwell Publisher.

Szelenyi, Ivan. 1989. "Eastern Europe in an Epoch of Transition: Toward a Socialist Mixed Economy?" In *Remaking the Economic Institutions of Socialism: China and Eastern Europe.* David Stark and Victor Nee, eds. Stanford, Calif.: Stanford University Press.

Tarkowski, Jacek. 1989. "Old and New Patterns of Corruption in Poland and the USSR." *Telos* 80: 51–63.

Taylor, Michael. 1976. *Anarchy and Cooperation.* New York: Wiley.

Theil, Henri. 1976. *Econometrics.* New York: Wiley.

Thoma, Richard. 1988. "On the Ideology of Parliamentarism." Appendix to Carl Schmitt, *The Crisis of Parliamentary Democracy* (1923). Cambridge, Mass.: MIT Press.

Tollison, Robert D. 1982. "Rent Seeking: A Survey." *Kyklos* 35: 575–602.

Torańska, Teresa. 1985. *Oni*. London: Aneks.

Ullman-Margalit, Edna. 1977. *The Emergence of Norms*. Oxford: Oxford University Press.

van der Veen, Robert, and Philippe van Parijs. 1986. "A Capitalist Road to Communism." *Theory and Society* 15: 635–57.

Verney, Douglas. 1959. *Parliamentary Reform in Sweden, 1866–1921*. London: Oxford University Press.

Vernon, Raymond. 1988. *The Promise of Privatization: A Challenge for U.S. Policy*. New York: Council on Foreign Relations.

Verou, Pablo Lucas. 1976. *Crítica jurídica-política de la reforma Suárez*. Madrid: Editorial Tecnos.

Vickers, Douglas. 1987. *Money Capital in the Theory of the Firm*. Cambridge: Cambridge University Press.

Walicki, Andrzej. 1990. "From Stalinism to Post-Communist Pluralism." Manuscript, Notre Dame University.

Walras, L. 1874. *Eléments d'économie politique pure*. Paris: Guillaumin.

Ward, Benjamin. 1957. "The Firm in Illyria: Market Syndicalism." *American Economic Review* 48: 566–89.

Weber, Max. 1968. *Economy and Society*. 3 vols. G. Roth and C. Wittich, eds. New York.

Weffort, Francisco. 1989. "Incertezas de transição na América latina." *Lua Nova* 16: 5–47.

Weil, Philippe. 1990. "Nonexpected Utility in Macroeconomics." *Quarterly Journal of Economics* 104: 29–42.

Wiatr, Jerzy J. 1983. *Polska szansa*. Krakow: Wydawnictwo Literackie.

1989. "Nie sposób zatrzymać lawiny." *Zdanie* 11–12: 2–14.

Wilk, Marian. 1988. *Człowiek i Stal*. Warsaw: PIW.

Williamson, John, 1990. *Latin American Adjustment: How Much Has Happened?* Washington, D.C.: Institute for International Economics.

Wnuk-Lipiński, Edmund. 1989. "Nierówności, deprywacje i przywileje jako podłoże konfliktu społecznego." In *Polacy 88*, pp. 18–80. Warsaw: CBPB.

Wood, Gordon S. 1969. *The Creation of the American Republic, 1776–1787*. Chapel Hill: University of North Carolina Press.

Zaleski, Edward. 1984. *La planification stalinienne: Croissance et fluctuations économiques en URSS, 1933–1953*. Paris: Economica.

Zalyguine, Sergeuei. 1987. "Le 'projet du siècle': Détournement des fleuves, détournement de la science par la bureaucracie." *Les Temps Moderns* 42: 171–92.

Zaslavskaya, Tatyana I. 1988. "Friends or Foes? Social Forces Working for and against Perestroika." In *Perestroika, 1989*, pp. 255–80. Abel G. Agabegyan, ed. New York: Scribner.

Zaslavsky, Victor. 1987-8. "Three Years of Perestroyika." *Telos* 74: 31–42.

# Author index

# Subject index